The 360° Video Handbook
Michael Wohl

Second Edition, 2.01

🌐 Vrrrynice.com
📍 Los Angeles, CA
✉️ 360VideoHandbook@gmail.com
📷 #360Video_Handbook
🐦 @360Video_book

© Copyright 2019 by Michael Wohl

👥 Research, permissions: Jonathan Stein
Additional research, permissions, indexing, layout,and a million other things: Hamish Briggs
Illustrations: Robert Jencks

Edition 2.01, Published February, 2019

For Greta and Eli
and the magical worlds
you will inhabit

ACKNOWLEDGMENTS

I would like to thank the following people who were instrumental in the creation of this book. Many of them graciously allowed me to interview them (some, multiple times), some shared footage, techniques, or sample hardware or software to test with, and some participated in the shoots I performed to explore and verify the various ideas and concepts described and proposed herein.

Sameer Agarwal, Google
Niclas Bahn, FXFactory
Nick Bicanic, Rvlvr Labs
Dane Brehm
Hamish Briggs
Michael Booth, Radiant Images
Matthew Celia, Light Sail VR
Eve M. Cohen, Cinematographer
Scott Connolly, The Astronauts Guild
Tim Dashwood, Dashwood Cinema
Bob Degus, VR Filmmaker
Amanda Drain, Kodak PixPro360
Bryan Eliacin, Screenifest Destiny
Achim Fell, DearVR
Ian Forester, VR Playhouse
Kevin Friel, Symphonic Filmworks
Richard Furse, Blue Ripple Sound
Daniel Gamburg, Enlightened Pictures
Carra Greenberg
Jason Goodman, 21st Century 3D
Matt Gordon, 360Fly
Sarah Hill, StoryUP VR
Christina Heller, VR Playhouse
James Kaelen
Jessica Kantor

Alx Klive, 360 Designs
Aaron Koblin, Within & HereBeDragons
Melissa Koujakian, Republique
Sarah Kroll-Rosenbaum
KC Lai, iZugar
Jon Landman, Teradek
Morris May, Specular Theory
Michael Mansouri, Radiant Images
Garrett McCullum, Dysonics
David McGriffy, VVAudio
Len Moskowitz, Core Sound
Liza M.S. Patnoe, Google
Winslow Porter
Aaron Rhodes, Pixvana
John Root, TSL Products
Celine Tricart, Lucid Dreams Productions
Joey Santana, Jaunt
Amanda Shelby, Radiant Images
Duncan Shephard, Immersive Media
Amy Sezak, 8i
Joseph Szopa, Google
Nakul Sood, Embrace Cinema, Brahma Mic
Jonathan "Yoni" Stein
Nav Vasudevan, Google
Milica Zec

And special thanks to Radiant Images for not only supplying us with a variety of cameras and equipment to test and experiment with, but for the exhaustive and intimate knowledge of the equipment, workflows, and idiosyncrasies of the various equipment.

The 360° Video Handbook

Prologue

You may think of virtual reality as new technology, but in some ways VR has been one of mankind's oldest and most persistent dreams. The idea of creating an alternative constructed reality to share one person's unique experience is ancient. It was perhaps one of the fundamental motivators for the invention of language, and certainly for the concept of story. From cave paintings to medieval scrolls to YouTube videos played back on an iPad, the effort to share our experiences is one of the most basic and most human of activities.

And throughout history, we have invented newer and newer technologies to make that shared experience more and more realistic, more and more immersive, and more and more effective at sharing those deepest feelings.

A good book can be delightfully, even overwhelmingly immersive—and it doesn't require a head-mounted display or a late-model graphics card. A well-made film can do the same; communicating emotional truth and eliciting genuine feelings in the viewers by fooling their brains into thinking they are having the same experiences as the characters on screen.

It's an exhilarating feeling to let yourself be tricked like this. And of course, this is why so many of us have fallen in love with books and with cinema. To be fully immersed in a fantastic world different than the banal one we inhabit in our daily lives is irresistible to most humans.

Still, if the mountain is there, we humans are compelled to climb it, and while novels and movies (and video games, and music, and many other art forms) are effective at transmitting an emotional experience to another person, we are perpetually searching for an even more effective way. Virtual reality technology is the next step in this inevitable evolution.

My first experience with virtual reality was in 1990 at an underground event hosted by the Whole Earth Institute and LSD pioneer Timothy Leary. It was called the Cyberthon and it was a 24-hour party to celebrate all things VR.

I was 19 and drinking beer with my roommate at a party in San Francisco's Lower Height. We were deep in discussion about whether or not Wintermute (the AI villain in William Gibson's *Neuromancer*) was self-aware or not when a striking young woman with thick-framed glasses (years before "nerd" was hip) overheard us, and joined the exchange.

She quickly bettered our shallow arguments and pitched a much more comprehensive theory evoking Hegel's concept of sublation, Dante's Inferno, and the mating habits of whiptail lizards. We were clearly outranked.

The conversation turned to Data from Star Trek, and then to the Holodeck, which we all agreed was the ultimate tech fantasy. As if we had passed some secret Turing test, our new friend squinted at us and then invited us to join her at a special "after party." Moments later the three of us eagerly squeezed into the back of a taxi and sped off.

As we neared our destination, I realized we were in Hunter's Point—a neighborhood that I had never dared set foot in, near the housing projects and notoriously run by gangs. The taxi dropped us off on an eerily deserted street surrounded by warehouses and the driver sped away. Standing there, my roommate and I shared a concerned look, but our beguiling chaperone seemed unfazed by the danger. She consulted a folded up scrap of paper and led us around the corner to a big warehouse humming with activity. I exhaled a deep breath.

She knew the guy working the door and we were issued laminated guest passes on colorful lanyards. We stepped into what felt like the party of the decade, maybe of the century. The warehouse was vast and dark, punctuated by swirling colored lights and flooded with loud thumping music. There were scores of people milling around purposefully in twos and threes, some with dark sunglasses, some with colored LEDs woven into their clothes. Drinks were free and flowing, and it wasn't totally clear what substances we might have been imbibing.

The space (which I later learned was the home of a successful animation studio) was divided into a dozen little sections and booths. It was a virtual reality trade show, except that VR technology was so nascent that the people interested in it tended to be more idealist dreamers and artists, rather than venture capital-backed entrepreneurs, so the whole thing felt much more art-fair or proto-rave than SIGGRAPH or CES.

We followed our new friend around the exhibits put up by companies with clever and optimistic names like Ascension Technology, Dreamworld Inc., and FakeSpace Labs. We saw demonstrations of primitive CG renderings of multiplayer games displayed on 19" televisions and powered by hand-modified Amigas.

The huge braided snakes of cables running behind the tables looked as much like an art project as the work on the screens themselves.

In one darkened room, we were guided, one by one, to step onto a replica of a section of the Golden Gate Bridge, where fan-blown fog and sound effects and video projection were used to make the environment feel convincingly real. You were urged to step out to the edge and feel "virtual vertigo." And then, a chorus of voices began berating you and encouraging you to jump off the bridge. I wasn't particularly moved, but I took the leap anyway, and was disappointed to find solid floor just a few inches below the structure.

Still, while it all had the distinct whiff of "the future," there was nothing that was anything like the fanciful descriptions of cyberspace in the science fiction of the day. There certainly was nothing like the Holodeck.

As the drinks kicked in and we explored deeper, we were drawn to a boisterous throng crowded into one corner of the main room. As we got closer we saw what the fuss was about—not an actual virtual reality demo as we had hoped, but instead, it was Tim Leary himself and he was engaged in a lively impromptu dialogue with an animated young guy in shoulder-length dreadlocks pulled back into a ponytail. This was Jaron Lanier and he wore a perpetual smirk like he knew an incredible secret that he couldn't quite keep in. Tim probed, Jaron parried and the crowd giggled and cooed with each retort, a percussive soundtrack to accompany their dance.

Eventually we moved on and followed whispers in the crowd to a waiting area for a van that was shuttling people a dozen at a time to a small tech office a few blocks away. Supposedly an actual head-mounted display unit was set up for people to try out real VR for themselves. It was already after 1am and we were told that there was at least a two-hour wait, but that the demo would be going on all night. We immediately scribbled our names on the list.

Two hours turned into three and a half, and along the way, the alluring girl who brought us to the event had long vanished into the crowd. Disappointed, but too deep in to go home, we endured, and finally, around 4:30am we were ushered onto the shuttle and were driven all of five minutes away to a nondescript brick building marked with the letters VPL. Jaron was there and when it was my turn, he helped me into a giant, heavy helmet called an "EyePhone" (no joke) and a single "DataGlove" for my right hand. Both were tethered by a thick complex of wires to a huge Silicon Graphics workstation. He typed something into the indigo keyboard and suddenly I was "jacked in" to a fully computer-generated world that fully responded to my movements and actions. I could look around, move forward and back by tilting my hand in a certain way, and explore this colorful, intriguing dream space.

I was connected for all of about 3 minutes before I had to hand over the equipment to the next eager participant. To be honest, it wasn't all that impressive. The "world" I leapt into was made up of flat, unskinned polygons, and while a virtual arm stuck out in front of me that accurately mimicked the movements and actions of my gloved hand, there wasn't much to do other than marvel at the technology's potential.

Fortunately, Jaron and the other evangelist there (speaking in a mesmerizing French accent) were eager to stimulate our imaginations with their visions of the incredible future this achievement heralded: A revolution in entertainment, but also in medicine, space exploration, and even an end to real war where soldiers could wage virtual bloodless battles that could usher in a whole new phase for humanity.

We left giddy and exhausted, overwhelmed and over enthused. When I woke up, head aching and slightly nauseous the following day, it was hard not to feel like the whole thing had been a dream. I dug the white laminated entry badge out of my jeans pocket to prove to myself it had really happened. I still have that laminate to this day.

Unfortunately, despite the hype and the hyperbole, VR didn't penetrate the mainstream that decade nor the next. But fast forward twenty-five years, and VR may finally be having its moment. Technology has advanced exponentially and now most of us keep a device capable of displaying 360-degree, photorealistic, virtual worlds right in our pocket. The biggest and most powerful companies in technology and entertainment have invested billions of dollars into bringing it into the mainstream, and slowly, very slowly there is content emerging that shows off the real promise of this immersive, interactive experience.

New 360° video cameras have made at least one type of VR available and affordable for anyone to create their own content. And you don't have to be a computer scientist, game designer or Holodeck dreamer to jump in and give it a try. And hopefully, this book will serve as a trusty guide as you learn how this new medium works.

I don't know if this technology can end war as we know it, or even if it will supplant traditional movies and video games as a form of popular entertainment, but I do know that every time someone experiences it for the first time, just as I did as a teenager back in 1990, they feel that peculiar lightness in their stomach and they are struck with the unmistakable feeling that this technology might just expand the possibilities for human experience. And that is truly something to behold.

Introduction

Spherical video allows you to transport an audience into a new world, surrounding them in an immersive photorealistic environment where they truly feel like they are there—inside the movie alongside the other characters. And each individual viewer gets a unique experience, able to freely look around and focus on whatever catches his or her eye.

And it's no more difficult to create than it is to shoot regular video. Okay, it is a bit more complex in some ways (though arguably easier in others). But just like with traditional video, you can keep it extremely simple, shooting with a handheld camera and sharing it directly on Facebook, or you can go through an elaborate multi-step process, employing a large professional crew, and continually refining your work until you achieve a result that feels perfect. Most creators likely fall somewhere in the middle of that spectrum, and that's exactly who this book was written for.

This book is intended to be a practical, hands-on guidebook for the creation of 360° video. I have purposely designed it so you can also skip around and jump right to the topic or section you're most interested in. There are frequent cross-references to help you skip right to related or complementary topics.

Of course, you can also read the book straight through. Reading it that way, you may find some important concepts are mentioned more than once as I explain them from a variety of different contexts and perspectives.

Whenever possible I include tips, tricks, shortcuts, and the occasional anecdote to help enhance your understanding of the concepts presented.

What this book is not

This book does not cover the development or scriptwriting phases nor the marketing and publicity aspects of distributing your 360° video content. The former are still too nascent and varied for me to attempt to catalogue a set of rules and guidelines, and the latter are essentially the same as for any other media project.

Note that in some ways those tasks that occur before the steps covered in this book are the most important of all—as with traditional film and video production, the more planning you do before jumping into production will almost always determine the level of success you achieve on set.

A good plan can certainly be ruined through poor execution, but even flawless execution won't salvage a poorly conceived idea. And effective budgeting, scheduling, and other preparatory steps will ensure that a project actually gets finished—and that the process of making it is fun and invigorating, instead of a miserable exhausting (and expensive) slog.

And finally, knowing what kind of content you're trying to make, and to whom you're hoping to deliver it is the best way to ensure that the project ultimately reaches its intended audience.

My pledge to keep it simple

My aim is to keep this book as non-technical as possible. The technology that enables VR to exist is incredibly complex and intricate. It's easy to get overwhelmed, confused, or distracted by that minutia and in doing so, to lose sight of the bigger creative task. I strive to focus on that higher-level objective of effective communication and to keep jargon and technical descriptions to a minimum.

When I do include technobabble, be it common VR terms such as HMD or stitching, or abstruse terms such as equirectangular or interpupillary distance, you will find definitions in the margins of the page where the term is first used.

Painting a moving canvas

I want to stress that VR is a new and rapidly evolving medium, and the language of communicating using 360° video is still being formed and refined. Inevitably, some of the ideas and tools that are in wide usage today might be totally obsolete within a very short time.

I'll endeavor to update this book regularly to account for these changes as they occur, and as much as possible I'll strive to put the most emphasis on the aspects that are more likely to remain relevant, even as technology evolves and as audiences get more familiar with this amazing new form of communication.

Is it really VR?

This book is limited to techniques associated specifically with 360° video. Though I (and many others) occasionally use the terms "360-degree video" and "VR" interchangeably, in fact, 360° video is a subset of virtual reality; Full VR typically incorporates computer generated images and environments instead of (or in addition to) video elements, and more importantly, it allows the viewer to move about in a virtual space, or at the very least it allows for six degrees of freedom. 360° video (also called *spherical* video) only enables a viewer to turn or tilt her head to look around within a virtual world from a fixed spot. (Though there are some exciting technologies such as volumetric video recording, that will eventually change that.)

HMD (head-mounted display): goggles or a headset designed to optimize 360° video viewing.

Stitching: Combining multiple images/ videos into one panoramic image/video (also sometimes refers to a seam in a panoramic image).

Abstruse: difficult to understand or obscure.

Equirectangular: Stretching a spherical image into a flat, rectangular format. (i.e. the way a world map represents the spherical Earth).

Interpupillary distance: The distance between the pupils of the eye / lenses of a camera in stereoscopic photography.

Six degrees of freedom: The ability to move left-right, up-down, and forward-backward (in addition to being able to rotate around the x, y, and z axes). Provides significantly more immersion than basic 360 video.

Volumetric video recording: A method of capturing a scene in which the spatial layout is recorded instead of just the light that comes through the lens, enabling representation of the scene in a digital, 3-dimensional space.

As 360° video gets more sophisticated there may be ways to incorporate more interactivity, but at least in terms of the techniques described in this book, I'm talking about content where the user's interaction is limited to choosing where they want to look.

While full VR unquestionably has the potential to be more immersive and engaging than mere 360° video, the affordability and ease of use of the 360° video creation tools exposes this new medium to a vastly greater audience. And as more and more people begin using and experimenting, creative innovators will inevitably expand the potential of 360° video beyond anything we can imagine right now.

Part I: Preparing to shoot

Like any project, a 360° production requires a lot of work before the camera ever turns on. In addition to the obvious logistical issues of defining what, where, and when you'll be shooting, there are some differences to consider in terms of cast and crew, equipment choices, and of course budgeting and scheduling. This section introduces many of the factors that will guide these decisions including an examination of the many varied types and styles of cameras that you need to choose between when preparing for your 360° production.

Chapter 1: Conceiving an Idea

There are differing opinions as to how much a 360° concept should be defined by the medium. Some creators believe that any video idea can be made better by shooting it in the round. Some argue that unless you take full advantage of the added dimension, it isn't worth taking on the limitations and challenges that spherical video brings.

It's undeniable that in some ways shooting in 360° is more challenging than shooting flat, but at the same time, the limitations of 360° video can actually make shooting easier and quicker. There's no coverage, there are no lenses to decide on, and you typically need only one setup for any given scene. This can speed up your daily workflow and efficiency. Because the camera sees in all directions all the time, rigging, lighting, and even crew must be kept to a minimum. A lean production can help keep budgets down, and a smaller team can often work faster and more proficiently than a large one. And because you're limited in how many different shots you can take of a scene, editing is (in some ways) greatly simplified too.

On the other hand, without close-ups, over-the-shoulders, reverse-angles, montages, and the many other tricks of the film-making trade, your storytelling palette is severely restricted, and this can make some kinds of content especially hard to communicate effectively.

It's up to you to decide (as early in the process as possible) what it is you're trying to communicate and why you're doing it in this new creative medium. The sooner you know your goals and your expectations, the more effectively and successfully you'll be able to execute your vision.

Coverage: Multiple shots from multiple angles to capture the events in a scene (i.e. master shot, medium shots, close-ups, inserts, etc).

Setup: A camera position for a given scene. You might shoot more than one shot from a single set-up (wide shot and close-up).

Some VR creators believe that the medium is fundamentally incompatible with traditional narrative structure. They argue that the viewer is effectively the director—deciding what elements within a scene are important and worth watching—and so any directorial attempt to lead viewers through a story (for example, by requiring that they pay attention to specific details or elements) will inevitably fail as viewers look in the wrong directions at key moments.

In that worldview, the best pieces are purely experiential, and are filled with enough varied elements that every viewer has a unique experience as they venture about and explore on their own volition.

Others believe that a rich narrative is still possible, and it's more a matter of subtly guiding the viewer's point of focus with carefully spatialized sound, choreography, and lighting cues (as well as through traditional editing). To these creators, VR is simply an expansion of traditional cinema, but one where familiar rules (and tools) still apply.

Spatialized sound: A soundscape where audio is positioned from specific locations within a sphere around the listener.

Neither of these approaches is right or wrong; they're clearly both points on a continuum, so you may find yourself somewhere between these two extremes. I believe that as the medium matures over the next few years, some content will stand out, and a new language will begin to emerge; a visual grammar that takes advantage of the strengths of the new medium. As that happens, the stylistic overlap between 360° video and traditional media like cinema and videogames will become more clear.

In some cases, you may consider VR180 as an alternative that offers many of the immersive qualities of spherical video but that alleviates many of the technical obstacles inherent in true 360.

VR180: A subset of spherical video where only the front half of the sphere is recorded. Learn more in Chapter 30: VR180.

Chapter 2: Location, location, location

In flat cinema, setting is always an important consideration. In VR, choosing your environment thoughtfully is even more critical. After all, the experience of being thrust into another place is the essence of VR. For many viewers that sense of physical transportation to a different space can be more memorable than the characters or actions in a piece.

Consequently, you should treat the location as if it were a character in your story. In other words, your setting should be motivated, justified, and essential.

Furthermore, because your viewers are able to direct their gaze wherever they want, you need to pay close attention to every detail of every direction in the space before you begin shooting. Get in there and look around, focusing on every facet of your environment. This preparation will also lay the groundwork for your choices for camera placement (covered in more detail in Chapter 20: Placing the camera).

Here are some aspects that you should always consider when selecting a location:

Specificity

The key to a good location is finding (or creating) a space that communicates something specific to the viewer. The nuances and details of the location will give your audience clues about the tone and timbre of your story. And this begins with the script. Remember that the feeling of presence in a space is one of the most fundamental aspects of watching VR. Be sure that the spaces you choose for your scenes are as specific as possible.

Uniqueness

Hand in hand with *specificity* is the goal of creating a location that feels unique and memorable to your audience. When you think of your location as another character in your story, think about "casting" it with the same rigor and care that you use to choose an actor. Good casting is about finding an individual that brings her own inimitable traits to the role and makes it her own. Hold your locations to the same test.

Richness

With VR, there's no room for skimping on minutiae. You want your viewers fully immersed, and that means filling your scenes with realistic details. This is why it's a good idea to get a great production designer and do the prep work to ensure you have all the necessary elements in place to create a realistic scenario.

Production designer / PD: Crewperson responsible for all visual aspects of what is seen by the camera; (i.e. sets & locations, props, wardrobe etc.

Exposure variations

Bright windows or dark shadowed corners can't be framed out of a shot. Everything in the room appears in every shot. An exposure drastically different in one direction because of a bright light source or an unlit doorway can complicate or potentially ruin the overall exposure for the scene. In some cases, this may be unavoidable, and you'll just have to live with the imperfection. You can always try to manage this issue by Chapter 15: Guiding the viewer's focus.

Exposure: The measurement of the brightness and range (latitude) of light being captured by the camera. Exposure is governed by camera settings that either control the overall amount of light that reaches the sensor (using aperture and shutter speed), or directly adjust the sensor's sensitivity to the light that reaches it (ISO).

Parallax issues

Stitching the footage together requires matching images from lenses that see the world from different physical locations; consequently, having many layers of objects at different distances from the camera (such as trees in a forest or beams and windows in an office conference room) can be a nightmare when it comes

Stitching: Combining multiple images/videos into one panoramic image/video (also sometimes refers to the seams in a panoramic image).

time to assemble your shots. Learn more about parallax problems (and what to do about them) in the Sidebar: Understanding parallax.

Depth of action

At present, cameras that shoot 360° video use extremely wide-angle lenses. As a result, the sharpness and readability of details in a scene fall off rather quickly the farther they are from the camera. So elements close to the camera are very noticeable (and therefore seem very important to the viewer). Elements that are even 5 or 6 feet away yield much less attention. Keep this in mind when choosing camera positions and when dressing a set.

Additionally, the factors you'd plan for in a flat video shoot apply to a VR shoot, as well, including:

- *Facilities:* Does the location have adequate electricity, bathrooms, and so on?

- *Sound:* Is the space quiet enough to capture good sound?

- *Time of day:* Does the sun's movement change the lighting in the space and are you shooting at the same time of day as you scouted?

- *Bogeys:* Is there evidence of the crew or equipment visible in the scene?

- *Ancillary space:* Is there room for makeup, staging equipment and for the crew to eat lunch? Remember, when you begin shooting in the round, the entire crew will need to hide somewhere!

Bogey: Adapted from military slang, a bogey a person or object who accidentally appears in the frame during a shot.

Chapter 3: Cast and crew

VR requires a thoughtful approach to on-camera talent. The dirty secret of traditional cinema is that a great many performances are made or saved in the editing room. Unfortunately, 360° video doesn't afford you that luxury. In VR, you can't cut away from a shot, so your talent will need to remember their lines; your interviewees must be naturally succinct; and your actors will need to vary the intensity of their performances based on their relative distance to the camera. (This is covered in more detail in Chapter 17: Working with actors.)

Much of the below-the-line crew is essentially the same as a crew on a traditional set. However, the above-the-line jobs can be substantively different.

Below-the-line: The budgetary field that accounts for 'non-creative' crew in film production (e.g. everyone except the producer, director, writer, cinematographer, composer, editor, etc.).

Director

Directing for 360° video requires a very specialized approach (so much so that six chapters in Part II: Production are dedicated entirely to that job).

Cinematographer

The Director of photography's role changes too. And don't be fooled into thinking you don't need a DP at all. Despite the reduced camera-related options, a cinematographer experienced with shooting in 360° can contribute essential creative guidance, and can prevent visual or technical issues that the director shouldn't be worrying about.

Director of photography / DP: Crew-person responsible for designing the shotlist and lighting state, advising on camera selection, and directing the camera and lighting departments on set.

But because you can't have an operator sitting beside the camera while it rolls, the job of the DP and camera operator shifts. After configuring the cameras and lights, they'll need to run and hide (along with everyone else) when the camera begins recording.

Production designer (PD): Crewperson responsible for all visual aspects of what is seen by the camera; (i.e. sets & locations, props, wardrobe etc.).

DIT (digital imaging technician): is responsible for managing workflow of a production, ingesting and labeling footage from takes, monitoring image quality and color, and troubleshooting digital issues.

2nd AC (2nd assistant camera): is responsible for operating the slate, keeping a camera log, and managing the raw film stock and footage shot.

Dailies: The accumulated footage shot in a day on set (traditionally reviewed at the end of each day).

Assemblies: An extremely rough edit of shots that places them in the order they appear in the script.

Production designer

The role of the production designer becomes especially important in a 360° production, even for nonfiction or ordinary real location sets that wouldn't require such attention on a flat shoot. In VR, the set is unquestionably a character that influences the story in significant ways. Viewers can look anywhere they want, and focus on any detail, anywhere in the room. So it's crucial to have someone dedicated to the set.

Some PDs have begun assuming the title "world builder" and it's an apt name; so much of the VR experience is about being present in another space. The more you treat the set and setting as a full-fledged world where every detail is considered and is consistent, the more effective an experience you'll create. See also: Chapter 2: Location, location, location.

360° Camera technician

Modern (flat) productions (above the most bare-boned of budget) usually include a DIT (a digital evolution of the 2nd AC role from the days of celluloid film). This person keeps track of all the media cards and individual files being generated by the camera and sound equipment; creates essential backups; and sometimes generates dailies, assemblies, or other reference content the director needs in order to ensure her vision is accurately captured.

With the current crop of 360° cameras, such a role is more essential than ever. Consider that spherical cameras record to as many as 18 or 24 SD cards simultaneously; even with a minimal three-camera rig, it's crucial that the data on all those cards is tracked, labeled, and organized with precision.

With the more sophisticated 360° rigs (such as the Z CAM V1 Pro or YI HALO), each device comes with custom dedicated software for configuring the unit, previewing and monitoring, and managing and backing up the copious footage generated when you shoot. Each software package works very differently than the others and none is particularly user-friendly or easy to master at first glance.

You certainly don't want to be wasting precious minutes on set trying to figure these systems out yourself. Hiring a technician experienced with the camera you're planning to use is highly recommended. In addition to configuring the camera and managing and backing up your recorded files, a dedicated 360° camera tech can likely help with monitoring and building quick stitches so you can ensure you're recording exactly what you hoped.

Quick-stitched: Rapid, albeit potentially imperfect, stitches of 360° footage. In multi camera rigs, this may be achieved without utilizing information from every camera's lens.

Livestream: Distribute video playback in real time.

Color fidelity: The accuracy with which a digital camera captures the color of the photographed subject.

Resolution: The number of pixels in an image, typically presented as a ratio of the total pixels on x axis to the total pixels on the y axis (i.e. 1920 x 1080 for HD).

Field of view: The angle of space viewable from a given lens position.

Stitching: Combining multiple images/videos into one panoramic image/video (also sometimes refers to the seams in a panoramic image).

Stereoscopic: Video shot with two parallel cameras (or in the case of 360° video, multiple pairs of parallel cameras) Commonly referred to as 3D.

VR180: A subset of spherical video where only the front half of the sphere is recorded. Learn more in Chapter 30: VR180.

Chapter 4: Choosing a camera

Whether you're shooting traditional video or VR video, having the "right" camera will never make a crappy script or idea great. In fact, spending extra on a fancy camera can complicate your workflow. If you're new to VR video, consider using one of the relatively inexpensive consumer-oriented 360° cameras designed to simplify the production process and make it easy to quickly shoot and upload content. Many even allow you to livestream your 360° video directly to the web! (Learn more in Chapter 64: Livestreaming.)

Of course, the more expensive and more complicated cameras exist for a reason; they offer a number of non-trivial benefits. For starters, high-quality cameras and lenses produce sharper, more accurate images with higher color fidelity and fewer distortions.

Different high-end cameras offer different features. Some cameras perform better in low-light situations—an important quality given how hard it is to light for spherical productions (see Chapter 24: Lighting for 360°). Some cameras employ a larger number of photo sensors, increasing overall resolution and creating more overlap between each camera's field of view, thus dramatically improving stitching quality. And some cameras can generate stereoscopic output. (Learn more about stereo [3D] versus mono in Chapter 29: Stereoscopic recording.)

The next few chapters in this book describe the categories of cameras: consumer, prosumer, multicam-rigs, professional, and specialty. But before reading up on the pros and cons of each category, take a moment to assess your needs. It's important to understand how the options stack up for your personal situation. Also, consider the virtues of VR180 as an alternative format.

Fast, cheap, and good—pick two

This old maxim applies quite well to evaluating 360° cameras: Consumer cameras are fast (easy to use) and inexpensive, but their quality is questionable. Multi-rig cameras are cheap(ish) and have good quality, but they require much more manual control, making them slower to deploy. Professional systems are fast and good, but they sure ain't cheap! Depending on your needs, your expertise, and your budget, you'll need to decide which direction to pursue in choosing the camera that's right for you.

Different cameras for different situations

When it comes to 360° video, the best option may be to use a variety of cameras for different aspects of your shoot. For example, a professionally oriented camera like the Yi Halo may be suitable for static, well-lit spaces. However, it's large and must be tethered to an external battery, so it may not be ideal for moving shots. The Z CAM V1Pro is smaller and lighter, plus it has a global shutter, which means moving shots won't have rolling shutter issues. However, a global shutter also means reduced dynamic range, so the Z CAM V1 Pro may not be the best choice in variable lighting scenarios (like the view from a moving car).

Additionally, because both these cameras are stereoscopic (3D), no action can be closer than 3 feet from the front of the lens; so neither is the best camera for scenes in cramped quarters. Other cameras may be great for small spaces, but may have poor overall image quality. The best recommendation I can make is to consider a wide range of different cameras, and be prepared to break out different rigs for different shots and situations.

Global shutter: A shutter that opens and closes all-at-once, exposing the entire sensor simultaneously (as opposed to a rolling shutter which opens a little at a time like a door opening).

Dynamic range: The varying degrees of brightness that can be captured by a camera or displayed by a playback device. You can think of it as the number of grays that can be represented before areas of the image appear all-black (in the shadows) or all-white (in the highlights).

Consider renting

There are many reasons to consider renting rather than buying a 360° camera. First of all, camera technology is changing at an incredibly fast clip. The sad truth is, the camera you buy today will more than likely be obsolete before your next production. Another reason to rent: unless you're planning to shoot continually, one project after another, purchasing an expensive 360° may not make the best economic sense. Another thing to consider: renting gives you access to better cameras that might be cost-prohibitive to buy. You'll get better results and spend less money doing it.

If you do go the rental route, there's currently few players in the rental space: Radiant Images and AbelCine are two of the largest. As specialists in VR and spherical cameras, they're likely to be among the very first to know about new equipment and updates to existing gear. Fortunately more and more camera houses are adding 360 gear to their repertoire, so hopefully even filmmakers in smaller markets will soon have myriad options.

Sidebar: Understanding parallax

Before we get to camera specifics, let's take a closer look at a fundamental concept: Parallax is a phenomenon that occurs whenever you observe something in three-dimensional space from two or more vantage points. Hold a finger in front of your face and close your left eye. Notice what is behind your finger in the background. Now, open your left eye and close the right. Your finger appears to move in relation to the background. That perceived shift is parallax. Our brains know how to interpret this optical discrepancy, and in fact this is one of the main ways we judge distances between objects.

Because the cameras in a 360° rig each view the world from different locations, objects appear to move in space depending on which camera's view you look at. In this example, the letter carrier appears to be to the right of the tree in the left image and directly in front of the tree in the right image. This is because Lens A is seeing the action from further to the left.

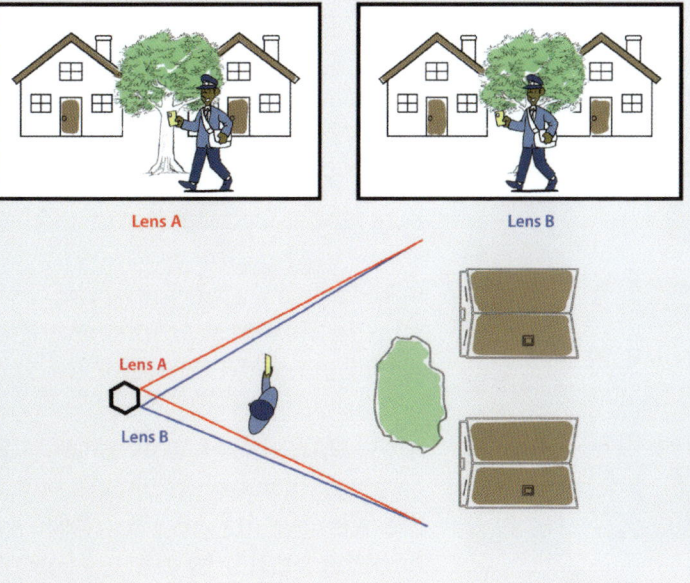

Unfortunately, when stitching together a spherical video frame from the output of multiple cameras, we have to manually do what our brains do automatically.

The farther the camera sensors are from each other, the more discrepancy there will be in the cameras' viewpoints. For this reason, a larger rig will inevitably create more parallax than a small one.

Shooting in 3D exacerbates the issue even more; stereoscopic spherical video displays two side-by-side images that deliberately include this parallax discrepancy. Depending on how and where the cameras are positioned, the stitching of the left and right video streams must be done differently (and with great precision) in order to preserve natural looking depth—not just when looking in a single direction, but also when turning your head.

Stitch: Combine multiple images/videos into one panoramic image/video (also sometimes refers to a seam in a panoramic image).

Video assist: A mechanism to watch in real time what is being recorded by the camera.

A sampling of consumer cameras: (from top-left) GoPro Fusion, Kodak Orbit 360, 360 Penguin, Insta360 One X, Ricoh Theta V, Samsung Gear360, 360Fly 4k, Rylo.

Chapter 5: Consumer cameras

There are countless cameras in this category—many from familiar vendors like Nikon, Samsung, and GoPro. Plenty are already on their 2nd or 3rd iteration and others have already disappeared. Over the next year, another batch will come to market. Of course, the year after that, two thirds of them will probably be discontinued, so keep in mind that purchasing one of these is best considered a short-term, expendable cost.

These consumer-targeted devices mostly incorporate two or three sensors into a single camera body[1] conveniently activated by a single "record" button. What's more, most automatically stitch the resulting videos into a single output file for you to work with (often this requires processing in a companion app). This is a huge benefit that removes the biggest barrier to shooting 360° video: stitching together the footage from multiple cameras.

Most consumer cameras provide wireless uploading, either to your companion phone or computer or directly to video file-sharing sites like YouTube or Facebook. This removes yet another barrier to entry—but only if you just want to post your raw, unedited footage rather than refining it first.

Remote monitoring is another benefit provided by many consumer cameras. That means you can watch the content while it's being recorded, via a smartphone or other device connected to the camera using Bluetooth. This is a terrific feature, and some professionals have taken to clamping one of these consumer cameras to their pro rigs as a type of video assist.

---

1   Some cameras such as the VSN Mobil and the Fly360 use a single camera; however, they don't capture a full 360° spherical image.

Shot with Samsung 360 Camera

stitch line   stitch line

So, consumer cameras are impressively tiny, dead-simple to use, and cost under $500. If that sounds too good to be true, you won't be surprised to learn that they have certain drawbacks.

Topping that list of disadvantages is poor image quality. Even cameras in this group that boast 4K resolution typically use cheap, tiny image sensors that suffer from noise (especially in low light), and other quality issues. Additionally, the lenses tend to be cheap, which can result in color aberrations, soft focus in areas of the image, and other mild image distortions. Furthermore, those less-than-perfect video images are then highly compressed to make the files small enough to store and upload wirelessly. This reduces quality even more, and can cause blockiness and dramatic color inaccuracies, compounding any flaws in the sensor or lens.

Even auto-stitching, one of the main benefits of these cameras, has a downside. Because most consumer cameras consist of only two or three linked cameras, there's not very much overlap between the images (and the lenses required are exceedingly

Noise: Undesirable variations of brightness and/or color in an image that typically occur when recording at high ISOs in digital cameras.

Color aberrations: The optical consequence of a lens that fails to handle color waveforms equally. It can result in blurred images or noticeable colored edges or "fringes."

Blockiness: An artifact of data compression whereby areas of the image look pixelated.

Low light scene reveals blockiness on consumer-level camera.

Wide-angle: A expansive view that takes in the entirety of a scene or location.

Stitch lines: The seams in a 360° video where footage from one camera has been combined with another.

wide-angle, which further degrades image quality). Consequently, the computer-generated stitching has minimal data to work with. In some cases, you can get surprisingly good results. But in other cases, the stitch lines are glaring, and because these cameras build this data into the saved file, there's nothing you can do about it. (However, check out Chapter 14: Working with the medium for tips on minimizing stitching errors.)

Another benefit—the consumer cameras' tiny size—comes with some drawbacks, too: battery life is typically under an hour, and the amount of video you can store in one session is similarly limited. Additionally, consumer cameras tend to have limited options when it comes to clearing the memory card or deleting bad files without offloading the content to a nearby phone or computer.

When it comes to consumer cameras, there's a lot to like. And some have distinctive features that may be perfectly suited for particular use cases. For example, the ALLie Cam has infrared

Chapter 5: Consumer cameras

LEDs, making it a great night-vision camera. The VSN Mobil is set up to easily capture time-lapse scenes. Other consumer cameras are waterproof or otherwise designed for sports or action use.

There's also a whole category of consumer-level cameras created specifically for VR180, which don't shoot a full 360° sphere, but they are stereoscopic and compatible with Google's VR180 initiative. Learn more in Chapter 30: VR180.

One useful quality that all consumer cameras tend to share: the amazing ability to "just work," which can't be overrated.

The quality (and especially the price/performance ration of all these cameras is bound to improve over time, and I expect that very soon subsequent models of one or another of these devices will advance toward that Goldilocks price/performance point to emerge as the perfect camera for a critical mass of users.

VR180: A subset of spherical video where only the front half of the sphere is recorded.

Stereoscopic: Video shot with two parallel cameras (or in the case of 360° video, multiple pairs of parallel cameras) Commonly referred to as 3D.

Chapter 6: Prosumer cameras

A number of vendors are already aiming for that market sweet spot where quality, features, and affordability come together.

A few of these are quickly becoming the most popular cameras for independent producers, including models from Z CAM, Insta360 and Kandao. Each of those vendors has a variety of cameras available at a range of price points, These cameras generally represent their lower cost options--with the exception of Insta360 which has a number of consumer level cameras as well.

The cameras in this category range are generally between $1000 and $4000 and generally provide 6K or better resolution. A few of them offer stereoscopic recording And best of all, most include software to take care of the stitching for you too (at a higher level of quality than the consumer cameras afford).

These devices may lack all the manual controls or highest-caliber image quality that a professional DP might demand, but the manufacturers are hoping that the results will be good enough for most users.

Unfortunately, some of these devices are still (as of our publishing date) unfinished or available in limited form. As they get evaluated and verified by the market, I'll endeavor to add more information in subsequent revisions of this book.

You can cameras listed here for sale from vendors like B&H Photo & Video, or for rent from houses like Radiant Images and Lens-Rentals.com.

Stereoscopic: Video shot with two parallel cameras (or in the case of 360° video, multiple pairs of parallel cameras) Commonly referred to as 3D.

Stitching: Combining multiple images/videos into one panoramic image/video (also sometimes refers to a seam in a panoramic image).

A sampling of prosumer cameras: (clockwise) Insta360 Pro, Detu F4 Plus, Sphericam 2, Z CAM S1, Kandao Obsidion Go, Aurovis 360, and (center) Vuze+

Fisheye: An extreme wide-angle lens, with image distortion occurring at the edges of the frame.

Wide-angle: A expansive view that takes in the entirety of a scene or location.

Stereoscopic: Video shot with two parallel cameras (or in the case of 360° video, multiple pairs of parallel cameras) Commonly referred to as 3D.

Stitch lines: The seams in a 360° video where footage from one camera has been combined with another.

A sampling of multicamera rigs.

Chapter 7: Multicamera rigs

Until very recently, most pro 360° video producers have relied on multicamera rigs. The most common devices employ a custom-made harness that houses a number of small cameras equipped with fisheye lenses (or at least very wide-angle lenses) pointing in different directions. There are rigs for 3, 4, 5, 6, 7, 8, 12, 16, and even 32 cameras (those larger numbers are generally for stereoscopic recording).

The more cameras you use, the higher the resulting resolution. Plus, you get more overlap between cameras, which makes it easier to hide stitch lines. Unfortunately more stitch lines means more opportunities for stitching errors, or at the least, more work to prevent those errors.

With a basic device that uses only two cameras, such as on the Ricoh Theta, there's only one stitch line.

A two camera rig generates 1 stitchline.

With six cameras, you've got 12 stitch lines, like all the edges on a die.

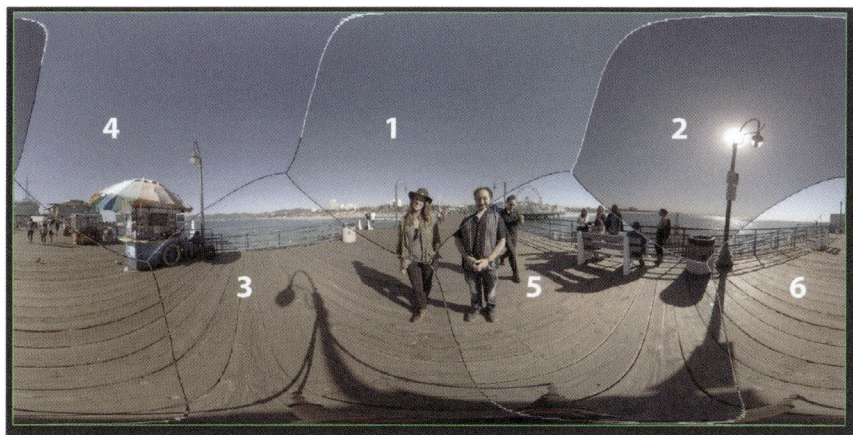
A six camera rig generates 12 stitchlines.

While each stitch line covers a smaller amount of the resulting sphere of video, the more stitch lines there are, the harder it is to prevent action in your scene from falling on, or crossing over, one of those seams. And fixing one edge can negatively impact the other related edges. So the enhanced resolution you get with more cameras comes with a trade off: The more cameras you use, the more complicated your stitching becomes.

Furthermore, the more cameras you use, the more problems you're likely to encounter. Each camera must be started and stopped independently, and each needs its own memory card. After shooting, all those memory cards must be collected and offloaded to a computer. Then the footage must be coordinated, synchronized, and ultimately stitched. And that's all before you even get a chance to view the footage and decide which shots you want to use.

There are myriad things that can go wrong along that journey, and at the very least, it's a lot of extra work, especially with very high numbers of cameras. Plus, each additional camera makes the rig that much more expensive. Oh, and there's always the low-level risk that one of the cameras (or memory cards) fails, a lens gets smudged, or some other unexpected mechanical problem arises.

GoPro rigs

Most multicamera rigs on the market today are designed to work with GoPro Hero cameras. The Hero is ideal for this purpose in some ways: It's quite small, very durable, optically stabilized, and armed with a fairly wide-angle lens. The sensors are small, but you can shoot with high frame rates and high resolution.

Optically stabilized: Includes mechanics that counteract camera-shake.

A modified GoPro rig from iZugar.

One significant drawback to GoPros is that they have poor low-light performance. Given the difficulty of lighting a scene where the camera is looking in every direction at once, this is not a small issue. Also, on a GoPro, the lenses are permanently attached to the camera, limiting your options (and quality) to the plastic lenses provided by the manufacturer (unless you permanently modify the camera as described below). See Chapter 22: Camera Settings to learn how to get the most out of a GoPro (or any) 360° camera.

Some VR producers have taken to replacing the stock lenses on the GoPro with a wider-angle version to create more overlap with fewer cameras—aiming for the perfect middle ground of sufficient overlap to stitch effectively with only three or four cameras. One vendor, Izugar.com sells a kit with new lenses and instructions for hacking the stock lens off of your GoPros and attaching their alternative.

The GoPro Omni camera rig

Ingesting: The process of capturing, transferring, and storing media in an organized manner in preparation for editing and output.

GoPro released their own proprietary six-camera rig—the GoPro Omni—and with it, software to automate the ingesting process.

The result is a very painless path to a quick-stitched image for offline editing. Unfortunately, the Omni is designed for mounting at a 45° angle, which can sometimes make it difficult to prevent subjects from sitting on or crossing over stitch lines. .

Higher-quality camera rigs

Some multicamera rigs are designed to work with higher-quality cameras than GoPros, including the Blackmagic Design Micro Cinema Camera and the Sony A7 DSLR. It's a promising idea, because these cameras have better low-light performance than GoPros; have full manual settings for exposure, white balance, and other essential controls; and have better dynamic range, resulting in a far superior-looking image. Plus, they accept third-party lenses, which gives you more choices for higher-quality glass.

The main downside here is primarily cost. Also, since these cameras (outfitted with appropriate lenses) can be significantly bigger than a GoPro, there may be additional issues in terms of parallax and proper framing. Ultimately, these cameras may make the stitching process more challenging and therefore more expensive.

To combat this, one intrepid team at production company Perception Squared deconstructed their GoPros to pull the lens and sensor apparatuses out of the camera bodies so they could arrange the sensors even closer together (thus reducing the parallax error as much as possible).

Quick-stitched: A rapid, albeit potentially imperfect, stitch of 360° footage. In multi camera rigs, this may be achieved without utilizing information from every camera's lens.

Upgraded camera rigs: 360 Designs MiniEye 4 uses four BlackMagic Micro cinema cameras and the "Dark Corner" rig uses four Sony A7s.

Dynamic range: The varying degrees of brightness that can be captured by a camera or displayed by a playback device. You can think of it as the number of grays that can be represented before areas of the image appear all-black (in the shadows) or all-white (in the highlights).

Parallax: The optical effect where an object's position appears to differ when viewed from different positions, i.e. the left eye vs. the right.

The "Periscope" rig.

This idea grew into a custom camera system created by Radiant Images called the Periscope.

Massive rigs

At the other end of the spectrum, some producers have experimented with elaborate and huge multicamera rigs. 360 Designs makes a rig that ties together 42 Blackmagic Micro Cinema cameras (and 24 microphones). The wizards at SuperSphere created a custom rig with eight RED Dragon cameras to capture the highest possible image quality, and Headcase makes a head-mounted rig featuring 17 Codex action cameras.

These rigs are not likely for everyday use, but it's important to remember that anything is possible, and unique circumstances may require you to consider constructing your own camera rigs to achieve certain results.

Massive rigs: 360 Designs "Eye" rig and the "Headcase" rig.

Chapter 8: Professional cameras

Another class of 360° cameras is designed to provide both ease of use and the highest possible quality. These devices include perfectly synchronized cameras that capture high-resolution images with full customization and a single-button to start and stop recording. Furthermore, the manufacturers try to take the pain out of the stitching process, delivering fully synched and stitched files at the end of the production—ready for editing and output.

The only catch is that all of these cameras are very expensive. These vendors are going after professional producers where cost is less important that quality and ease of use. Also, If you're working in a public environment, these cameras are large enough (and weird-looking enough to be highly conspicuous). This is opposite of showing up with a smartphone or DSLR and stealing a location.

The landscape of professional cameras remains in flux. Two highly regarded cameras (featured in the first edition of this book) the Nokia Ozo, and the Jaunt One, are now both discontinued. Google's Jump (which is a framework that works with multiple cameras) remains a reliable option, as does the Facebook 360 system, though the cameras these systems rely upon cost $50k or more. Meanwhile, Z CAM, Kandao, and Insta 360 all sell professional cameras for 1/2 to 1/3 of those prices, and there are a number of other players including established brands like Panasonic and Samsung that are entering the field. Each of these provide proprietary stitching software, some employing computational stitching, and some using a simpler approach.

Stitching: Combining multiple images/videos into one panoramic image/video (also sometimes refers to a seam in a panoramic image).

DSLR (digital single-lens reflex): A digital camera that uses a mirror to reflect the view coming through the lens onto the camera sensor, which enables the viewfinder to see the exact image the camera will capture (i.e. a professional still camera like the Canon 5D or Nikon D-series).

Stealing a location: Shooting in a location without first obtaining permission and/or the requisite permits.

Jump

Jump is Google's cloud-based computational stitching service. In order to use it, you must shoot with a "Jump-compatible" camera. Footage can be loaded into the Jump Manager software, which uploads the footage to Google's servers and can spit out computational stitched stereoscopic 360° content at up to 8K x 8K, plus it creates a depth map and stitching metadata to aid with compositing and other visual effects. As of now, two companies are offering Jump compatible cameras:

GoPro Odyssey camera

GoPro Odyssey: GoPro introduced the first Jump-compatible camera: the *Odyssey*, which sells for $15,000.

The field of view captured by the Odyssey is limited to a (115° vertical) cylindrical region, and not a true sphere of video. Jump 's stitching service fills the top and bottom with blurred circles based on the surrounding pixels. If you want to capture the top and bottom of the sphere with live video, you need to manually add a couple of additional cameras, or fill in the gaps with still images as described in Chapter 53: Rig removal and nadir patching.

YI HALO camera. Photo credit: Yi Technologies

YI HALO: Yi Technologies' YI HALO camera was built in close collaboration with Google around the Jump framework, and has a number of features that should improve both ease of use and the quality of the end results. For one thing, it includes a 17th camera —pointing upwards, but sunken into the body of the camera so the periphery of its view aligns with the edges of the horizontal cameras to optimize stitching. It also has a companion app to control the camera remotely and monitor the output prior to shooting. Plus it has a comprehensive internal diagnostic system to detect camera errors, battery errors, heat issues, and so forth.

And the kit even comes with a couple extra camera bodies in the event one individual unit fails.

Facebook Surround 360 camera

Facebook Surround 360

The Surround 360 is Facebook's mimic of Google's Jump, using Point Grey cameras instead of GoPros, and with the addition of (mono) up-facing and down-facing cameras.

Facebook claims that its stitching software can export 4K, 6K and even 8K video *per eye*. Additionally, the computational stitching software is open-source, so it will continue to improve.

Other Professional Cameras

Z CAM sells a line of professional 360 cameras, ranging from the *V1 Pro* (stereo) to the *S1 Pro* (mono). Kandao's *Obsidion S* camera offers 4k stereo at up to 120 frames per second , allowing you to capture 360 video in super slow motion. The *Insta360 Pro II* camera is another popular option, offering 8k capture with a special wireless monitoring device that can work at up to 1000' away. All of these offer professional level features such as high-resolution capture through high quality lenses, synchronized shutters and good dynamic range/low-light sensitivity—though each has drawbacks too, from non-intuitive interfaces to cumbersome software with limited control for stitching or live monitoring, modest battery life, and confusing file management. None of these issues are dealbreakers, but no one device seems to have broken away from the pack as the favorite in the professional 360 community.

Samsung 360 Round, Insta360 Titan, Kandao Obsidian S, Z CAM V1 Pro

There are other manufacturers competing with the ones above and by the time you're reading this, there are probably several new ones. In many ways the best camera to use is the one that you, or your DP is already familiar with.

The "Moibus" rig.

Chapter 9: Specialty cameras

There are a number of additional camera types that may be worth considering for very specific situations.

Head-mounted rigs

For creating authentic, first-person, subjective point-of-view (POV) VR footage, a few vendors have developed specialized rigs meant to be worn on a camera operator's head. The idea is that an operator can walk around a scene, and even use her hands to interact with objects, and the viewer will be able to relive that same, very subjective experience.

These rigs are basically identical (in terms of workflow) to the those described in Chapter 7: Multicamera rigs. However, in actual practice, they require a bit more care during shooting. For one thing, you don't want the rig to turn when the wearer turns his head; if that happens, the camera POV may conflict with the viewer's POV. For example, if the rig wearer turned right during the shoot, and at that same moment during playback the viewer looks left, that's a recipe for instant motion sickness.

Also, as explained in the sidebar on camera height, small changes in camera height can have a big impact on a viewer's experience. An average-height camera operator wearing a head-mounted rig (with lenses that sits slightly above her own eyes) might wind up with a point of view taller than most viewers—which can undermine the intended experience.

Drone-mounted rigs

Another popular idea is to attach a 360° camera to a drone. This way, you can fly around a scene and film the entire environment from above. Later, during stitching, the drone can be digitally removed from the image. Since looking up isn't very common (unless something in the story encourages it) and since the sky (or most ceilings) are fairly uniform and uninteresting, it's fairly easy to hide evidence of the drone.

Stitching: Combining multiple images/videos into one panoramic image/video (also sometimes refers to a seam in a panoramic image).

Underwater rigs

Shooting 360° video underwater is surprisingly tricky. Because the background is often very uniform with no straight lines, there's nothing to provide reference when stitching, and the software can easily get confused.

Nausea alert: After you've got the footage stitched, it can still be disorienting for viewers. For example, if the camera is pitched forward slightly, and you're watching while sitting up in a chair, the disconnect may not be visibly obvious, but your inner ears may get triggered that something is askew. Add to this that virtually all underwater footage is handheld (though movement is smoothed by the viscosity of the water) and you may be at risk of nauseating your audience. One simple remedy is to keep the ground or a stationary object visible in the sphere at all times.

Additionally, you've just got the same waterproofing issues that occur with standard cameras, except that remember you've got to hold the camera in some way, and if you're too close to it, it may be difficult to successfully stitch you out of the shot. For best results extend the camera in front of you on a pole by several feet. The Abyss GoPro rig and the VRTUL 1 stereo BlackMagic Micro Cinema camera rig are specifically designed to facilitate this.

Note: Head-mounted, drone-mounted, and underwater are all primarily designed for recording moving shots. If you're considering using any of these, be sure to read Chapter 26: Moving shots.

Volumetric capture devices

There are additional ways of capturing spherical video that I want to include here, even though these cameras and methods are not really available for widespread use yet. Volumetric capture refers to the idea of capturing not just the light coming into a camera lens, but also a map of where objects are within the space in a room. The result is a representation of the volume of a room in digital, three-dimensional space.

RED Cinema's (promised) Facebook-360 compatible volumetric camera.

When so captured, the data can be used to create an experience significantly more immersive than 360° video—though not as fully immersive as fully-computer generated VR, at least not yet. There are several companies working on volumetric solutions, and they're taking very different approaches.

Comprehensive capture: Facebook has announced a partnership with RED Cinema to create a new camera that promises to capture volumetric data simultaneously with 360° video. This camera don't exist in the field yet, so I can't comment about it in detail, but if they achieve what they advertise, this could be a game-changing improvement, and if the technology is available I'd expect to see most of the major 360° camera manufacturers follow suit. But until then, it's merely an exciting possibility.

Inverse 360° capture: Whereas 360° cameras are placed in the center of an environment, looking outward to record in every direction from one spot, these technologies do the opposite. 8i and Uncorporal Systems are two companies who place a subject (such as a person) in the center of a 360° green screen stage and surround her with an array of cameras.

Green screen: A subject shot against a background of a particular shade of green so the background can be removed and replaced in post-production.

The resulting data captures the subject from many different angles, and through interpolation and engineering magic, they construct a virtual hologram. That hologram can then be placed into an environment (created using computer graphics or with photogrammetry).

Photogrammetry: The use of photography to survey and map a location from a variety of angles.

Viewers can then watch the hologrammatic video from any direction, close or far, walking around to different angles, even kneeling down and looking up. The effect is striking and surprisingly engaging. The hologram could even potentially be placed into an AR environment so you could see that recorded person appearing totally realistically right in your living room!

AR (augmented reality): The superimposition of video images onto a user's view of a real-world setting.

Currently 8i and Uncorporal Systems are primarily using their recording systems for proprietary projects, but someone will soon offer this service more widely to independent VR producers.

LIDAR Capture: Another way to capture the volumetric information in a scene is with a LIDAR (Light Detection and Ranging) device. LIDAR is similar to RADAR or SONAR, but it uses laser light instead of radio waves or sound waves. A LIDAR device emits lasers in all directions, and records how the light is reflected back to the device. It doesn't record any photographic information, but you can combine LIDAR data with the output of a 360˚ camera (or even a single, flat video camera) in a game engine to generate a VR experience where the viewer sees a fully photo-realistic scene but can also move around in six degrees of freedom. Hype VR is a production company employing this technology presently.

Six degrees of freedom: The ability to move left-right, up-down, and forward-backward (in addition to being able to rotate around the x, y, and z axes). Provides significantly more immersion than basic 360 video.

Intel's Realsense Depth Camera captures depth data that can be combined with video to create volumetric content.

Chapter 10: Planning for output

It's important to keep your intended delivery method in mind as you're planning for your production. Are you aiming for a casual, on-the-go viewer—someone unlikely to put on headphones, let alone watch while in range of a PC on a desk. Or are you building a deeply immersive experience to be shown exclusively at festivals in a customized watching environment? Or are you aiming for one of several options in between?

If you know that the vast majority of your viewers are likely to be viewing your show in a magic window on a smart phone, you shouldn't waste the tremendous effort and cost of building your show to be watched exclusively in an HMD like the Oculus Quest or VIVE Cosmos.

This decision impacts which camera you should use, how you record audio, how far you place the camera from the subject, how long you should let the camera run, and other techno-aesthetic aspects of your shoot. And of course, there are specific resolution and field of view differences among the different viewing devices that need to be addressed when outputting your final delivery masters during post-production.

The following tables show the basic attributes of several potential target categories. Choose one—or at least choose a primary one and a secondary one.

Magic window

Imagine you're looking at a video image on your smartphone, but when you tilt or rotate the phone in physical space, the screen reveals more of the scene; move the phone to your left and you see what's on your left (in the scene), tilt upwards and

Magic window: A method of viewing 360 content where a rectangular frame acts as a portal to the larger, spherical recording. The viewer can navigate to a different perspective by scrolling (on a computer), or by tilting the viewing device (on a smartphone or tablet).

HMD (head-mounted display): goggles or a headset designed to optimize 360° video viewing.

Resolution: The number of pixels in an image, typically presented as a ratio of the total pixels on x axis to the total pixels on the y axis (i.e. 1920 x 1080 for HD).

Field of view: The angle of space viewable from a given lens position.

Magic window on a smartphone: Tilt or move the phone to see different parts of the environment.

Magic window on a computer: Drag the image within the playback window to see different parts of the environment.

1. While the field of view in a magic window is fixed, some software allows you to zoom in or out on the image, effectively changing the FOV.

Magic window specs	
Breadth of audience:	Very high
Immersiveness:	Very low
Point of access:	Desktop, laptop, tablet, smartphone
Software required:	YouTube, Facebook, Twitter (Periscope), and many, many more
Ease of setup:	Very easy
Additional hardware required:	None
Cost of additional hardware:	n/a
Headphones:	Unlikely
Audio format:	Mono or stereo
Video resolution:	Varies per device
Field of view:	Fixed[1]
Likely cost of content:	Free

you see what's above you (in the scene). It's as if your phone's screen is a portal into this other world. It really does feel a bit like magic the first time you try it, and it's commonly referred to as a "magic window."

The idea of the magic window has expanded to also refer to the similar (but admittedly less magical) experience of looking at a traditional rectangular window on your computer screen, but where you can drag the image with your mouse to pan and tilt the view within the scene.

The magic window is the easiest way to display 360° video. Its primary advantage is that it's ubiquitous: your video can be viewed on any modern computer, smartphone, or tablet and it's easily shared via social media, blogs, and websites. Unfortunately, it's the least immersive way to experience your content—challenging the justification for the added effort and expense of 360° over flat video.

Cardboard

"Cardboard" refers to a smartphone-powered HMD, from the strapless Google original to elaborate plastic mechanisms with built-in earphones. They are entirely "dumb" devices, with no sensors or electronics, so set-up relies on configuring the phone properly—which often means taking the phone in and out of the device several times before you can watch a clip.

Some devices include buttons to perform navigation or to pause and play a video, but many do not, and therefore require an additional Bluetooth controller that adds cost and configuration headaches. All of which dramatically reduces the number of people willing to watch more than one or two examples before leaving the device to collect dust somewhere.

Because these devices work with a wide range of smartphones the quality of the experience is widely variable based not only on the phone's capability, but on its physical condition. (How often do you wipe the smudges and fingerprints from your screen?)

Cardboard viewer specs:	
Breadth of audience:	Moderate
Immersiveness:	Low
Point of access:	Smartphone
Software required:	YouTube, Facebook, and others
Ease of setup:	Moderate (see above)
Additional hardware required:	"Dumb" HMD
Cost of additional hardware:	$20–$50
Headphones:	Unlikely
Audio format:	Mono or stereo, spatialized
Video resolution:	Varies per device
Field of view:	80° – 90°
Likely cost of content:	Free

A selection of cardboard viewers.

"Smart" mobile headsets

HMDs like the GearVR and Daydream View are not much more expensive than their dumb cardboard brethren, but they provide a significant jump in immersiveness. They still rely on your smartphone to do the work of playing the video back, but the headsets include motion sensors that communicate with the software in the phone.

Smart mobile viewers: Samsung Gear VR and Daydream View HMDs.

Smart mobile headset specs

Breadth of audience:	Low
Immersiveness:	High
Point of access:	Specific smartphone
Software required:	Dedicated software
Ease of setup:	Easy
Additional hardware required:	Samsung Gear VR or Daydream View
Cost of additional hardware:	$100
Headphones:	More likely
Audio format:	Spatialized
Video resolution:	4096 x 2048
Field of view:	90° – 100°
Playback frame rate:	30 or 60 fps
Likely cost of content:	Free

The manufacturers limit their use to specific phone models that are tested to ensure a satisfying response. Also, users who have bothered to step up from the cardboard style HMD are usually more thoughtful about their viewing habits and are much more likely to use headphones, which dramatically improves the overall experience.

PlayStation VR

Harnessing the power of a late-model Sony PlayStation, Sony's HMD provides a quality of experience that is a dramatic jump over the smartphone-based viewers. It costs a lot more, and so the installed base remains relatively small. Still, it's a very promising market for VR, though it remains to be seen whether most users will use it exclusively for gaming, or will also embrace other content including the 360° video you're likely producing.

PlayStation VR headset.

Smart mobile headset specs

PlayStation VR specs	
Breadth of audience:	Low
Immersiveness:	High
Point of access:	Sony PlayStation 4
Software required:	Dedicated software
Ease of setup:	Easy
Additional hardware required:	PlayStation VR
Cost of additional hardware:	$300
Headphones:	Required
Audio format:	Spatialized
Video resolution:	4096 x 2048
Field of view:	90° – 100°
Playback frame rate:	120 fps
Likely cost of content:	~$50

Standalone HMD

In 2018 a new type of HMD arrived with built-in displays and the graphics processors to run them. They are not as powerful or robust as the HMDs that are paired with a full-fledged PC (described on the next page) but these standalone HMDs offer a significant improvement in user experience from those that require you insert your cell phone.

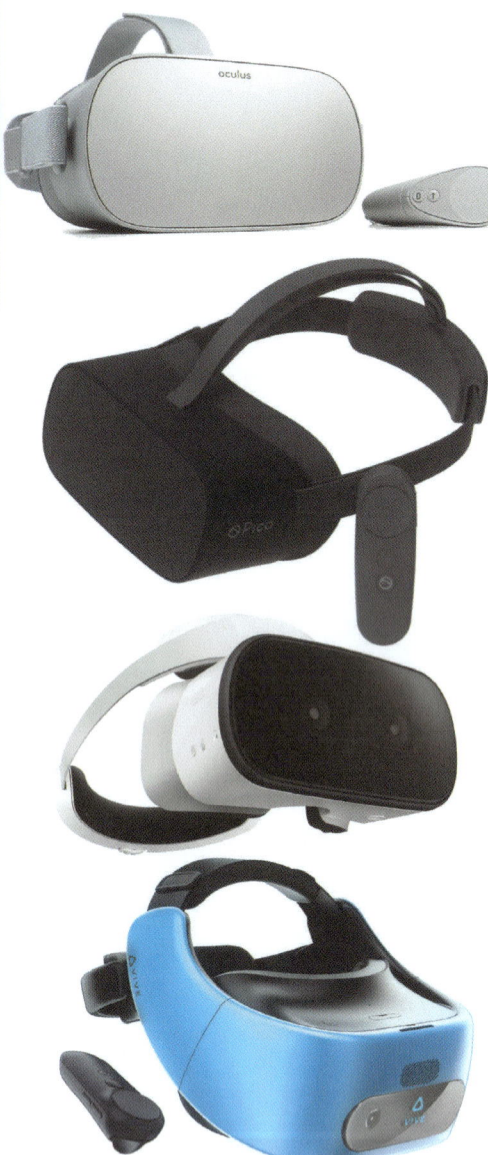

These devices are comparable in quality and usability as the Google Daydream View and the Samsung Gear VR, however they don't require you to insert your phone, which means you don't have to constantly refocus and re-setup the playback system every time you want to use them. You just put them on and "go." (Hence the name for the leading brand, Oculus Go.)

These devices lack the sophisticated tracking and hand-controllers that you find on the more expensive, computer-driven HMDs, but those features aren't actually necessary for watching 360° video, so they may be quite suitable for your needs.

Standalone HMD specs:	
Breadth of audience:	Low
Immersiveness:	Very high
Point of access:	Direct
Software required:	Daydream/Oculus Home
Ease of setup:	Easy
Additional hardware required:	None
Cost of hardware:	$200 – $350
Headphones:	Required/Built-in
Audio format:	Spatialized
Video resolution:	1280 x 1440
Field of view:	95° – 110°
Playback frame rate:	60-75 fps
Likely cost of content:	~$15

Standalone HMDs (from top to bottom):
Oculus Go, Pico G2, Lenovo Mirage Solo, VIVE Focus,

Computer-driven HMD
The most advanced HMDs in the market are laden with multiple motion sensors to track your every tilt, lean, and nod, and the latest generation even do that without external hardware. They come with robust, trackable hand controllers, and they boast

high video quality in terms of resolution, color fidelity, frame rate, and field of view—all the things required to ensure a highly immersive experience.

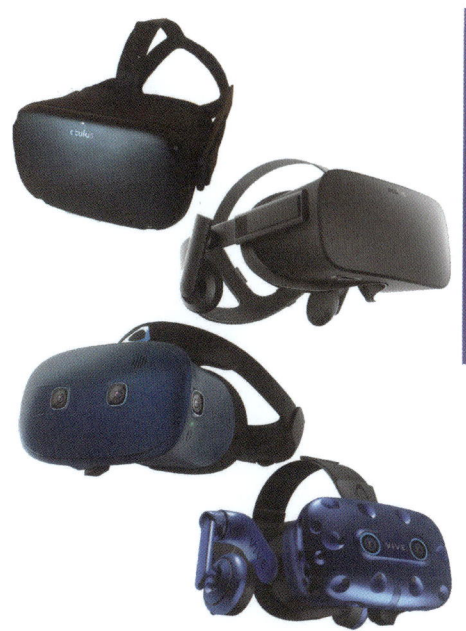

Unfortunately, in order to deliver all this, the devices must be connected (either wirelessly or via a cable) to a high-end graphics card inside a PC. This limits where the devices can be used, though at least in the latest generation headsets there is no cumbersome cable tethering you to the computer!

Computer-driven HMD specs:

Breadth of audience:	Very low
Immersiveness:	Very high
Point of access:	High-end PC
Software required:	SteamVR, Oculus Home
Ease of setup:	Easy
Additional hardware required:	PC with robust graphics card.
Cost of additional hardware:	$400 – $1500
Headphones:	Required/built-in
Audio format:	Spatialized
Video resolution:	4096 x 1080 and higher
Field of view:	110° – 210°
Playback frame rate:	90 - 120 fps
Likely cost of content:	~$15

From top to bottom: Oculus Quest, Oculus Rift, HTC Cosmos, HTC VIVE Pro Eye

While Oculus and HTC have the most popular devices in this category with good specs and the most access to content, they are not the only options StarVR and Pimax are two startup HMD developers selling 5k and 8k resolution HMDs which are far more powerful than HTC or Oculus.

Also, Microsoft has created its own mixed reality version of Windows that has enabled many popular PC manufacturers (Samsung, Dell,

Top: StarVR 8k HMD
Bottom: Pimax 8k HMD

Windows Mixed Reality headsets

Acer, Asus, HP, and others) to build VR-capable hardware without having to create their own software to drive it.

By following this model that is so similar to traditional PC development they may be able to commoditize the VR headset market, lowering prices and improving quality at the same time. Alternatively Valve's SteamVR drives the HTC VIVE products, Pimax's HMDs and can be used on others. There are also open source VR operating systems (OSVR, OpenXR, etc.) that are vying for hardware manufacturer's support. The next few years will likely see the market consolidate as it matures.

> **Note:** While many of these HMDs can track your movement in six different dimensions (up-down, side to side, and back and forth), most 360° video can't take advantage of all of that data. Because your camera is at a fixed point in space when shooting, viewers can only turn their head to see different parts of the image.

Still, these are the most pleasant viewing options currently available, offering the largest field of view. And perhaps because these devices are more expensive and delicate, viewers are that much more likely to watch content enthusiastically, tolerating longer durations and more complex game-like stories and structures.

Specialty hardware

Some creators have been working with customized viewing displays or environments to enable an even greater level of immersiveness and control over the audience's entire experience. One obvious example of this is site-specific content like the New Revolution rollercoaster at the Magic Mountain amusement park: Each rider on the coaster dons a VR headset that plays a video coordinated to take advantage of the coaster's movement and provide the experience of flying through a city.

In the narrative realm, an example of this is the film *Giant*, which requires not just an HTC VIVE headset, but also a special vibrating chair that's activated at certain points during the film to complement the visual and audio data pouring in through the HMD. In *Birdly*, your body is physically suspended in a winged contraption, complete with flappable wings and a fan blowing air on you while an HMD transports you into the body of a pigeon flying around New York City.

These custom-made viewing environments limit your potential audience to film festivals, museums, and other dedicated gatherings. Still, they afford a level of immersion that potentially exceeds any other method. And as VR arcades, theaters, and dedicated viewing rooms become more common, there may be new opportunities as yet unexplored.

Headset-less VR

While this isn't yet widespread, and it's significantly more expensive to deploy than the other methods discussed, it remains an interesting technology to keep in mind for certain types of projects.

There are a number of systems designed to display 360° video on the walls of a room, so multiple viewers can experience the scene without requiring headsets at all. Barco Escape is a system that projects video onto all the walls of a rectangular theater. And there are a number of companies projecting 360° video onto the inside of a dome, where a group of users can share the immersive VR experience without any need for individual hardware.

Part II: Production

At first glance, a spherical video production may appear similar to a traditional video shoot. However, as you examine the nuances and details of the work required, you'll begin to see that nearly every aspect of your production must be adjusted or adapted to accommodate the special requirements of working in this new medium. From crew functions to camera positions to directing actors to monitoring the video feed, there are technical, aesthetic, and organizational considerations to make. This section catalogs the production workflow and provides tips and guidelines to help ease your transition to shooting 360° video.

Chapter 11: Shooting 360° video

Some creators argue that because the audience *can* look in any direction, the VR filmmaker is obliged to stage action "in the round," that is, not just directly in front of the viewer but all around her. In fact, some VR creators reward viewers for rubbernecking, providing surprises or extra bits of content that are only discoverable if you fully explore the space.

This approach can be used to incorporate background or "side-ground" B stories that might otherwise be cut from a traditional narrative—action that adds to the story if you catch it, but isn't crucial to the main narrative.

That doesn't mean that you should you fill the screen with swarming activity, like a Hieronymus Bosch painting or a Richard Scarry drawing. Too much unfocused action happening everywhere at once can be distracting and annoying. If your scene encourages viewers to gape in all directions, they're likely to find your video a literal pain in the neck.

It's better to give viewers a clear place to look within the sphere. That point of focus can move around within the 360° space, but shouldn't be too "twisty." Forcing your audience to frequently shift focus is uncomfortable, unnerving, and guaranteed to pull them out of the experience. (This is discussed in more detail in Chapter 15: Guiding the viewer's focus.)

Personally, I believe that the sense of immersion in 360° video derives mostly from having your peripheral vision filled while watching the main action. Add a spatialized sound mix and you'll have generated an experience dramatically more engaging than could ever be possible with flat video.

Spatialized sound mix: A soundscape where audio is positioned from specific locations in space around the listener.

In other words, spherical storytelling is a weapon in your communications arsenal but one that should be used sparingly.

Tip: Consider always giving your viewers an establishing beat at the beginning of each scene so they can get a sense of where they are before the action begins in earnest.

Sidebar: participant vs. ghost

One important creative decision you need to make for your 360° project: Will your onscreen talent "break the fourth wall" and directly address the camera? It's long been common practice in traditional video to avoid acknowledging the camera. But the notion is still up for grabs in the 360° world.

Watching immersive 360° video, viewers feel as if they're "in" the same space with the people on the screen. So it may seem odd if the onscreen characters *don't* acknowledge viewer presence. This makes sense: In the real world, when someone makes direct eye contact with you, your body responds involuntarily. The same thing happens when watching a 360° video, and can result in a more engaged, immersive viewer experience.

On the other hand, acknowledging the viewer can also have distancing effect. When characters directly address the audience, and the audience can't respond or react in any natural way, the artifice of the whole experience in emphasized.

To break the fourth wall or not: different creators have different opinions on which approach is better.

A related issue: Should your 360° video "incorporate" a stand-in body for the viewer? In other words, if your viewer looks down and doesn't see a physical person where her torso or legs ought to be, will the sense of personal presence in a scene be diminished? Or is the converse the more distracting choice? If your viewer looks down and *does* see a body, but it's a body different than expected (she sees a he, for example), isn't that even more unnerving than having no body at all? Again, creator opinions differ.

Nausea alert: If you do attempt to put a simulated body under the camera (either by having an operator wear a head-mounted rig or by adding a body during post-production), take great care to get the distance and angle right. If the body seems too far away or at the wrong angle, you can create an effect where the viewer's neck feels too long or is set too far back on her shoulders. Unfortunately, humans are enormously sensitive to small errors in this area, and getting it wrong can cause more than just mild disorientation in your audience.

Whether or not to break the fourth wall all comes down to your intent as a filmmaker: If your goal is to encourage viewers to experience a sense of presence in a scene, looking around, lingering here or there while action unspools around them, then it may make sense to have onscreen people ignore the camera. In this way, the viewer becomes a voyeur or "ghost" who can see everyone else, but can't be seen herself.

If your goal is to create a scenario where the viewer is more actively engaged in the story as a participant, then it may make sense to have the people onscreen (interview subjects, actors, and so on) look directly into the camera lens. There are some interesting projects that have pushed the boundaries of this technique. For example, pieces where some characters in the room can see you, but other characters can't. Or scenarios where at first people ignoring you, but later in the story suddenly take notice.

One early VR short called *Defrost* tells its story from the point of view of a woman who's just awakened after 30 years in a cryogenic freeze. When watching it, you can look down and see "your body" sitting in a wheelchair, and the fact that you can't speak (even as other characters look at, and talk to you) is justified in the story as a side effect of the de-freezing process.

G&E (grip and electric): The production departments on set responsible for the operation of grip and lighting equipment. They work under the director of photography.

Coverage: Multiple shots from multiple angles to capture the events in a scene (i.e. master shot, medium shots, close-ups, inserts, etc.).

Chapter 12: Running the set

The management of any film or video shoot involves coordinating the work from disparate departments (camera, sound, G&E, set design, and so on) so the overall production can get through the schedule smoothly and efficiently. Traditionally, this job falls to the assistant director (AD), and bigger shoots rely on an entire *set operations* department consisting of multiple ADs. But even on the smallest shoot, having a dedicated AD focused on keeping the day's schedule running on time frees the director to focus on the creative aspects of the job—namely, ensuring that what's recorded on camera achieves the intended goals.

A 360° shoot is no different in concept, but in execution, the details of the AD's job do vary somewhat. 360° video requires more time to be spent preparing to shoot and less time actually rolling the camera. Although a traditional AD may spend a lot of time worrying about coverage, on a 360° set she's likely to focus more on honing rehearsals so that everyone knows their roles cold when it's time to roll. This includes ensuring that actors know their lines and marks, but also means the AD will be involved in rehearsing lighting or sound cues, camera movement, or any other dynamic elements in the scene—just like a stage manager in a theater production.

Also, because everyone needs to run and hide before the camera starts rolling (or else be caught by the all-seeing spherical lens), the AD must work more like a theater stage manager, calling the cues for sound, lighting, and actors live from a hidden position.

Here are some guidelines for running a successful set on a 360° shoot:

Work methodically

Film sets can be overwhelmingly chaotic if they're not managed well, and good management requires sticking to a clear, consistent plan. One of the best plans is to follow the basic four-step process of *block, light, rehearse, shoot*—or *BLRS* for short.

Begin by walking through the scene without any equipment on set. Have the director observe the scene as it plays out and block it to work in the actual space *before* determining where the camera should best be placed. Then, based on the blocking, place the camera, set up any microphones, and add any lights or other needed equipment. Then, when all the equipment is ready, rehearse the scene and run it over and over again until everyone involved has every aspect perfectly coordinated. Then (and only then), turn on the cameras and roll the scene.

Block: Position and choreograph actor movements in a scene.

After the scene is successfully shot, repeat the process for each subsequent scene.

Review the stitch

As described in more detail in Chapter 23: Monitoring on set, you may need to do some test shots to ensure that you don't have critical action occurring on or crossing over a stitch line.

Stitch line: The seam in a 360 video where footage from one camera has been combined with another.

This means injecting an additional step after rehearsals and before shooting: Record one of the rehearsals, then quick stitch the footage and watch it. If you discover that some of your action will cause stitching problems, you'll need to adjust the blocking and/or camera position and go through the process again.

Quick stitch: A rapid, albeit potentially imperfect, stitch of 360° footage. In multi camera rigs, this may be achieved without utilizing information from every camera's lens.

Depending on the type of camera you're using, this process can be somewhat time-consuming, and it may require multiple iterations before you're actually ready to shoot.

Use a slate

Any serious 360° production will likely use double-system audio; recording sound to one or more secondary devices that will later need to be properly synchronized with the picture during post. While there are many ways to automate the syncing process, it's always a good idea to use an old-fashioned clapper—audible by all sound recording devices and visible by at least one of the cameras. That way you can always sync manually if necessary.

Slate: A card or device positioned in front of the camera at the beginning of each shot to document all relevant shot information for easy identification during post. Usually operated by the 2nd AC, who reads the relevant information aloud and then activates the clapper bar to provide a synchronization point for audio and video files.

Furthermore, using a slate forces you to stop and identify every shot before you begin rolling, giving it a name and take number. This can help tremendously if there are ever any media management issues (as described in Chapter 32: Ingesting footage). In fact, if there's any way to move the slate around and hold it for a few seconds in front of each of the different camera lenses on your 360° rig, that will ensure that the name and number will be visible in the footage from every lens. Then you'll be able to identify any given camera-original file in the event your footage ever got mixed up or mislabeled.

> **Note:** There's are specific instructions on using a slate in Chapter 27: Recording audio for 360˚.

Use walkie-talkies

It's very common for crew on film sets to rely on two-way radios (aka walkie-talkies) for inter-department communications. On a 360° set, walkies are indispensable, even for very simple productions. It's the best way to effectively communicate quickly (and without yelling) when the crew is spread out and hiding from the camera.

Slow your roll

You'll need to allot extra time after the camera and sound recorders are turned on to allow the crew to run and hide before any action can safely begin. If you don't factor in "scatter time" during rehearsals, you may wind up spoiling the first few takes as cast and crew adjust to this change in timing of the scene.

Sidebar: Where's the crew?

One of the tricky aspects of shooting in 360° is that when the camera starts rolling, all of your crew and all of your equipment must be hidden. Consider this fact when choosing your locations. Make sure there's a separate room or area where the crew can hide and the equipment can be stashed. This is also a reason to keep your crew size as small as possible!

You also need to consider what this means when shooting in real-world or public locations. For a shot on tourist-mobbed Hollywood Boulevard, we had to set up the camera and walk away from it, but we needed a way to ensure that no one bumped into it and ruined the shot (not to mention, protecting against someone walking away with it). So, our DP bought an ice cream cone, donned her sunglasses, and stood nearby, pretending to be a tourist herself. Hiding your crew among extras in a scene can work in some settings, but make sure that every shot doesn't have that same annoying extra who always seems a little too close to the camera.

Close-up (CU): A limited view that narrows in on a key feature of a subject: an actors face, a smoking gun on the floor, etc.

Wide-shot (WS): A expansive view that takes in the entirety of a scene or location.

2-shot: A camera angle that encompasses two people in a scene.

Chapter 13: Directing 360° video

In many ways, directing 360° video is more like theater directing than film directing. Film directing requires you to deconstruct a scene into many fragments, with each shot focused on a particular element of the story. A close-up reveals nuances of character—who the story is about. A wide-shot gives a sense of the location—where the story takes place. 2-shots define relationships between characters, and so on.

Focus on the big picture

In theater directing, you must consider the piece much more as a whole. Sure, the audience can be guided to pay attention to one part of the stage at a time, and you can highlight specific elements. But ultimately the whole stage exists simultaneously. The story progresses in real time, without the interference of an editor choosing which shots to serve up in a predetermined order.

Rehearse and run

And as in theater, you must prepare all elements in rehearsals so that the show can be run straight through (at least scene by scene), rather than in the piecemeal fashion of traditional cinema, where individual moments are run and re-run until the perfect version is captured on film. Theater direction also requires more flexibility and spontaneity in the moment of production. And 360° video is much the same.

See it from afar

Another important similarity between 360° video and theater: stories that rely on the subtlety of human facial expression don't really play. The combination of limited camera positions (discussed more in Chapter 20: Placing the camera) and low resolution during playback (at least with current technology) means that you must forgo one of the most effective devices in the film-maker's toolkit for creating empathy and connection between your viewer and the character onscreen: the close-up.

Get interactive

On the other hand, the theater analog only goes so far. Though you can't cut to a close-up the way you do in film, your audience is not sitting twenty (or two hundred) feet away from the stage in neat rows. They're right there in the midst of the action. Perhaps the better comparison is to immersive theater (sometimes called interactive theater).

Experimental works like *66 Minutes in Damascus* or *Sleep No More* put the theater audience amid the actors playing roles. The result is a very different experience from that of traditional shows; interactive theater makes the audience participants in the action, rather than merely observers. In *66 Minutes* the audience takes on the role of hostages held by corrupt Syrian militants. The actors prod and interrogate audience members, forcing them to stand against a wall with hands up, simulating the experience of being held against your will. In *Sleep No More*, the audience is led into a sprawling multi-floor hotel, where they can explore the rooms on their own—going up and down stairs, opening trunks and bookcases and encountering lurid and sometimes unsettling scenes featuring the murderous characters from Macbeth.

Not only do these productions break the "fourth wall" that traditionally separates the audience from the cast, but each audience member has a different experience—choosing on their own which aspects of the "show" to observe. This is similar to the experience of watching a (well-made) 360° video.

Direct for different perspectives

When directing a piece in 360° video, you need to keep in mind that different viewers will take in different aspects of the scene, but that ultimately everyone should be able to take away something meaningful and memorable. This might mean rehearsing the space one quadrant at a time, so that each area works on its own. You might envision different possible threads of story, and ensure that each thread is coherent by itself but also compatible and complementary with the other threads.

It's a lot to keep track of, but if done well, orchestrating multiple perspectives can be far more exciting and effective than anything possible in traditional video. And unlike a show such as *Sleep No More*, a 360° viewer can stop and start the narrative, or watch it over and over again, witnessing different elements each time.

Abandon your expectations

Because of this multiplexing potential, many of the ways we think about traditional storytelling go out the window. This is one of the reasons I think traditional filmmakers may be at a disadvantage when it comes to embracing this new medium. You need to approach your piece with the understanding that each viewer can effectively *tell* the story as they watch, by choosing which elements to pay attention to. Rather than focusing on telling a linear narrative, it may be better to think of 360° storytelling as world building: Creating a rich, realistic environment where a viewer following their own interests will still achieve a meaningful and worthwhile experience.

Chapter 14: Working with the medium

360° video introduces both challenges and opportunities that a director must account for throughout the production process. Ignoring these things and just treating the 360° camera like a fancy traditional camera can yield distracting visual errors that are nearly impossible to eliminate. Worse, discounting the ways in which 360° is different than flat cinema means forfeiting the transformative promise of the medium.

Mind the stitch lines

As much as you'd like to think your job is primarily creative, 360° video introduces a technical obstacle that the director must account for at every stage of the project: those pesky stitch lines. Do whatever you can to avoid having critical action sit on, or cross over a stitch line during your scene. The closer to the camera, the more noticeable stitching errors are, so if you need an actor to cross a stitch line, do your best to have it occur farther away from the camera, as swiftly as possible, and ideally not while they're in the middle of an important line.

In this image, the subject is directly on a stitch line. While you may be able to clean it up, it would be far easier to work with if the camera had simply been rotated slightly.

In many scenes, it's impossible to avoid having some action cross the stitch lines, especially for non-fiction work where you can't necessarily tell people (or animals) where to stand. Still, if the main point of focus for your scene is straddling that boundary between cameras, it's going to be terribly distracting to your viewers. Try to use the tools in Chapter 15: Guiding the viewer's focus to keep your audience looking away from those stitch lines during moments when someone has to cross over from one camera view to another.

And, remember (as mentioned in several other chapters), if at all possible, watch a quick-stitched test shot or two before you commit to your scene to observe where the action is falling in relation to those stitch lines, and adjust the choreography or the camera position as needed.

Use the rear as a "trick shot"

Most scenes do have a primary point of focus, but it's important that you're considering what's happening throughout the rest of the sphere too. This needs to be handled deftly (you don't want to overdo it as described in Sidebar: Managing your 'spin budget'), but it does provide a powerful storytelling tool that's simply not present in flat cinema.

How you use that space (behind, or above, or below the viewer) is up to you, but I recommend thinking of it as a type of "trick shot"—like a rack-focus or a zolly shot in traditional filmmaking—something that can be uniquely effective when used judiciously for a key moment (like when the murderer suddenly appears behind you and whispers in your ear) but beware that the effect will quickly grow tiresome if overused.

Rack-focus: A shot where the camera focus is shifted during the scene (while the camera is rolling) to shift attention to a different subject or track a subject as it moves.

Zolly: A shot where the lens is zoomed (focal length is changed) at the same time as the camera is physically moved (dollied) creating an optical effect where the background appears to shift around the subject.

Chapter 14: Working with the medium

Reward disruption

On the other hand, it's also important to have enough going on in areas other than directly in front of the viewer to warrant shooting in 360° in the first place. You want your environment rich enough that there's some encouragement for your audience to explore. Your show will be that much more compelling (and warrant repeated viewings) if there are rewards for viewers who are adventurous enough to look beyond the most obvious places.

You could include additional non-critical story elements occurring away from the main action and that complement the main focus. You could include cute or clever "easter eggs" hidden somewhere in the frame that reveal something about you the creator or about how the video was made. You could even include secret hot-spots that take the viewer on a whole new journey that they might have never seen if they weren't poking around.

Hot-spots: An active, or interactive area of the frame.

Sidebar: Managing your 'spin budget'

Just because spherical video allows you to fill a location with action and activity in every direction doesn't mean you should always do so. Use the periphery of your scene thoughtfully and sparingly.

Making your viewer spin around and look behind her to see an important detail in a scene can be effective if it happens once, or for a specific and deliberate reason. However, if you do it too often, it quickly becomes tiring and annoying. I call that being too "twisty" because I feel like I'm constantly twisting my neck around. Even if I'm sitting in a swiveling office chair (so I don't have to hurt my neck), the experience can be disorienting and ultimately disengaging.

Similarly, placing the camera in the middle of a scene full of action encourages the viewer to frantically swing her head around trying to catch all the various points of interest. Not only can this be physically uncomfortable, it can also leave her feeling like she's missing out on important details.

Making your scenes complex, engaging, and filled with enough activity to keep your viewers' attention is a good idea. But if you go too far, you'll lose them and they'll take off the goggles feeling overwhelmed at best, or angry (or nauseated) at worst.

In real life, we don't swing our heads more than 5–10 degrees very often. Forcing viewers to do so in a VR experience doesn't improve presence and immersion; on the contrary, it reminds your audience that they're in a simulated experience, not a real one.

Chapter 15: Guiding the viewer's focus

One of the most critical aspects of your job creating a 360° experience is deciding how to guide the viewer's point of focus. Where in the sphere should the viewer look? Some creators reject the idea that the filmmaker should impose any directorial agenda, preferring that viewers direct their own journey. This, they argue, allows each audience member to create a unique and personalized viewing experience.

But I would argue that for most pieces, you as creator have something you're trying to communicate, and it's your job to convey that something, whatever it is—an experience, a sensation, a theme, a message, or something else. To do that, you've got to be able to lead your viewers through the piece somehow.

Traditional filmmakers employ myriad tricks and techniques to "direct" attention to what they want the audience to see. (There's a reason the person in charge is called the *director*.) Camera position, focal length, focus, movement, composition, editing, sound (and many other elements) all combine to deftly guide audiences through a story, often in ways so subtle and organic, viewers don't feel led at all.

Focal length: A lens property; i.e. wide-angle or telephoto; different length lens lengths frame the subject differently, creating a different experience of a scene for the viewer.

Composition: The layout and relative position of the objects within a shot.

As you've probably realized by now, most of these techniques are not tenable in 360° video. For example, in VR video, you can't cut to a sudden close-up of a time bomb ticking under the dinner table—at least not without jarring your viewers out of the experience. But that doesn't mean there aren't powerful and effective mechanisms you can use to help lead your viewers through your piece.

Just remember: In traditional film as well as in 360° video, no audience appreciates a heavy-handed director telling them where to look. It's always better to provide subtle cues that encourage viewers to pay attention to certain things, in a way where they feel like they're doing it of their own volition. Let them believe that they are exploring the space entirely randomly, following their own intuition, and that they just happened to have come upon the important details at just the right time.

When it comes to subtly guiding your viewers to these hot spots, here are some tools you can use:

Spatialized sound cues

Perhaps the most organic way to encourage someone to look at something is through sound. If you hear a door open behind you, you're likely to turn around to see who came in. If you hear a dog barking as it runs rightward, you'll probably turn to the right to follow its movement. And if someone is speaking, you're likely to look at their face. In 360° video, you can position sound in specific places within your sphere to encourage viewers to look toward areas where critical plot elements are unfolding. See Chapter 51: Spatial placement for more details on how to do this.

Spatialized: A soundscape where audio is positioned from specific locations in space around the listener.

Naturally, this tool has its limitations; spatialized sound cues only work on viewers who are wearing headphones. Plus, having sound elements occur in different locations simultaneously will merely confuse your viewers. And even you don't overlap your spatial sound cues, having too many such triggering cues over the course of the project will likely overload your viewer.

Eyeline

One of the most effective tools used by traditional filmmakers works extremely well in 360° video, too. It turns out when someone onscreen turns their head, or looks intently at something offscreen, you feel pretty compelled to see what they're looking at. The effect is amplified when the onscreen subject also displays a reaction to what they're seeing: horror, humor, confusion, lust—whatever it is that makes sense for that moment. The vast majority of viewers will be unable to resist looking to understand what caused the reaction.

With traditional film, the viewer is stuck captive, wondering what the onscreen subject is looking at, until the editor cuts to reveal it. But in 360°, the viewer can turn her head on her own volition. This can really enhance the sense of presence and agency within a scene, and you get the bonus of tricking your viewer into looking where you want them to without them realizing that you guided them there.

Lighting cues

In many ways, 360° video is similar to theater. In theater, the audience can see the entire stage all the time, but you can lead their gaze to one or another section of the set with the lighting board. 360° video affords a similar technique.

For example, imagine a scene that opens in an apartment at night. Moonlight shines through a window, illuminating a wrapped gift on a table. Because the gift is the only object on the table, all eyes will be on the package. Then, a door opens, and light streams in from the hallway, silhouetting two figures as they enter the doorway. Most viewers will now turn their attention away from the wrapped gift and look toward the doorway. As the couple stumble into the room and cross (away from the package) towards the kitchen, viewers will follow their progress. The package is still visible in the room, but few viewers will still be looking at it. Instead, they'll focus on the kitchen, where the couple, having turned on a light, begin to kiss.

But now a lamp flicks on near the wrapped package; most viewers will turn to see the source of the light and only then notice the woman who has been sitting in the shadows beside the gift the whole time, waiting for her partner to arrive home.

Live lighting cues like this are an effective way to direct audience attention in 360° video. But constant lighting (or even color correction that adds or removes certain shadows) can also guide viewer attention toward (or away from) parts of the scene.

Camera position

The physical placement of the camera can also serve to guide the viewer's focus. For example, if you put the camera in a corner or against a wall, you effectively force the viewer to ignore a significant portion of the 360° space. Or, if you position the camera near a post or a table, you can deliberately obscure certain objects or elements that might otherwise distract your viewer from your intended subject. We'll cover these techniques in more detail in Chapter 20: Placing the camera.

Composition and depth

The arrangement of elements in your scene can help viewers make sense of the environment, and help you direct their focus. For example, you can:

Incorporate classic architectural elements such as diagonal lines (like the edges of a room as you peer into it) to lead a viewer's eye toward important objects in the scene.

Diagonal lines (highlighted in red) draw your eyes towards the back of the room.

Use doorways, windows, a car's windshield, or other structural elements in your environment to create a "frame-within-the-frame" to give a sense of the boundaries of the principal action.

The rectangular opening (highlighted in red) draws your attention to part of the sphere.

Take advantage of depth, placing important elements close to the camera so that they appear much larger in the sphere, or using layers of objects at different depths to create a complex and dynamic set that begs viewers to explore it.

Objects at different distances from the camera invite the viewer to explore the scene.

Add a dash of bright color to an otherwise monochromatic scene to attract viewer eyes to an area of interest.

A burst of color draws the viewer's eye to that part of the sphere.

Chapter 15: Guiding the viewer's point of focus

Position people and objects in the scene

If the people or subjects in a scene move around within the space, most viewers will follow their movement, even if it requires turning their head at times.

You can even use one subject's movement to lead to another subject, "handing off" the point of focus from one place in the scene to another. For example, imagine a scene in a suburban backyard. There's a flock of noisy parrots roosting in a tree, leading most viewers to look at the tree. Then, the flock takes to the air and heads across the yard, passing a bear that is climbing over the fence and into the yard. Viewers will follow the movement of the birds until the more surprising or compelling subject of the bear is introduced. At that point most viewers will stop following the birds and follow the bear instead, even if it's moving in the opposite direction.

Theater directors have long understood the power of blocking: Who's in the foreground? Who's is in the background? What's the power dynamic as they interact? Is one stalking the other? Are they coming together on equal footing? The power and importance of how and where your subjects move in the scene is critical to successfully telling a story in VR. We'll cover this subject in more detail in Chapter 16: Blocking and choreography.

Onscreen graphics or arrows

Another way to guide where your viewers look is to explicitly tell them via text, graphics, or arrows on the screen. This is less likely to be appropriate in a dramatic narrative piece; but for instructional videos, sports videos, and nonfiction videos of all types, there's little harm in a little bit of overt communication.

While it might disrupt a deeply immersive narrative piece, many projects can take advantage of graphics added directly to the video.

All of the techniques described above can help you direct your viewer's attention in the 360° frame. Just don't overdo it. Try to resist the desire to hold the viewer's hand too tightly. The beauty of the medium is the freedom your audience has to explore a space. Be sure to give them the flexibility to experience that sense of discovery.

Chapter 16: Blocking and choreography

In traditional filmmaking, the director's standard toolkit includes swappable lenses, camera angles, and coverage. Unfortunately, those methods are simply not available to the VR filmmaker. To control a scene and communicate a story sequentially in 360° video, you'll need to reach for other tools and techniques. Chief among those tools are blocking and choreography.

Because takes are typically longer in VR video than in flat video, you have an opportunity to guide your audience through a space slowly and organically. You can use sound, lighting cues, and people moving around the room (or entering and exiting) to encourage viewers to examine the location fully over the course of a scene.

Using these same methods, you can also organically control the emotional arc of a scene. For example, have your subject move closer to the camera for more intimate or internal moments, and then have her move farther away for events that are more external and physical. If this feels at all familiar, it's because this is one of the techniques employed in theater; bring your actor downstage for an intimate soliloquy, or upstage for group scenes.

Experienced dramaturges can explain how entering stage-left conveys different meaning than entering stage-right, and so on. You need to begin to look at the space of your set as a stage, and then decide how to choreograph your subjects' movements through it (and/or your camera movements through it). The goal is to keep your viewers engaged and following your story, and to prevent them from getting confused or missing important actions.

Coverage: Multiple shots from multiple angles to capture the events in a scene (i.e. master shot, medium shots, close-ups, inserts, etc.).

Blocking: The positions and movement of actors in a scene.

Choreography: Prescribing movement for actions that require precise execution, such as dance or combat

Takes: Individual instances of a shot; a take = each time the camera is started and stopped.

Downstage: Closer to the audience/camera.

Upstage: Further away from the audience/camera.

This work is just as critical for nonfiction/documentary-style projects as it is for fiction/narrative ones. No matter what your subject, you need to think about where to place your camera and how to manage movement within the scene to convey clearly the details and nuances of that subject.

Wide shots: A expansive view that takes in the entirety of a scene or location.

Close-ups: A limited view that narrows in on a key feature of a subject: an actors face, a smoking gun on the floor, etc.

I've long taught a shooting and editing technique based on the fundamental questions of *who, what, where, when, why,* and *how.* I describe how different specific shot types routinely answer each of those questions (for example, wide shots answer "where," close-ups of hands answer "how," and so on). I believe that if you can include the right mix of each of those shots in a given scene, you'll effectively communicate the intent of the scene. If you leave one of those elements out, you risk disengaging your viewer—like the way an action sequence with too few close-ups can feel boring because you aren't engaged with the character.

Medium shots: A view sized from an actor's waist up to the top of her head.

In 360° video, you need to answer all of those questions—*who, what, where, when, why,* and *how*—within a single, spherical shot. By choreographing the action to flow and move throughout the space. There should be moments of close-up to give a sense of "who" the protagonist is; medium shots to answer "what" the scene is about, and so on. If you leave out certain elements, you risk your viewer not fully understanding the scene.

Here are some important "stage management" tips to help you succeed:

Keep critical action away from stitch lines
This is especially important when the action is close to the camera. If there's a clear main subject in your scene, do your best to frame that subject so that it (or he or she, if the subject is a person) appears entirely within one camera view.

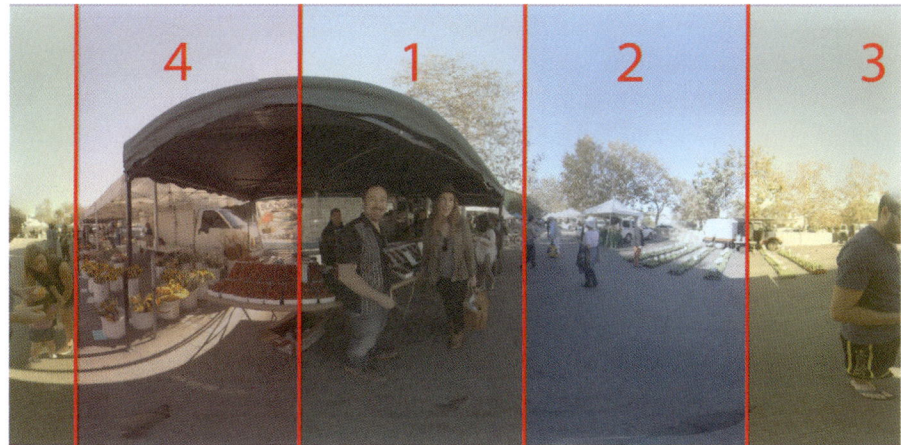
Do your best to keep the subject limited to a single camera lens.

The closer the subject or movement is to the camera, the more difficult it is to get a clean stitch across that area. If you have movement that must pass across stitch lines, try to choreograph it so it occurs farther away. Worst of all is to create blocking where you've got an actor who passes back and forth across a stitch line.

Also, some cameras and rigs make it very difficult to accomplish this. For example, the GoPro Omni rig is designed so when the camera is mounted to a tripod, no one camera is pointing "straight ahead." This means that the stitch lines appear diagonally throughout the sphere. If you've got a subject (such as a person standing up vertically) it may be useful to deliberately mount the camera at an angle to contravene this design.

With cameras like the Facebook 360, or YI HALO which have many lenses, it's impossible to avoid some action crossing stitch lines, but these cameras are designed to have enough overlap between lenses to mitigate stitching problems.

In some cases, you can rotate the camera to avoid action occurring on a stitch line.

Allocate extra time for blocking

Because blocking is such a critical element in a VR scene, allow yourself extra time to figure it out and get it right. First, stand at the camera location and watch the action from there. Finesse the action to ensure that important information happens at the right time, that subtle emotional details occur when an actor is close to the camera, and that you are using the entire space effectively.

Action going on in many directions at once can improve immersion, but it also complicates blocking and timing. Coordinating and timing the actions of multiple people becomes exponentially harder with each new variable you add.

When you're satisfied that things look right, set up the camera and review a quick stitch in an HMD to see how things play in the goggles. Make more adjustments and finesse marks and any other cues your actors need to get their performances perfect.

Rehearse actors until they hit their marks precisely

With a traditional camera, the operator can pan slightly to the left or right if an actor doesn't land in the right spot, but in 360° productions, the camera doesn't move. If an actor in the foreground steps in front of an important action in the background, or if they're turned slightly away from the camera at a critical moment, there's no way to fix it.

To make things even harder, you probably can't just slap some tape on the floor to help an actor know where to stand—because viewers can look down at the ground anytime they want! You must hide all evidence of your filmmaking or risk your viewer becoming distracted and disengaged from your piece.

Quick stitch: A rapid, albeit potentially imperfect, stitch of 360° footage. In multi camera rigs, this may be achieved without utilizing information from every camera's lens.

HMD (head-mounted display): goggles or a headset designed to optimize 360° video viewing.

Marks: A position on set (defined during blocking) where an actor is supposed to be at precise moments during a scene. On set, a mark might be a piece of tape on the ground to indicate where an actor should be standing.

Cues: A trigger for a action or line of dialogue.

Chapter 16: Blocking and choreography

Instead of tape, you'll have to use markers that are organic to the scene, such as sticks or leaves in an outdoor set, or perhaps subtle smudges on the floor or carefully positioned shadows in an indoor set.

And because in VR video, there's (generally) no intra-scene editing, you can't just cut to another shot or edit out a bit of wasted time. All your takes will likely be much longer than those in traditional video. A single mistake at the end of a two-minute take can mean starting all over again. You can count on shooting many takes over and over again, even after extensive rehearsals.

Inserts: Close-up shots of an object or detail previously seen in a wider angle.

Beats: Units of action within a scene.

Close-ups: A limited view that narrows in on a key feature of a subject: an actors face, a smoking gun on the floor, etc.

Wide shots: A expansive view that takes in the entirety of a scene or location.

Chapter 17: Working with actors

Acting for VR is in some ways a hybrid between traditional film acting and theater acting. In standard (flat) film or television, most scenes consist of multiple shots with an edit every 3–5 seconds. The ability to cut to another shot gives the traditional director great flexibility on set. She can start and stop shooting a scene dozens of times to finesse performances, experiment with different reactions, hinge a scene on a subtle gesture that can be highlighted in an insert, and so on.

In a spherical scene, there are no edits. Consequently, the entire scene is usually shot in a single take. For a director, this is extremely challenging. You can't take the best beats from three different takes of a particular shot. You can't cut to close-up for a deep emotional moment and then out to a wide shot for a big, physical confrontation.

Your actors must perform the whole scene, flowing from one emotional beat to another in an organic and fluid way—just as they would on a theater stage. Some actors prefer this approach, as it allows them to build up to moments and to react to one another in a natural and realistic way. It also requires the actors to more thoroughly embody their characters—fully understanding the backstory and motivations that underlie their actions big and small.

And although 360° video is like theater in many ways, it's also inherently a filmed medium. Performances must be intimate and subtle, presented for a camera placed a mere meter away from the actors.

In fact, what's really required is a fusion of film acting and theater acting: When performers are close to the camera, they should dial back their performance to the understated naturalism of a filmed close-up; but as they walk deeper into the room, they've got to dial it up, integrating larger gestures as they would on stage. However, because they're (most likely) close-miked, performers need to keep their vocal performances subtle and understated throughout, even as the scope of their physical movements vary depending on their proximity to the camera.

Close-miked: Audio recorded with a mic placed very close to the subject (often directly attached to the clothes or body).

Bad performances on a theater stage can be viscerally uncomfortable for the audience to watch, and with VR the same thing can happen. Your viewer is virtually "in the room" with the performers. So if the acting rings false or feels inconsistent with the environment or the tone and style of the scene, it will be impossible to ignore. Fortunately, the converse is also true: When a performer nails her role, it can feel exceptionally moving and intimate.

So as a director, it's vitally important to evaluate your actors' performances effectively. As detailed in Chapter 23: Monitoring on set, it's very challenging to judge performance on a 360° shoot. You can't be in the room with your performers, and even with top-of-the-line monitoring equipment you simply can't look in every direction at once. However, there is one element that you *can* track all at once: the sound.

As flat video editors know, the audio of a scene is often a better indicator of performance than the video. Personally, I often close my eyes while watching dailies to get a better sense of the nuance of a performance. When it comes to judging the emotional undercurrents of a scene, the subtleties of timing and

Dailies: The accumulated footage shot in a day on set (traditionally reviewed at the end of each day).

intonation and the intricacies of vocalization are often more telling than the picture. For example, someone can "sound like" they're smiling, even if their face remains relatively stoic; or vice versa.

Also, when listening to the sound on a 360˚ set you can hear all the performers simultaneously even if some are behind you. Just be sure everyone is miked properly (as described in Chapter 27: Recording audio for 360˚.

Chapter 18: Interviewing in VR

With interviews, you face a different set of challenges. First of all, there's the issue of where to conduct the interview. In a traditional video interview, you need to consider the background, making sure there aren't distracting elements like flashing lights or brightly colored or moving objects to pull attention away from the subject. And of course the background should subtly provide additional context for the content of the interview.

In 360° video, you need to think about the entire environment—and not just because your viewer may look around and see different things. In VR, viewers feel as if they're standing near the subject, in a shared space. That makes it even more important to pick an appropriate environment, one that complements (or perhaps deliberately contrasts) the content of the interview.

Next, there's the question of whether or not the subject should address the camera directly. In traditional video, most creators opt to have the subject look just past the camera lens. However, in 360° video, most creators prefer to their subject to look directly into the lens. (The reasons for this are discussed in more detail in Sidebar: participant vs. ghost.)

In either case, the tricky question persists: Where should the interviewer stand?

To avoid distracting the viewer, your interviewer could ask the subject a question, then run and hide while the subject answers. This may be great exercise for you, the interviewer, but then how do you ask follow up questions?

Lavaliere mic: A small microphone attached to a lapel or discretely hidden in an actors wardrobe.

Composite: The post-production process of combining two or more images. Could be as simple as a title superimposed over an image, or as complex a digitally generated explosion rotoscoped over a filmed miniature spaceship in front of a hand-painted painting of outer space. Also can refer to the result of that process; a composite, or a composite image.

Post: The phase of production that occurs after filming completes.

Plate: A part of a composite, usually intended as a background, though here it refers to a duplicate version of the main shot with the offending objects removed. The name comes from old-fashioned analog visual effects where the background was painted onto a sheet of plate glass.

One solution is to outfit your interview subject with a wireless earphone, then ask your questions from a separate room or otherwise out of the camera's view. This can work well, although you'll need to rent a wireless transmitter, which will then be subject to interference from other devices on the same radio spectrum—including the wireless lavaliere mic you may be using to record the subject's voice. (This option becomes even less practical if you're using a translator to interpret a foreign language.)

The wireless earpiece solution has another drawback that's potentially more damaging than equipment complications: Without the eye contact and subtle nonverbal feedback an interviewer provides during the conversation, your interviewee may become stiff or unnatural and may be less able to give the human, empathetic performance that you're probably after. Good interviewing is an art, and doing it remotely while the subject stands all by herself in front of a bizarre-looking camera is especially difficult.

An alternative is to stand behind (or beside) the camera just as you would for an old-fashioned video interview, and then composite yourself out of the image in post. If you know you're going to do this and plan ahead, it doesn't have to be a difficult or expensive fix. Place your camera so that you can find a place to stand where there's no moving action behind you. Make sure you're not straddling a stitch line, and shoot a plate (a version of the scene where you're not in the shot). You can learn more about this compositing trick in Chapter 53: Rig removal and nadir patching.

During the interview, the interviewer sits behind the camera (with his laptop), but below, you can see the background has been replaced, removing him.

If your journalistic ethics are tweaked by the idea of removing someone from the sphere while still trying to claim that the scene is "real," there's a third option: Just leave the interviewer there in the scene. This may not work in every situation, but there are plenty of scenarios where it works just fine.

First of all, the vast majority of viewers will choose to focus on the interview subject—the person talking and communicating to the audience—rather than the interviewer (especially if the interviewer is standing directly behind the camera). And if a viewer is so interested that they make the effort to pivot and peek over their shoulder, they may consider it a reward to see the interviewer's reactions to what the interviewee is saying.

Chapter 19: Spherical composition

As I describe in Chapter 2: Location, location, location, one of the most special aspects of watching VR is the experience of being transported to a different place. The degree to which your piece achieves that transformative feat depends on your decisions about what is visible to the user, and how environmental elements are revealed over time. Composition is a way of thinking about how and where the objects in the image appear in relationship to each other.

The rule of thirds: The concept that divides a traditional film or television frame into nine squares to guide the optimal composition of subjects.

Leading lines: Subtly stimulating invisible lines that direct attention or convey meaning in a frame's composition.

Directing action inward: Framing'a subject with action, people or objects that draws your attention to the center of the frame.

Field of view: The angle of space viewable from a given lens position.

The notion that there's an ideal way to compose an image first emerged centuries ago with the advent of painting as an art form. Than, as now, composition was largely predicated on there being a frame around the image. Common composition techniques like the rule of thirds, leading lines, directing action inward and many others depend on the presence of edges around the image. In fact, a common synonym for composition is *framing*. But in VR, there are no clear frames, edges, or borders. When there's no frame, how do we decide where to position objects in relation to the camera (and vice-versa)?

Well, for one thing, while 360° video is filmed without any frame lines, it is nevertheless *viewed* within a frame. But that frame is *dynamic*, determined by the field of view of the viewing device (and beyond that, by our peripheral vision). If you, the VR director, can identify a point at the likely center of the viewer's gaze, then you can extrapolate an effective frame around that point.

Even though the VR frame is dynamic, shifting as your viewer turns her head and looks at different things on the screen, it can help to think about your basic composition.

Sidebar: Understanding field of view

Field of view (or FoV) is simply how much you can see at any given time without moving your eyes or turning your head. Before considering how FoV works in VR, first just think about your own two eyes.

LEFT EYE: 160°
RIGHT EYE: 160°
BINOCULAR: 200°
STEREOSCOPIC: 120°
VERTICAL: 135°

Monocular FoV (with one eye open) is about 160° horizontal x 135° vertical. Binocular FoV (with both eyes open) is about 200° horizontal x 135° vertical. Of course, at your periphery, the quality of your vision is significantly reduced. The area where your two eyes' FoV overlap in the middle is about 120° horizontal x 135° vertical. This is called stereoscopic FoV.

So how does VR hardware affect FoV? The current generation of HMDs is more limited than our natural vision; the broadest FoV commercially available in a headset provides only about 110° horizontal x 100° vertical[1], and most of the headsets out there provide closer to 90° horizontally.

This means that your eyes still see the black edges of the inside of your goggles at their periphery.

Nonetheless, because you can turn your head you still feel as though you can see the entire world projected around you.

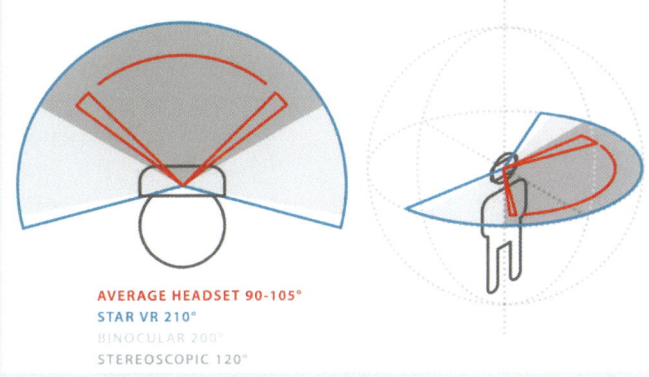

AVERAGE HEADSET 90-105°
STAR VR 210°
BINOCULAR 200°
STEREOSCOPIC 120°

1 The StarVR and Pimax headsets offers 210° of horizontal FoV.

As you plan your VR composition, consider the following guidelines:

Use the "spherical compass"

One useful way to think about VR composition is to establish a point in the sphere that is "straight ahead." Think of this direction as your *north*. Even though you can adjust that center point later in post, it helps immensely to have a sense of "north" when you set up the camera.

The diagram on the left reflects the relative positions of the people and other objects in the scene.

In some cases, north may be very obvious: an interview subject, a concert stage, a cook sautéing a fish, and so on. But in other cases, your north may be less certain; there could be relevant action in multiple directions, including up and down. Remember, when you set-up your camera, there's no inherent front—It sees in all directions all the time.[2] So, it's helpful to declare a center point during production. Doing so can help inform where you position the camera in the room or even how to orient it (rotating or tilting it). Setting a north can also guide your decisions about choreography and element placement.

2   Some cameras like the GoPro Odyssey clearly mark a camera 1, but this doesn't mean that must be the center point.

Compose in quadrants

Even in settings where there's clearly no single point of focus, it can still be helpful to establish a north, even if somewhat arbitrarily. That way, you can effectively divide the space around the camera into four quadrants (north, south, east, and west) and you can think about each quadrant individually.

For example, if you're shooting a rock band in a recording studio, you might define the guitarist's position as north; directly behind the camera, where you can see into the mixing booth, becomes south; the singer in her isolation booth to your left is west; and the bassist and keyboard player to your right are east.

Of course, your eventual viewers can (and hopefully will) turn and look around at all the different elements in the room. But for the sake of communicating with your crew and preparing your shot, you can now all be on the same page. Furthermore, you might adjust the positions of the various musicians (or adjust the camera position) to ensure that no matter which direction the viewer faces, he'll see a clear, well-composed subject.

Note: In some cases, you may want to add two additional quadrants for up and down (thus making each section a sextant). In many environments there's not a whole lot to look at above or below you, but sometimes critical action or interesting details may reside in these less-used areas of the image.

Positional microphone: A mic that employs multiple sensors to capture a 360 sphere of sound.

Sync them up (synchronize): Match to play back at the same time (and space) as the video.

Post: The phase of production that occurs after filming completes.

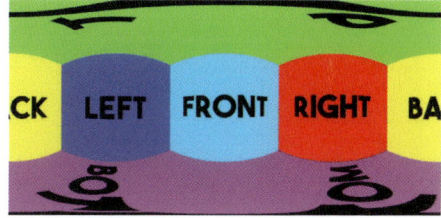

This image shows where the different parts of the sphere appear when viewing a latlong (equirectangular) frame.

Center around the subject

Just because your viewer can turn her head and choose what she wants to look at doesn't mean you don't have any ability to control the aesthetic appearance of the image. If you have a specific subject likely to draw the viewer's attention (such as a talking dog or a laser beam eating away at a truck tire), you can consider how the image unfolds around that center point.

Field of view: The angle of space viewable from a given lens position.

Unlike a traditional rectangular frame where you can deliberately place your subject off-center or near the edge of the frame, in VR if you give your viewer something specific to look at, that thing will become the center in her field of view.

You can take advantage of this to determine which other elements should lie within the approximately 100° field[3] that appears peripherally to the left and right. This way, when your viewer is looking at the talking dog, you can take advantage of many of those classic composition tenets.

For example, if 50 degrees to the left of the talking dog, there's a window where cars are visible racing by outside, those movements in the viewer's peripheral vision will nag at her attention, tempting her to turn away from the dog. If instead you had the dog and the window closer together, both can be taken in at the same time. Or, by moving the dog a bit farther away from the window, the viewer won't see the window at all unless she deliberately turns her head away from the dog.

Leading lines: Subtly stimulating invisible lines that direct attention or convey meaning in a frame's composition.

Alternatively, by adjusting the camera position, you can use leading lines in the room's architecture to guide your viewer from the talking dog to a gun conspicuously sitting on a nearby table.

3   Human peripheral vision is actually more like 200°, but the current generation of HMDs limit field of view to a much smaller range.

Chapter 20: Placing the camera

How do you decide where to position the camera to best capture a scene? In traditional film and video, filmmakers shoot most scenes using a technique called *coverage*. Coverage simply means shooting a scene multiple times from different camera angles (covering all the angles).

Later, during editing, the scene is assembled using these different shots, which allows the filmmaker to control the point of focus. For example, a scene might begin with a wide-angle showing a room and two characters, then cut to a profile shot of the two characters conversing, then cut to a shot of one character from over the other character's shoulder, and so on.

However, in spherical projects, intra-scene editing like that is usually not desirable, because in a VR environment sudden cuts to new angles can be jarring and destroy the immersive effect—reminding the viewer that she's not really in the same room as the characters.

Consequently, 360° projects are rarely shot using the coverage method. Instead, 360° filmmakers typically shoot each scene as a single shot, from a single camera position (albeit with multiple lenses recording "in the round"). Shooting from a single camera setup may sound simple, but in practice figuring out where to place the camera can be challenging.

If you're familiar with traditional coverage, you can think of every 360° shot as a master shot. And because there's no such thing as a close-up or an insert in spherical video, important details must be integrated into that master set-up via clever blocking, choreography, and camera placement.

Master shot: A shot, typically wide, that captures all the action across the duration of a scene.

Close-up: A tight shot that narrows in on the key feature of a subject: an actors face, a smoking gun on the floor, etc.

Insert: A close-up shot of an object or detail previously seen in a wider angle.

POV (point of view) shot: A shot that represents a character's perspective within the scene.

Your camera positions should be highly motivated and subjective. Every shot is a POV shot. Every shot should be a deliberate and justifiable choice about exactly where you want your viewer to be as she witnesses the events. Think of shooting 360° video as literally placing your viewer into the scene.

That sense of being "in the scene" can be highly persuasive. When you're watching VR and a character walks toward the camera, you feel as if that person is really approaching you. This triggers all of the subconscious and nonverbal reactions you might feel under similar circumstances in real life. POV immersion in VR is much more potent than it is in traditional cinema. Someone pointing a gun at the 360° camera (or to give a gentler example, seductively winking at the camera) will trigger involuntary physical reactions in the viewer. Where you place your camera to create a sense of POV immersion can have a powerful dramatic effect. But take heed and use these effects sparingly. For more on this, see the Sidebar: Managing your 'spin budget'.

Hostess tray shot: A shot captured by a camera rigged to the outside of a car's driver side, or passenger side window, supported by a device reminiscent of the trays used at drive-in restaurants in the '50's.

Furthermore, remember that wherever you set up the camera, you're positioning your viewer's "head" in that space. So, for example, a hostess tray shot may be a classic way of filming dialogue in a moving car. However, mounting a VR camera outside the window of a moving car may make your audience feel as they're suctioned to the side of the car, probably not the effect you're hoping to achieve. Similarly, placing the camera too close to a rotating ceiling fan will likely create an inescapable distraction, prompting your viewers to flinch every time the blade comes around. And that means they're likely not paying enough attention to the scene going on below.

Nausea alert: Naturally, there are exceptions to every rule, and there are situations when an odd or uncomfortable camera placement is exactly what you're after. But unlike something like a Dutch angle that gives viewers of traditional cinema a slight subconscious sense of unease and can be employed for dramatic effect, challenging camera positions in VR can quickly lead to very strong reactions including dizziness, nausea, and headaches that linger long after taking off the goggles. While it may be fun and valuable to occasionally confront your viewers' expectations, you probably don't want to make anyone physically ill.

Dutch angle: When the camera is tilted slightly left or right, so the horizon appears to be diagonal.

Here are a few guidelines to help you decide where to place the camera:

Keep a safe distance from the subject

This advisory presumes you've got a clear and singular subject for your scene, and there are arguments against that. But if you intend to focus on a person, object, action, or activity as the primary subject of a scene, you must decide how close or far to place the camera from that subject. Remember, the viewer experiences the world exactly as though her head is where the camera is placed, so err on the side of giving your viewer a little bit of breathing room.

Close-up using traditional "long" lens.

Close-up using a spherical camera.

Long lens (telephoto lens): magnifies objects in the distance, narrows the field of view, and optically 'flattens' an image.

Parallax error: The phenomenon that occurs when the position of an object viewed from slightly different positions is inconsistent.

Stitching: Combining multiple images/videos into one panoramic image/video (also sometimes refers to a seam in a panoramic image).

Wide-angle: A expansive view that takes in the entirety of a scene or location.

HMD (head-mounted display): goggles or a headset designed to optimize 360° video viewing.

Keeping a bit of distance is especially crucial when the camera is relatively close to a human subject. In traditional film and video, a close-up shot using a long lens simulates the effect of standing extremely near to someone. However, in VR, where viewers feel like they're sharing a room with the people onscreen, being "close-up close" is just a little bit creepy.

It's much safer to keep your subjects no nearer to the camera than a meter or so, even during intimate moments. The audience will be able to read the subtleties of facial expressions, but they won't feel so awkwardly close to the person that it becomes distracting. (This also helps with avoiding parallax errors while stitching.)

Remember that objects are closer than they appear

Because 360° cameras view the world through wide-angle lenses, when monitoring on set, it can seem like objects more than a few feet from the camera are tiny and insignificant. But you must remember that in an HMD, the wide-angle effect is removed. Objects appear the actual distance they are from the camera while shooting. And, while that wide-angle lens makes everything appear in focus (even objects dangerously close to the lens) putting objects too close can still create the experience of having to focus too closely for comfort.

Dotted area shows the area visible in an HMD.   The view inside the HMD.

Don't place the camera in the middle of the room

Because the camera sees in all directions, it may be tempting to always stick it in the middle of every action. This can work in some instances—like, for example, in the midst of a swarming school of fish or on a factory floor where machines are whirring and buzzing all around. But for many scenes it's better to pick a deliberate point of view where you want the viewer to witness the scene from.

Remember, you're "pinning" the viewer's head to the location where you place the camera. If you stick the camera on a plate in the middle of a thanksgiving dinner table, your viewers will feel as if they are on the platter with the turkey—a very unnatural (and unsettling) experience. A far more comfortable camera location would be at the side of the table, alongside the diners in the scene, thus creating the experience of actually sitting at the dinner table. (Unless your goal is to make the viewer feel like a roasted turkey!)

Furthermore, if there's action occurring all around, the viewer may not know where to look. She may lapse into "rubberneck mode," desperately attempting to take in too many actions. The only aspect of the experience she's likely to remember is the lingering sore neck—and she'll be disinclined to put on the headset again anytime soon. (Where to direct the viewer's gaze is discussed in more detail in Chapter 15: Guiding the viewer's focus.)

Keep a safe distance from distracting elements

Remember my ceiling fan example above? Even if the main action is clearly only in one direction, don't place the camera so close to a wall or boundary object that if a viewer turns her head she'll feel like she's going to bump into it; she'll likely wince, and then when there's no impact she'll be reminded that the whole experience is an illusion.

Don't obscure the subject with walls or objects

Because your viewer can't walk around in the space (at least not yet), avoid placing the camera behind a table or around a corner from important action in a scene. Pick a perspective where the viewer can see all the relevant information in the scene.

Stay out of the "helpless distance"

Remember, your viewer really feels like she's physically in the space where the scene is set. And yet she can't actually interact with the elements in the scene (at least not using current technology). This conflict can undermine presence and immersiveness. If your camera is so close to, or surrounded by, the action in the scene that the viewer feels compelled to interact—for example, standing within arm's reach of a child teetering on the edge of a subway platform as a train approaches—she's likely to become acutely aware that grabbing for the child's arm doesn't work. This, in turn, will remind her that she's not actually present in the scene. However, if you place the camera ten feet further away from the child, the viewer will still be riveted to the action in the scene, but less likely to involuntarily flail her arms.

Chapter 21: Camera mounting considerations

In 360° video, how you mount the camera is important. Whereas in traditional video, you can simply place the camera on a tripod, most 360° cameras record video not only "in the round," but also above and below. Consequently, a tripod under the camera will likely be seen in the shot. You can digitally remove the tripod in post-production (to learn how, see Chapter 53: Rig removal and nadir patching), but your choices on set can impact how easy or arduous that compositing work will be.

Here are few useful techniques to keep your camera rigs as inconspicuous as possible:

Minimize the tripod footprint
The less space the tripod takes up, the easier it will be to digitally "paint out" later. So whenever possible, reduce the spread of your tripod's legs or use a monopod with a small-footprint spider base. However, be safe! It's vital that your camera is supported sufficiently and doesn't fall over. So, especially for heavier cameras, be sure your tripod legs are wide enough to provide a stable base. (You can hang a sandbag from the tripod's center hook to improve stability). For smaller, lightweight cameras, you may be able to completely skip the rig removal step, simply by using the right kind of camera support—a monopod, or other narrow stalk will often disappear (at least partially) during stitching with no special effort required.

Suspend the camera from above
Sometimes the best way to mount the camera is from above. Mounting from above is a good option if you expect viewers to look down more often than up.

The monopod here mostly disappears automatically during stitching.

Paint out: Digitally remove an object from a scene.

Sometimes it's necessary to mount a camera from above.

Stitching: Combining multiple images/videos into one panoramic image/video (also sometimes refers to a seam in a panoramic image).

Stereoscopic 360° video: Three-dimensional 360° video, captured using multiple cameras arrayed for stereoscopic capture.

Always use the level bubble on your tripod to ensure a straight horizon.

North: The point of origin where a viewer enters a 360° scene, also serves as a frame of reference for orienting discussions about the scene.

Level the camera

Don't ever begin shooting without taking a moment to ensure that the camera is level with the horizon. In 360° video, a level camera makes stitching easier. (Correcting the horizon after the fact is doable, but it may require compromises in how the cameras are overlapped and introduce additional parallax or stitching errors.) What's more, a level camera is absolutely essential for stereoscopic 360° video. If the horizon is off even slightly, the stereo effect can be severely compromised when the viewer attempts to turn her head—and the ability to turn your head is arguably the most basic difference between 360° and flat video.

Most tripods have a level bubble, so you can quickly ensure that your horizon is straight. But even if your tripod doesn't have a level bubble, there are many apps that turn your smartphone into an instant level.

Position the camera thoughtfully

In general, think of the camera as your viewer's head; treat it gently and position it somewhere that won't make your viewer feel uncomfortable or confused. Thoughtful camera placement is important just for the shot as it stands on its own, but also for how well it integrates into the rest of your piece.

For example, during a restaurant shoot, I thought it would be interesting to suspend the camera above the expediter's station where plates of food are garnished and moved from the kitchen into the dining room. We mounted the camera on a post about 12 inches from the ceiling, and treated straight down as north.

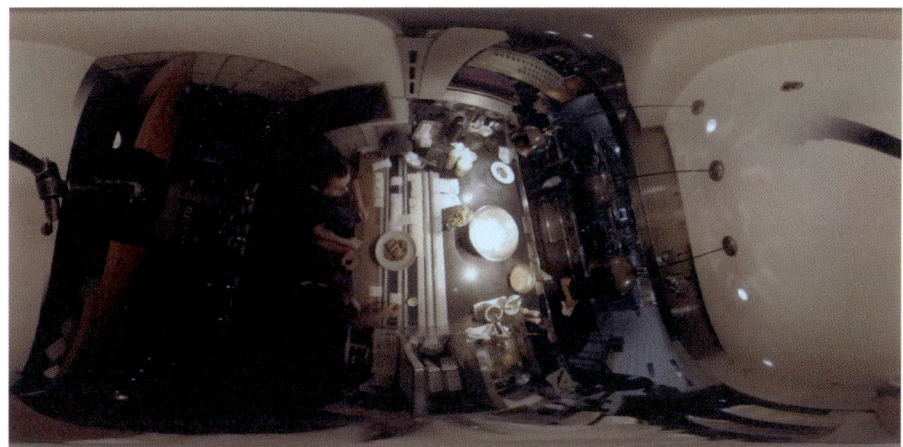
A shot rigged looking down on the restaurant's expediter station.

The resulting shot was very cool, successfully capturing the careful precision required to make every dish look perfect, as well as the high-pressure stakes of delivering food to diners quickly and efficiently. On its own, the shot was fun to look at, but when edited into the piece, between shots staged from a more familiar, grounded perspective, the overhead view was enormously distracting. In fact, the God's eye view caused some test viewers to lurch forward when they suddenly found themselves floating above the room and looking down. Sadly, we had to cut the shot the final piece.

Sidebar: Camera height

The height of your spherical camera has a surprisingly dramatic impact on the experience of the viewer. Even a few inches can make a big difference in affecting comfort or disorientation.

Whereas in traditional video you can employ a wide range of camera heights to generate a variety of effects, most 360° video creators are very careful to set the camera precisely at the eye-height of the main subject in the scene and to keep it consistent throughout the piece. Setting the camera too low or too high (even by a small amount) can undermine presence and immersion in a scene, or in the very least can weaken your viewers' empathy with the subjects of the shot.

Camera height has also long been used in cinema to establish power dynamics between characters in a scene or to enhance or diminish a person's stature. This effect can still be used in 360° video, as long as you keep it subtle. Putting the camera slightly below a subject's eyeline makes that subject appear more powerful, positioning it slightly above makes the subject appear weaker. Because in VR everything feels so subjective, these adjustments go even further, making the viewer herself feel more or less powerful in a scene. Beware though—go too far and rather than creating a subtle psychological effect, you merely distract your viewer and pull them out of the experience.

With stereoscopic images camera height can be combined with interpupillary distance (IPD) to create even more creative effects; if the camera is close to the ground and the IPD is smaller than a typical adult you can authentically simulate the point-of-view of a child (or go even more extreme, and you can simulate the point-of-view of a squirrel). With the camera five meters off the ground, a small IPD might simulate a true bird's-eye view, but with a large IPD it might suggest a giant's point of view.

Consider whether you expect your audience to watch your program sitting or standing, and try to keep the camera height consistent all the way through your program. A sitting person watching a show filmed at standing height will feel slightly ill at ease throughout the program (and vice versa). Consider adding a title card before the program starts, instructing viewers to stand or sit (or sit on the ground) to ensure the best experience.

Chapter 22: Camera settings

To capture professional-quality spherical video, you need to make sure that several important camera controls are properly configured: resolution, frame rate, exposure, white balance, image quality, sharpness, and (for GoPro cameras) Protune.

Some cameras and rigs have default settings that match the configurations described in this chapter. In many cases, that's great news: You won't need to think about all of these parameters and variables—you can simply begin recording! However, even in mostly automated systems, there are usually a few settings that require adjustment. Carefully checking these settings can help you elevate the quality of your work.

Important: With 360° rigs that comprise multiple individual cameras, it's vital that all the devices are configured identically. One camera with an inconsistent setting can ruin the whole shoot.

Note: If you're planning to combine or integrate the live action footage you're capturing with animated or computer generated (CG) elements after the shoot, some of these settings may be even more critical. Consult with your visual effects coordinator before you begin shooting.

Resolution

With a spherical camera, there are two resolution values (frame dimensions) to consider:

- *The resolution of each camera within the rig*
- *The resolution of the final stitched output*

Because stitching combines multiple camera views, the stitched output is likely higher than the resolution of any single camera. And the more cameras a rig uses, the higher the potential resolution of the final stitched output. But the math of adding together camera resolutions gets a bit complicated because during stitching the camera fields of view are overlapped, yielding a final resolution smaller than the combined sensor values. Plus, the more sensors there are, the more overlap there is likely to be between lenses. Consult the camera charts in the consumer, prosumer, and professional camera chapters to compare the resolutions of various cameras.

HMD (head-mounted display): goggles or a headset designed to optimize 360° video viewing.

Why is higher resolution so important? After all, HMDs and other devices for viewing spherical video have resolutions that generally max out at around 4K. So why even bother shooting at resolutions higher than 4K?

Color correct: The adjustment of color in post-production to match different shots and enhance the picture.

Well, first of all, next year's HMD technology will (hopefully) bring higher resolution, so a higher source resolution helps to future-proof your production. Also, a higher resolution increases your ability to color correct or sharpen your video and improve the overall image quality. Plus, because your final video will be heavily compressed for distribution, the higher your source resolution, the better your final video will ultimately look.

However, even though bigger is better when it comes to resolution, there are times when you might deliberately decide to reduce resolution. For example, GoPro cameras can shoot at 4K resolution, but only at 30 frames per second (fps). If you want to increase your frame rate to 60 fps, the resolution drops to 2.7K. To shoot slow motion at 120 fps, your resolution drops to HD (1920 x 1080).

The good news (at least in this example) is that six GoPro cameras shooting at 1920 x 1080 will, after stitching, still greatly exceed the 4k stitched resolution of the Samsung 360.

Frame rate

The higher the frame rate, the smoother motion appears during playback. Because smooth playback reduces motion sickness, most VR projects are shot at a 60 fps or at least 30 fps (a higher frame rate than traditional cinema which is still mostly shot at 24 fps).

Beware though; like everything, there are tradeoffs. Higher frame rates mean larger files, which means bigger hard disk requirements, longer transfer times, longer render times, and so on. So there's some pressure to find a reasonable compromise between the competing factors. That said, as technology marches forward, higher frame rates may become increasingly achievable with minimal downside.

When selecting a frame rate, consider what your intended delivery format is. If you're planning for all your viewers to watch on a high-end playback device, shooting at 60 fps may be worthwhile. However, if you're expecting most viewers to watch on a cell phone, you may be fine with 30 fps.

Note: Don't confuse frame rate with refresh rate. High-end HMDs like the Oculus Rift and the HTC VIVE advertise that they refresh their screens at 90 (or even 120) fps (which helps reduce motion sickness), but video shot at 60 fps (or even 30 fps) can be viewed perfectly fine at that higher refresh rate.

Refresh rate: The frequency at which an image is drawn on screen during playback, expressed as the number of cycles per second (hertz). For example: 90hz.

Exposure

Exposure refers to the light sensitivity of the camera. If exposure is set incorrectly, bright areas can appear as pure white, or dark areas can appear as pure black—in either case the content of the scene will be unreadable. Therefore, proper exposure is critical.

Most cameras offer an autoexposure setting that adjusts the camera dynamically, ensuring that the image is always visible, even if lighting conditions change during the course of the shot (like, for instance, if a window was opened, or a light was turned off). Autoexposure is great to make sure the resulting footage is watchable (and is better than overexposed or underexposed images) but it can also cause sudden brightness shifts that can be very distracting to your viewer. Plus, there may be good reasons to leave a portion of the image too bright or too dark; for example, by having an actor turn on a light, you can direct the viewer's attention to a formerly dark area of the scene.

With multiple-camera rigs, exposure is especially challenging. For example, if one lens is facing a sunny window and another lens is facing a dark corner elsewhere in the room, autoexposure will assign very different settings to the two cameras. This can complicate your stitching chores.

You have much more control over the scene if you manually set the exposure for your cameras and control the lighting in the environment instead.

You can control camera exposure in a number of ways:

Aperture (or iris): The size of the hole through which the light enters the camera. Higher aperture settings let less light in.

Shutter speed: Controls how long the camera sensor is exposed to the light. Unless you're after a special effect, when shooting video, it's best to keep the shutter speed configured to match the frame rate. And no matter what, you must ensure that all your cameras record at the same shutter speed.

ISO (or ASA): Controls the camera sensor's sensitivity. A higher ISO means increased sensitivity, so you can shoot in darker environments. Unfortunately adjusting the sensitivity in this way adds noise to your image, and because spherical video is viewed with your eyes only a few inches from the screen, even a little noise can be very distracting. For the cleanest images, set the ISO as low as possible and provide enough light (natural or artificial) to expose the image properly.

Noise: Undesirable variations of brightness and/or color in an image that typically occur when recording at high ISOs in digital cameras

Gain: A setting available in some professional cameras, effectively magnifies the ISO setting to make the camera more sensitive for darker environments. Gain can be useful when you want to leave the ISO at a constant setting for the bulk of the shoot, but quickly add a little sensitivity for one particularly dark shot. Like high ISO settings, adding gain can add a significant amount of noise to your image.

Exposure value compensation (EV): A kind of meta-setting that doesn't change the exposure directly (like each of the above settings). Instead, it forces the camera to expose higher or lower than the auto setting. So, for example, if you're shooting a night scene and you want the scene to feel appropriately dark you can use autoexposure and set EV to –2. This sets the exposure two stops darker than the setting autoexposure would otherwise use.

Stops: f-stops are the measurement of, and mechanism for controlling how much light is let through the lens to reach a camera sensor (i.e. f22, f16, f8, f4, f2, f1.4, etc. Larger numbers mean less light)

White balance

While you may think most light is "white," in fact all light has a color temperature based on the source emitting the light. Color temperature falls on a spectrum from orange to blue, where electric lights are generally orange and sunlight is more blue. Your brain compensates for these differences and continually adjusts as light changes when, for example, you walk through a doorway out of sunlight and into a room with electric lights.

But your camera needs to be told what color temperature you want to treat as white. Most modern cameras have an automatic white balance setting that guesses which color should be white. But there are some situations in which you might have two very differently colored lights in the same scene. For example, it's very common to have a scene set in a room illuminated with electric lights but that also has a window where sunlight is shining through. In this case, if the camera thinks the electric lights are "white," the light coming through the window will look very blue, and if the camera thinks the window light is "white," the table lamp will look like it's bright orange.[4]

Like exposure, auto-white balance is especially challenging in 360° video. With multiple cameras pointing in different directions, one camera might designate the color of the window light as white while another camera prioritizes the lamp as white. When it's time to merge the resulting images into a single file, you may have trouble avoiding a noticeable seam. This issue becomes even more complicated if the camera (or the light sources) moves during the shot.

---

4   The best way to solve this problem is to put a blue gel on the table lamp or an orange gel on the window so the color of the lights match up.

When all the cameras are set to an identical white balance (ideally a manually assigned value created by holding a white card in front of the cameras while enabling the custom white balance setting—see your camera's manual for more details), it's far easier to ensure that the group of cameras match up properly later.

Image quality
Some cameras offer the ability to select a quality setting. The lower the image quality, the more footage you can store in the camera (on the storage card or drive). The camera reduces image quality by lowering the bit rate used to compress footage as it's captured. In dire situations, you might consider making this tradeoff, but if possible, try to use the highest quality setting.

Sharpness
Not all cameras offer a sharpness setting, and/or it might be called something more generic like "enhancement." Sharpness increases the contrast of the image, especially around edges of objects in the scene. This creates a cleaner, more pleasing image, but in making this adjustment in-camera you're actually throwing away data and baking in corrections to the image; consequently, you won't have as much flexibility later to adjust or color-correct the image.

Consumer cameras (like GoPro) are built to provide the best-looking image possible directly out of the camera, so that no editing or color correction is required. This is great for many situations (even in 360° video), but if you're aiming for the best possible results, you're better off limiting the in-camera adjustments and making changes later, in post.

Flatter: Less contrast between the dark and light areas of the image.

Color correction: The adjustment of color in post-production to match different shots and enhance the picture.

Gen-locked: Using a signal generator to synchronize the shutters across multiple cameras so they all operate in precise alignment.

In post (post-production): Work undertaken, or scheduled to be undertaken, after principle photography wraps. Typically refers to digital corrections.

Protune

GoPro cameras have a special setting to limit the in-camera image tuning. The result (similar to shooting RAW files on a DSLR) is flatter-than-normal footage that retains more detail in the darkest and lightest areas of the sphere. As with RAW footage, footage shot with the Protune setting affords you more room to customize the images in post-production. Protune also uses less compression that ordinary footage, making the files slightly larger. By combining Protune with low ISO and low sharpness, you can get the absolute most (and highest-quality) data from your GoPro camera. Just remember, you have to do color correction in post to make those images look their best.

Camera sync

When you use multiple cameras, you need a mechanism to start and stop the cameras together and keep them synchronized. Some cameras can be gen-locked, which means linked together with a cable so they all start and stop simultaneously. Gen-locked cameras should be perfectly synchronized during the shoot; and linking the various video tracks together in post is effectively automatic.

Some rigs include a mechanism to start and stop all the cameras at once, often using a wireless connection to a companion app. This allows you to press one button to control all the cameras, but there are likely to be a few frames of discrepancy between the starting frames for each camera. If you're using this type of start/stop automation (but not gen-lock), you'll need to sync the footage from multiple cameras during post, before you can stitch the footage together into a single 360° video file. (Most stitching software includes a mechanism to perform this synchronization.)

To make this synching easy, ensure that each camera is recording audio (even if you're recording the master audio on a separate device—see Chapter 27: Recording audio for 360° to learn how). Recording "scratch" audio on each camera and using a slate makes it very easy to sync the footage using PluralEyes or similar software in the editing suite.

If you're after a perfect stitch between your different camera images (and anything less than perfect can undermine the illusion of immersion you're after), you'll want cameras that use a global shutter. Most cameras use a *rolling* shutter, which means that the camera records each frame pixel row by pixel row, from top left to lower right. A global shutter captures the entire image all at once, frame by frame.

Slate: A card or device positioned in front of the camera at the beginning of each shot to document all relevant shot information for easy identification during post. Usually operated by the 2nd AC, who reads the relevant information aloud and then activates the clapper bar to provide a synchronization point for audio and video files.

PluralEyes: Software that synchronizes audio and video files by aligning the audio waveforms of the different files.

The top row shows a global shutter and the bottom row shows a rolling shutter.

Rolling shutters work great in many situations, and allow cameras to record high quality images even in lower light. However, when stitching footage from multiple cameras together, if the camera shutters are rolling out of sync with one another, you can wind up with action in the overlapping areas that doesn't match.

By using cameras that employ a global shutter, you can avoid this potential mismatch. By combining global shutters and gen-lock, you can drastically reduce syncing issues when recording footage from multiple cameras.

HMD (head-mounted display): goggles or a headset designed to optimize 360° video viewing.

Chapter 23: Monitoring on set

Monitoring from a 360˚ camera is a tricky proposition. Depending on the camera, the monitoring options range from complicated to impossible. Ideally the director can watch the scene unfold in real time in an HMD, hearing live audio and seeing exactly what the eventual viewer will see. But for a number of reasons, this can be difficult to achieve.

Paint out: Digitally remove an object from a scene.

First of all, director (and crew) must remain far away from the action to avoid the camera's all-seeing view. Secondly, wearing an HMD takes you out of the real space in a way that many directors dislike, especially when working with actors. Thirdly, many rigs don't offer any easy monitoring options, or if they do, they add a hydra of additional cables, breakout boxes, and other conspicuous junk that you'll need to paint out in post.

Given these issues, some directors choose to find a place close to the action, but near a convenient hiding space—behind a wall or beneath a table. Lying low while the camera is running, they monitor performances by listening to the wireless audio (even if they can't see the actors). You'd be surprised how much you can gauge by just listening.

Stitch: The panoramic image/video created by combining multiple camera sources.

Monitoring is essential, if only to ensure that all the cameras are successfully recording. With complex multi camera rigs, it's not uncommon to have a camera or an SD card failure, and if this goes unnoticed before you leave the set, your footage may be all for naught. (Though Jump allows you to omit a bad camera and still get a complete stitch.)

What follows are a number of monitoring options. Consider which method might work best for your shoot:

Monitor live in an HMD

The most complete experience is to view the scene exactly as your audience will. This is especially important for shows where you want your viewer to feel like a participant in the scene. What does it feel like when the actor stares right at you? Are you stuck in the helpless zone where you feel compelled to reach out and touch something but can't? And so on.

To view live footage in a headset, you need to shoot with a camera that supports live HMD. That generally means tethering your camera to a computer and connecting the HMD device to the computer. Few cameras actually provide that option.

Many professional cameras can be configured to provide a live view of the scene (although it's usually just a mono quick stitch of a subset of lenses). Often the camera is tethered to a computer and that computer drives an HMD (usually a DK2 Oculus Rift).

Quick stitch: A rapid, albeit potentially imperfect, stitch of 360° footage. In multi camera rigs, this may be achieved without utilizing information from every camera's lens.

DK2: Developer kit version 2 of the Oculus Rift HMD, which works on Macs as well as Windows computers. The shipping "consumer version" (CV1) does not support Mac.

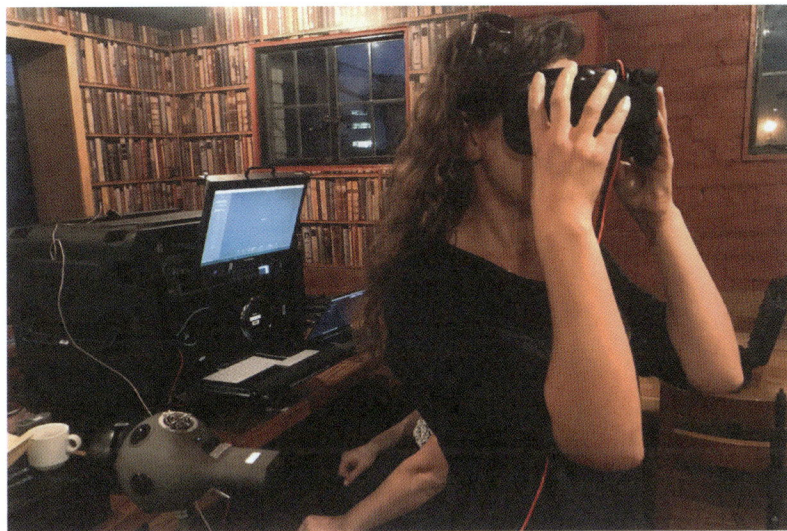

Monitoring the Nokia Ozo+ in a DK2 headset via a portable rack-mounted Mac Pro.

A Sphere connected to a four camera rig.

Equirectangular projection: Stretching a spherical image in a flat, rectangular format. (i.e. the way a world map represents the spherical Earth).

Magic window: A method of viewing 360 content where a rectangular frame acts as a portal to the larger, spherical recording. The viewer can navigate to a different perspective by scrolling (on a computer), or by tilting the viewing device (on a smartphone or tablet).

The Sphere interface on iPad.

Another option is to use the Teredek Sphere: a portable four-input H.264 encoding box[5]. There's an HDMI version which accommodates most cameras used in 360° rigs or an HD-SDI version (for $1k more) if you're shooting with HD-SDI cameras.

To monitor using the Sphere, connect it via Ethernet to a wireless router and transmit the video streams to an iPad or Mac over the air. The Sphere software on the iPad or Mac stitches the streams in real time and you can view the resulting image in a number of formats, from a four-up display of each camera's output, to an equirectangular projection, to a magic window view where you can swipe around with your finger to view different areas of the sphere.

On set monitoring using a sphere connected to a Dark Corner rig.

5   You can link two Spheres together to accommodate rigs with up to eight cameras.

If you connect the output of the Sphere to a properly configured computer, you can use that computer to drive an HMD.

There are a number of drawbacks to live HMD monitoring, one is the requirement for cables and equipment that need to be hidden on set or digitally painted out in post. Live HMD monitoring also requires you to be relatively close to the camera, making it more likely that you'll be in the shot. Adding equipment like the Sphere adds more cables and more batteries (or more draw from the cameras powering your camera), and more cost. Plus, it requires extra setup time before you can begin working.

Furthermore, wearing goggles, you won't be able to monitor all directions at the same time, and are more likely to miss a distracting detail or mistake happening in a direction where you aren't looking.

Also, let's not forget that cameras like the Z CAM V1 Pro or YI HALO are very expensive, and beyond the budgets of many productions. Even renting a Sphere can be costly, and the benefits are somewhat limited.

Due to these downsides, few directors regularly use live HMD monitoring throughout a shoot. They might don the headsets here and there for specific shots, or maybe just for rehearsals before recording begins. In fact, this approach is far more common, and so I've broken it out into a separate category:

Monitor in an HMD not in real time

By watching in an HMD during rehearsals or during setup before the camera starts recording, you get many benefits of monitoring this way, without most of the drawbacks described above.

Additionally, when you remove the need for real time preview, nearly any camera can be monitored in this way. Even if you don't have a Teredek Sphere or a rig that can be fed into a pair of goggles, you can simply run a take, then remove the SD cards, load them onto a computer, and create a quick stitch on set.

It takes a few extra minutes, but verifying that the scene is working as you hoped, that the blocking makes sense, and that no critical action is occurring on a stitch line is worth the extra time.

Monitor in a magic window

As noted above, live HMD monitoring can be impractical, for example, on an outdoor shoot, in a vehicle, in a hut in Antarctica with no AC power, and so on.

Monitoring the output of the Samsung 360 in real time.

Still, working without a monitor at all is taking a big risk, especially if you've traveled all the way to Antarctica! And even if you forgo the HMD (and the computer to drive it) you can still view the output of many cameras and rigs in a magic window on a tablet or smartphone. (You may still need hardware like the Sphere to combine the output of the various cameras.)

Another option is to mount a secondary camera to your primary rig. Tiny consumer cameras like the Ricoh Theta V or GoPro Fusion can transmit stitched output via Bluetooth directly to your phone or tablet.

The quality of that camera may not be sufficient for your final product, but it should be perfectly adequate for monitoring. Just try to get the lens of the monitoring camera as close as possible to the primary camera's lens height. (In the picture to the right, the Theta is so tall that its monitoring usefulness is undermined.)

A Ricoh Theta V mounted atop a GoPro Omni rig.

Monitor an equirectangular (latlong) view

The latlong view isn't all that useful for gauging performance, and even stitch line errors aren't as obvious as they may be in other views, but it does allow you to see everything at once. For that reason, while it may not be ideal for the director, your DP, or PD, or someone on your team should review the shots this way if at all possible.

A Latlong is a great way to gauge the overall exposure and color tone of the image; you can also see if there are any bogeys in the sphere; and identify technical issues, including whether your horizon is properly leveled.

Monitor unstitched output

With some rigs, you just may not have any way to create stitched output without tremendous effort. For example, footage from high-end rigs combining multiple RED Dragon sensors capturing 6K uncompressed video may simply be too cumbersome or too time-consuming to stitch on set. Although you can piggy-back a Ricoh Theta on top of the rig to get a quick view of the framing and prevent stitching issues, nevertheless you'll want to ensure that the main cameras are set properly. Especially with professional or highly customized rigs, it's critical that focus, exposure, and other settings are correct and that they're matched across each of the multiple cameras.

For a case like this, you can view the output directly from the individual cameras. You can wire the output of the cameras to a multi-monitor setup or use a specialized box (also from Teredek) that combines multiple inputs into an *n*-up display showing all the camera outputs at once.

Latlong (latitudinal-longitudinal): Stretching a spherical image into a flat rectangle (similar to the way a world map represents the spherical Earth). Also called equirectangular.

DP (director of photography): Crewperson responsible for designing the shotlist and lighting state, advising on camera selection, and directing the camera and lighting departments on set.

PD (production designer): Crewperson responsible for all visual aspects of what is seen by the camera; (i.e. sets & locations, props, wardrobe etc.

Bogeys: Adapted from military slang, a bogey is a person or object who accidentally appears in the frame during a shot.

Stand behind the camera

Another monitoring option is to stand behind the camera just as you would in a flat shoot, and then digitally paint yourself out later. This was mentioned earlier as one of the ways you can maintain the eye contact and essential connection with an interview subject. There are times when standing behind the camera can also work for monitoring any kind of action that's primarily focused in one direction. As long as you aren't obscuring some critical action, shoot the scene standing there, plainly in the shot, and then run the camera again—after you've moved out of sight—and stitch together that director-less version of the background with foreground of the primary shot.

Monitor audio only

And finally, as mentioned above, you may find that as long as you can monitor the audio of the scene live, you don't need to see the visuals at all. This method does require wireless audio playback transmission.

In this case, be sure to run some test shots to ensure that your action isn't on a stitch line, and that you've watched enough rehearsals to be confident you're not going to wind up with unpleasant surprises later.

Chapter 24: Lighting for 360°

Traditional filmmaking relies heavily on lighting and grip equipment to control the appearance of the images being recorded. If you've worked on (or just walked by) a professional film shoot, you've certainly seen multiple 18-wheelers filled with tons of G&E equipment. This heavy-duty gear isn't just a bunch of high-powered light fixtures, but also reflectors, silks, scrims, flags, filters, and other devices for sculpting the light to get precise results.

In recent years, cameras have become increasingly sophisticated, and more capable of working in low-light settings. But professionals know that to get the best-looking results (and to capture images that look consistent even when it takes many hours or days to complete a scene), you need to exert as much control as possible over the light that finds its way into the camera lens.

Controlled lighting is just as important in spherical video. But because the 360° camera sees in all directions, it's difficult—and sometimes impossible—to hide the heavy lighting gear used in traditional film and video production. For obvious reasons, exposed arc lights, reflectors, and other light-shaping tools would instantly destroy the illusion that the VR viewer is "present" in an unadulterated environment. Furthermore, because the VR camera sees in all directions at once, you need to ensure the entire environment is sufficiently lit simultaneously. Given these limitations, you have a limited number of options for lighting a VR production:

Use natural lighting

You can choose to forgo using any lighting equipment. You'll need to find locations and settings where the lighting is

Lighting and grip equipment: All the equipment required to rig and control the lights during production, including lights, lighting stands, C-stands, cables, silks, flags, sandbags, reflectors, etc. Grip equipment also encompasses auxiliary camera gear, such as dollies (& their tracks), cranes, jibs, etc.

G&E (grip and electric): The production departments on set responsible for the operation of grip and lighting equipment. They work under the director of photography.

Color temperatures: The apparent color of light measured in degrees kelvin (K), i.e. Daylight emits a blueish 5600K light, and Tungsten filaments (traditionally used in film lights) emit an orange 3200K light.

Practical lights: Lights that are illuminating a scene but that are part of the set, so they can be seen by the camera without revealing the artifice of the filmmaking act.

CRI (color rendering index): The measure of how close to true white a light bulb appears.

inherently attractive (or at least sufficient) and then live with whatever results you get. Although this approach can save a lot of time on set, it may yield uneven or unpolished results. For example, your location might have light bulbs of varying color temperatures, which can make some areas of the room appear strangely orange or blue. Another drawback to natural lighting: Sunlight moves over the course of a day, so a scene that might look great during rehearsal at 9 a.m. might look completely different when you begin recording at high noon.

Additionally, without the benefit of the professional lighting control we're used to seeing on TV and in movies, your 360° productions may look more amateur, with distracting shadows on people's faces, blown-out windows, or other imperfections. And you certainly sacrifice the subtle but effective ways in which deliberate lighting can contribute to effective storytelling.

Use practical lights

One of the easiest ways to add light to a set is to add fixtures that look like they're intended to be in the scene. Lamps and lighting fixtures that are part the set dressing are known as practical lights—they can be seen by the camera without disclosing any evidence of the filmmaking process. Practical lighting may be as simple as switching on lamps already in a location, or moving lamps around to illuminate areas that are otherwise too dark.

You might also exchange the bulbs in the lighting fixtures or lamps with special bulbs specifically designed for filming (sometimes called photo floods). These bulbs can be brighter than ordinary lightbulbs, or at least of a consistent color temperature. For fluorescent bulbs, be sure to use bulbs with high CRI ratings to avoid noticeable flickering or a green color cast.

Hide lights (and lighting control) in the set

Another trick you can try is to hide lights and other lighting equipment on the set: Tuck them around corners, under tables, and behind other elements in the scene. You can position a light outside a window, or align a flag with a column so the flag properly controls the light but is effectively invisible to the audience. You might even conceal a light behind one of your actors—as long as you're sure he's not going to move and expose the equipment to the camera. Just be sure to hide all the cables and plugs too!

You can cover windows with neutral-density (ND) gel to reduce the amount of light coming in, or with tinted gels to correct the color temperature so the blue sunlight matches the orange light emitting from the light fixtures inside the room. As long as the gel is applied carefully and the edges are trimmed and properly hidden, it will be invisible to the camera, but the results can dramatically improve the polish of your scene.

Digitally paint out the lights in post

Finally, if your budget permits, you can add lighting equipment to your set just as you would for a flat movie, and then digitally remove the gear from the scene after the fact. While this may seem less than ideal, if you're already planning to digitally paint out a tripod or some other element of the set, you may be able to remove the lights as well (if you're careful about where you place the lighting equipment).

In many cases, you'll use a combination of these techniques and every situation will ultimately require different choices.

Flag: a frame of solid black fabric used to partially block a light source.

Latitude: Similar to *dynamic range*; The range of brightness that can be captured by a camera usually measured in *f*-stops).

Dynamic range: The varying degrees of brightness that can be captured by a camera or displayed by a playback device. You can think of it as the number of grays that can be represented before areas of the image appear all-black (in the shadows) or all-white (in the highlights).

Regardless of how you decide to illuminate your set, there are a few additional lighting issues to consider:

Compensate for mixed exposure

Pay special attention to scenes with both light and dark sections. If your location has a wide range of brightness (lighter areas and darker areas), the camera may not be able to capture the full range of light. (This is one of the biggest limitations of GoPro cameras (as well as several other camera types used for 360° video: their relatively limited latitude or dynamic range.) You'll need to set the camera to properly expose either the bright areas or the darker areas. Consequently, one part of the scene will wind up improperly exposed, which can compromise the look of the finished product.

To deal with this issue, you can make adjustments to the settings of the camera (as described in Chapter 22: Camera settings). You can also reduce the lighting latitude of the scene, by adding lights to brighten dark corners and/or adding ND gel to windows to reduce their brightness.

Compensate for mixed color temperatures

Similar to the mixed exposure problem is the issue of mixed color temperatures, that is, when your location has light sources that vary in terms of color. Most often this occurs when daylight in a window is mixed with electric lighting on your set. Another example: Your set is illuminated by a mix of electric light and candle light (which is even more orange than electric lights) or moonlight (which can be even bluer than sunlight). Although you can adjust your camera's white balance setting to pick which color of light appears as white, your best bet is to eliminate the disparity by forcing all the lights to be the same color. You may need to cover windows or lighting fixtures with colored gels, or you may need to swap out some light bulbs with others that are configured to a specific color temperature.

All of this is to emphasize that even though your 360° video crew can be smaller than a traditional crew, you shouldn't skimp on the essentials. Even if you won't be using a lot of lighting and grip equipment, having a smart and experienced gaffer will go a long way toward making your production more professional and ultimately more successful.

Gaffer: The chief electrician on set, responsible for contributing to and implementing the director of photography's lighting vision.

Chapter 25: Visual room tone

When recording the audio for a scene, good sound recordists always capture a few extra moments of "silence" after the scene ends, it's not actually silence that they're recording. There are a host of subtle sounds in any environment: the hum of an air conditioner, the drone of distant traffic, and whatever other noises are unique to that location and microphone position. We call that extra recording of incidental background noise *room tone*. In post-production, when an editor removes or replaces snippets of dialogue from the scene, she can fill in the gaps in the sound with the room tone recorded at that location, thus creating a smooth-sounding audio track.

Similarly, when shooting a 360° scene, it's essential to record some "visual room tone" to fill in any gaps in the image. For example, when shooting with a spherical camera, you'll often need to remove the camera's tripod from the final shot and replace it with a clean shot of the ground. Think of that clean shot as your visual room tone.

Background plates

For each shot you capture using the 360° camera, you should also get one (or more) still background shots of the ground underneath the camera. That still image is called a *plate*. To capture a clean plate, remember the position of the 360° camera, move the camera and tripod out of the way, hold a still camera in the exact position where the 360° camera was, aim it at the floor, and then snap a shot.

Note: If you're using a cylindrical camera like the GoPro Odyssey, you'll need to use a still camera to capture images both above and below to fill in the missing areas and complete the sphere (Without that, Jump fills those areas with a blurred circle using the colors of the adjacent pixels.)

When you assemble the final composite (described in Chapter 53: Rig removal and nadir patching) the plate becomes the background, so when you cut out the tripod, the background plate fills in the holes.

Composite: The post-production process of combining two or more images. Also can refer to the result of that process; a composite, or a composite image.

Latlong shot with tripod visible at the bottom.

Plate (shot with still camera).

The finished composite.

A production still of the set.

Focal length: The distance between a lens and its point of focus

Ideally, you should shoot your background plates using a lens with the same focal length as that of the 360°camera (often a fish-eye lens). That way, the lens distortion in the background plate will more readily match the lens distortion of the foreground elements.

Chapter 25: Visual room tone

127

Tip: An even better way to match the lens distortion of the plate to lens distortion in the spherical footage is to shoot the ground plate with your 360˚ camera itself. This is doable only if your 360˚ camera captures truly spherical images (that is, if it has lenses pointing up and down, as well as around the sides). Just flip the spherical camera upside down, so the tripod is sticking up in the air and the ground is unobstructed, then snap your shot of the ground.

Note: If your 360˚ camera is mounted from the ceiling, you'll need a background plate of the ceiling instead of the ground.

Most of the time, a still image is sufficient for filling in the background area. However, if your scene includes movement in the area beneath the camera (such as feet walking by, or shadows that pass across the floor area), you should capture a video background plate rather than a still image. It may be somewhat tricky to match the movement in the plate with the movement in the foreground shot, but some movement is likely better than a totally flat, still image.

Advanced plate techniques

In addition to hiding a tripod, background plates can be used to replace other areas of the sphere—potentially hiding the director, the crew, lighting equipment, and other bogeys.

Bogeys: Adapted from military slang, a bogey is a person or object who accidentally appears in the frame during a shot.

The simplest example of this is a technique commonly used for interview scenes. First, shoot the interview with the subject on one side of the camera and the director standing behind the camera. The director can see and talk directly to the subject, which (as explained in Chapter 18: Interviewing in VR), can greatly improve the quality of an interview. Then, after the interview, the director hides, and the camera is run again for the same duration of the interview.

In this second shot, the area behind the camera shows only the background. In post, you can use the split screen technique to combine the interview subject from the first shot and the clean background (without the director) from the second shot.

The same technique can be used to hide almost anything—as long as the background behind the object you want to hide is relatively static and stable. You can still use this technique if people or objects move in the area you want to hide, so long as that action doesn't cross over the stitch lines to the area in front of the camera, where the interview subject is standing.

Stitch: Combine multiple images/videos into one panoramic image/video (also sometimes refers to the seam in a panoramic image).

Chapter 26: Moving shots

In traditional cinema, adding movement to a shot is a key way to build viewer engagement. The same can be true with 360° video; however, unless you're very thoughtful about how you do it, moving a spherical camera can very quickly make the resulting video unwatchable.

Nausea alert: Because a person watching VR can turn her head, essentially moving the "camera view" on her own, any physical camera movement during shooting can conflict with the viewer's later head movements, leading to confusion, disorientation, and often nausea.

The more you think of your camera as a stand-in for your viewer's head, the more success you'll have. Dragging a head across the floor, or bouncing it around on a selfie stick, or moving it too suddenly in any direction will not be a pleasant experience for the person attached to that head.

Because of this, many 360° productions completely avoid moving the camera at all—and the results are great! Well-placed camera positions and thoughtful, effective blocking allow you to create fascinating, engaging productions without any complicating camera movement. Plus, you get the added bonus of quicker productions, because even a simple moving shot invariably takes 3–5 times longer to complete than a locked-off shot (just as in a traditional production).

But I know you, gentle reader, and you wouldn't be reading this chapter if you were not a rebel and a risk taker. So here are some tips for how to make the most of moving shots:

Avoid acceleration

Perhaps the most important guideline to follow is to keep any movement as constant as possible. Speeding up or slowing down a camera in motion is likely to be less pleasant for your viewers than steady motion. And the faster the acceleration or deceleration, the higher the probability of discomfort. If you must accelerate or decelerate (for example, if your shot begins from a stationary position and then begins moving), try to ease into and out of the movement as gradually as possible.

Keep it smooth

Similarly, steady movement is far less unsettling for viewers than uneven movement. One of the reasons GoPros remain popular devices for recording 360˚ video is that they have excellent built-in camera stabilization.

Hand-holding a 360˚ shot is a recipe for making your viewers sick. Our heads are ordinarily fastened quite firmly to our neck and spine and thus restricted to very small and limited movements. Putting your viewer's head at the end of your arm (with its impressively flexible range of motion) creates a very unnatural and uncomfortable experience.

Maintain a level horizon

This is especially critical for stereoscopic 360˚ video, but it's a smart idea for all moving shots: Make sure any movement is carefully controlled so as to limit rocking or tilting the camera side to side or forward and back. This kind of movement is not only disorienting (and can be challenging to correct for in post), but it totally undermines the 3D effect for stereo images.

Slider: A tripod 'head' mounted on a fixed track that enables the camera to smoothly move left and right or forward and back.

Camera dollies: Wheeled camera mounts, either on tracks or fully mobile, that facilitate smooth camera motion.

Rig removal: The process of compositing or painting out the camera support (tripod, dolly, slider, etc.) visible in the 360 image.

Background plate: A duplicate set up of a shot with an unwanted object (tripod, interviewer, crewmember, etc.) removed.

An Ozo+ (discontinued) on a motorized Syrp slider.

North: The point of origin where a viewer enters a 360° scene, also serves as a frame of reference for orienting discussions about the scene.

Use a motorized slider

An effective way to keep motion smooth is to mount your camera on a self-powered, motorized slider, such as those made by Edelkrone, Syrp, Rhino, and many manufacturers. These are small camera dollies that can be programmed to move along a predetermined route. Because they're programmable, you can run and hide before they begin moving, thereby staying out of the shot. And because these devices are motorized, they guarantee smooth, consistent movement.

> **Note:** Shooting on a slider (or on any camera dolly) complicates rig removal. However, with an automated slider, you can potentially reposition the camera and re-run the motorized sequence, allowing the camera to record its own background plate. (The process of using the background plate to hide the camera support is discussed further in Chapter 53: Rig removal and nadir patching.)

Avoid contra-lateral movement

Almost as bad as accelerating the camera too quickly is setting up a shot where the camera moves from left to right at the same time your viewer tries to look right to left. The result is surprisingly disorienting and is one of the things most likely to trigger vertigo and nausea.

The thing is, in a 360° space, it's not always apparent what is a lateral move and what isn't. If the viewer is looking due north and the camera moves from west to east, that's a lateral move, but if the same viewer is looking east the whole time, it's not lateral at all.

The key is to think about the subject of a shot in relation to the camera position. The more accurately you can predict where your viewer is apt to be looking, the more likely you can avoid creating the contra-lateral situation. (See Chapter 15: Guiding the viewer's focus for tips.) Of course, you can never completely eliminate the risk because you can't control where your viewers look.

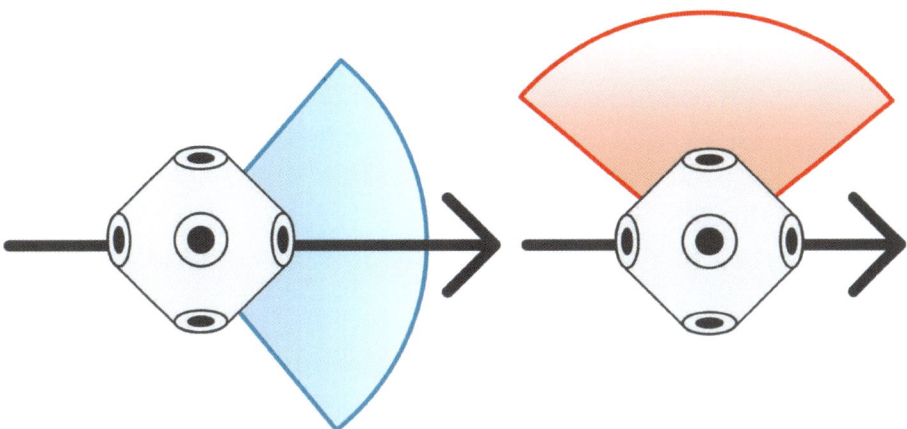

If the viewer is looking in the direction of the movement (blue), the camera movement will not be as disruptive. But if the viewer is looking in a different direction (red), the movement can be very disorienting or even nauseating.

Frame the scene

If you've ever been seasick, the boat captain may have suggested that you go to the helm and steer the boat for a while. Motion sickness happens when the movement your body feels is incongruent with what your eyes are seeing. Steering the boat helps align what you're seeing with what you're feeling. That's the same reason drivers in car are far less likely to get car sick than their passengers.

One way to implement a similar corrective effect in VR is to add a natural frame through which your audience views the movement. For example, if your scene is occurring in a moving car, the world whizzes by through the windows, but the inside of the car remains static (relative to your movement) and provides a (literal) frame of reference.

This is one of the reasons why flying or driving games (where you sit in a cockpit or driver's seat) are some of the most popular VR game titles. You get the thrill of fast and overwhelming movement, but you don't get motion sick because the cockpit itself provides a balancing reference.

Justify any movement

Even in flat cinema, camera movement requires justification or motivation to avoid knocking your viewers out of the story, and in 360° video this is even more true. Moving a 360° camera is rarely a subtle effect; your viewer—standing (or sitting) still in real life— suddenly feels as if she's moving through space. The disconnect between what she sees and feels will remind her of the artificiality of the experience, and reduce her feeling of presence. The only way to avoid this is to tie the movement something specific within the story.

Chapter 27: Recording audio for 360°

As any filmmaker knows, sound is often far more important than visuals when it comes to communicating to an audience. First of all, our ears are far more discerning than our eyes when it comes to noticing small errors or inconsistencies; most viewers will tolerate low-quality visuals as long as the sound is smooth and clear, but few people will endure watching a clip with bad audio, no matter how pristine the images.

Furthermore, when it comes to storytelling, sound is the key to our hearts. I like to say that *if seeing is believing, then hearing is feeling*; it's the sound that usually carries the emotional resonance of a film. And in the world of 360° video this axiom is even more true.

Sound makes VR

VR is about space as much as traditional cinema is about time. A properly crafted soundscape is the key to building an authentic and immersive space. And it is sound more than picture that what will create the feeling of presence you want to instill in your audience. If voices or sound effects appear to be coming from the wrong place in the screen, or if they don't appear to be coming from anywhere in particular, the immersive illusion is quickly shattered.

What's more, without the camera angles and editing techniques traditional filmmakers use to control the viewer's point of focus, sound is often your primary tool for helping to guide the viewer where to look. Given that your viewer is free to cast her gaze anywhere within the sphere, you may find that viewers are missing important elements that propel your story forward. If you want to be sure your audience notices that the door latch has suddenly come open, a properly positioned sound effect is the best way to get them to turn their heads.

In a documentary or nonfiction scene, sound is also the most effective way to gently guide your audience and ensure they don't miss important content. When you drop your viewer into a busy West African marketplace full of color, movement, and activity, there's so much to look at that it would be easy for people to miss the spice vendor who's surreptitiously selling hand grenades along with his satchels of hot chile powder. If the point of your show is to illustrate the weapons trade being conducted in broad daylight, you could highlight the sound of that transaction while dulling the conversations in the various other stalls. Viewers will subconsciously turn their attention to that important bit of content.

Without properly recorded and mixed sound, it's nearly impossible to affect what your audience is watching, and therefore to tell an effective story.

But recording quality audio is not always so easy. There are many types of microphones suited for different situations. And once you've determined the right mic, it's essential to position it correctly, set proper levels on the recording device, and monitor the sound in closed-ear headphones to ensure there are no problems during recording.

Perhaps most important is the positioning of the mic. It's essential for mics to be placed as close to the source of the sound as possible. Otherwise the sound you're recording may have unwanted reverb, or, if the level is too low, you have to turn

Levels: The adjustable sensitivity settings of microphones. Levels are set (and changed as necessary) to best capture the vocals of an actors performance.

Closed-ear headphones: Headphones that fully encompass the ear to reduce the interference of sound from the listener's environment.

up the recorder's input sensitivity which will amplify the background noise just as much as it amplifies the sound you're trying to record.

Camera mics

Nearly all 360° cameras include microphones that record audio along with the video. But an on-camera mic is very rarely going to capture adequate sound. As mentioned above, mics need to be placed as close as possible to the source of the sound, and the nature of 360° shooting means that your subjects are unlikely to be closer than 1 or 2 meters away.

Your subjects are also likely to be moving around the space (while the camera remains fixed). That means the volume of their voices will vary over the course of the scene, which will translate to uneven volumes for your viewers. This may seem desirable as it replicates the actual movement occurring in the scene but to create a natural sounding scene, you're far better off recording the audio at a constant (high quality) level and simulating any volume changes during the sound mix.

That said, you absolutely should let your 360° camera record audio along with its video. That audio is very valuable when it comes to helping synchronize multiple cameras; and in some cases, in-camera audio may be useful in the final mix as an ambiance element.

Some VR cameras record mono or stereo audio tracks in the same way as a traditional on-camera mic. Other 360° cameras record with multiple mics which may be saved as a surround sound format, or it may be formatted in a positional (ambisonic) format. Positional recording is covered in more detail in the next chapter: Positional audio recording.

Ambisonic: Pertaining to audio reproduction that captures the spatial acoustic qualities of recorded sound

Shotgun mics

In flat cinema, dialogue recording is done with a hypercardioid (or shotgun) mic. These are designed to record audio from a distance, but this comes with the compromise that they capture a narrower frequency spectrum and so they're not ideal for sounds other than human voices (for which they're usually tuned).

Also, while they can work from a distance, that means 5-10 feet and not much farther. Plus, the mic has to be manually pointed at whomever is talking. This is why you frequently see a person on a film set following the actors around with a mic at the end of a long stick (called a boom pole).

Just as the all-seeing eye of a VR camera makes it difficult to light and dress a scene, the same problem affects audio; those boom poles and shotgun mics are out of the question. Even for documentary or nonfiction work, the presence of a location sound mixer balancing a boom pole on his shoulders will make for a highly distracting element that you'll probably want to avoid.

Omnidirectional and cardioid mics

Secondary elements like sound effects, ambiances and sourced sound (like an onscreen dog barking) are usually recorded individually after the primary scene is completed using an omnidirectional or cardioid mic. These mics are more full-spectrum than shotguns, and by capturing sound in a wider pickup pattern, they record not just the primary source of the sound but also any reverberations or sound reflections created by the walls of the room.

Hypercardioid / shotgun: A microphone polar pattern that picks up sound primarily to the front, with less sensitivity to the side and rear.

Frequency spectrum: The range of sound wavelengths recorded up by the microphone.

Ambiances: Background sounds that capture an environment such as the general murmur of a crowd, birds and insects in a rainforest, or the pitter-patter of rain.

Sourced sound: Sound elements that are tied to a specific object or source onscreen.

Omnidirectional: Picking up sound evenly in all directions.

Cardioid: A microphone with a primary sensitivity in front of the microphone, but which also records audio to the left and right.

> **Note:** sometimes these non-primary sounds are added in the editing room, sourced from sound effects libraries or rerecorded as foley or ADR. Later, they're panned into stereo or surround sound mixes to link the audio cue with the source of the sound onscreen (or off-screen).

Lavalieres

For the bulk of your sound recording you'll probably be dependent on tiny mics that can be easily hidden called lavalieres (or *lavs* for short). Lavs can often be configured to transmit wirelessly, so that the audio is sent from the lav to a recording device somewhere nearby. The problem with wireless audio is that it requires radio transmission, which is frequently unreliable and subject to interference that can ruin the audio signal. And the likelihood of this happening is multiplied by the number of mics you use. They also eat up batteries like you wouldn't believe.

One trick is to hard-wire your mics to portable audio recorders that can be hidden in someone's pocket. Not only are there inexpensive portable recorders from Zoom and Tascam, but that smartphone already in your actor's pocket can be used too. And any recent model will likely give as high quality a signal as many of those standalone devices. Just be sure to enable airplane mode so text messages and other alerts don't interrupt your recording!

Lavs have drawbacks too. In addition to the interference that can occur when transmitting wirelessly, they can sound unnatural at times. Because they're usually placed so close to the speaker's body, lavs have very little natural reverberation. Also, unless you're using very high-quality mics (at correspondingly high prices) the frequency spectrum can be limited and require a bit of equalization to sound natural.

Foley: The process of reproducing sound effects in a controlled environment synchronized to actions onscreen. For example footsteps, or grunts.

ADR: Automated Dialogue Replacement is the process of re-recording dialogue by the original actor in post-production in a way that matches the recorded video. It is employed to correct sound issues or reflect dialogue changes (also called "looping").

Lavaliere: A small microphone attached to a lapel or discretely hidden in an actors wardrobe.

Also, they can fall off or move around inside someone's shirt creating unwanted noise or muffling the sound. And even when placed perfectly, they can be undone by a simple hug: For some reason all the shows I produce seem to include characters hugging as they say hello and goodbye, which always ruins the audio from both players during those brief embraces.

Plant mics

Another trick is to hide a microphone (or several) on the set near where your subjects might be talking (or otherwise making noise). You can use a lavaliere for this, though it's probably better to use a cardioid or other directional mic which might capture more natural sound. Hidden mics like this are called a "plant" mics, though I don't know if that's because they were routinely hidden in houseplants, or if "planting" is just a synonym for placing.

Slating and logging

One of the downsides of using multiple mics is that someone will later need to synchronize the recordings in the editing room so that the various audio tracks line up with the picture, and with each other. On set, you'll need a cue sound at the beginning of each take, loud enough to be audible to each of the recording devices.

A common way to do this is have someone clap their hands to make a loud, sharp sound at the beginning of each shot. But it's far more preferable to follow the systematic procedure described below using a slate (also called a clapperboard). By logging the scenes by number, and using the clapper on the slate, you'll dramatically reduce the likelihood of problems—both on set (such as forgetting to turn on one of the recording devices) or later, in post (where elements can get lost if they're mislabeled).

Take: Individual instance of a shot; a take = each time the camera is started and stopped.

Chapter 27: Recording audio for 360°

Here's the common order of operations when calling a scene:

1. *"Roll sound"*: AD or director instructs that all sound devices be turned on to record.
2. *"Speed"*: Anyone with a recording device turns it on, verifies that it's running, and verbally affirms.
3. *"Roll Camera"*: AD or director instructs camera operator to begin recording.
4. *"Rolling"*: Camera operator turns camera on, verifies that it's running, and verbally affirms.
5. "Shot 1, take 2": Holding the slate in front of the camera, 2nd AC (or someone) calls out the name and number of the shot.
6. *"Mark!"*: Slate holder creates a sharp, short sound, audible to all recording devices—typically using the clapper on the slate. (If your slate has no clapper, someone can clap their hands once sharply.)
7. [Run and hide]: Everyone who's not supposed to be seen on camera gets out of sight.
8. *"Action"*: Director instructs the performers to begin the scene.
9. *"Cut"*: After the scene is played out, director instructs everyone to turn off their recording devices.

Additionally, if you've got the time and resources, it's a great idea to keep a written log of every shot you record. Write down the shot name and number, a brief description, and perhaps a comment or two about the results.

AD (assistant director): The crew-member responsible for running the set during production, ensuring the production runs on schedule and all requisite shots are captured.

2nd AC (2nd assistant camera): is responsible for operating the slate, keeping a camera log, and managing the raw film stock and footage shot

Some common abbreviations for comments are listed below:

- **NG:** Take was no good
- **\ (Slash drawn through the item):** Take aborted
- **TECH:** Take had a technical problem
- **CAM:** Take had a camera problem
- **AUD or SND:** Take had a sound problem
- **(Circle drawn around the take number):** Take was good/director's favorite

Post: The phase of production that occurs after filming completes.

While keeping such a log may seem unnecessary or an expendable luxury on set, it takes just a few seconds to jot notes for each shot. A basic log will save you time in post, preventing frustrating and costly efforts to locate or identify a misplaced audio or video track.

Tip: There are a number of apps available for tablets or smartphones that make this logging process especially easy. Some of these apps even make the clapper sound. The Black and Blue[6] is a website for camera assistants that keeps a list of great apps for filmmakers including some great logging and slating apps.

Room tone

Don't forget to always record some ambient background noise (a few moments of silence, with no one in the crew talking or milling about). Known as *room tone*, this audio allows your editor to cut and replace unwanted noises and audio glitches recorded on the main mics. Without good room tone, when the editor removes a wayward sneeze coming from the director's

6   https://www.theblackandblue.com/cinematography-apps/

hiding spot under the table, you'll wind up with dead silence that doesn't sound natural at all.

Tip: Be sure to record the room tone with all the mics positioned exactly where they were during the scene. If you remove a lav from someone's shirt before recording room tone, the sound quality may not match the original sound you later need to replace.

One option for grabbing room tone is to just remind everyone to stop moving and hold still for 20 seconds at the end of the take, after the director calls "cut." That way the room tone is simply appended to the end of each shot. (There's no need to do this more than once per scene).

Documentary tip: Remember that room tone is just as essential for documentary recording as it is for fiction. If you want to remove an "um…" from your interviewee's recording, or if there's any other background noise you want to eliminate, you'll need that room tone track to make the resulting edit sound smooth.

Wild lines

If you're ever worried that you didn't get perfect audio while the camera rolled, record the scene again for audio only. Without the camera rolling you can position the mics at the best possible position to ensure an ideal recording. Because the audio is not synced to the camera we call it a "wild" recording.

Later, in post, you can attempt to sync up the audio with the best take from the camera. It may be impossible to line up the audio perfectly (if you need perfect sync, consider ADR). But fortunately, with 360° video the angle is often wide enough that your audio will appear to line up with the actors' lips even if you're a few frames off.

Chapter 28: Positional audio recording

To replicate the sonic experience of standing in a three-dimensional place, you can use a special microphone that records not just the soundwaves producing the audio, but also their relative position in space. There are several different types of mics that record this way.

Binaural microphone

Binaural mics replicate the hearing field of a human head, simulating the effect of two mics placed approximately ear-distance apart. In fact, binaural mics are often modeled to look like human ears so they can reproduce the aural response shaped by the contours of your head (called the head-related transfer function or HRTF, and no, I'm not joking).

When recording using a binaural mic, you can represent the sounds in a particular location with tremendous accuracy. However, a binaural mic can't be rotated without distorting the sound in a way that undermines the positional information.

Consequently, audio recordists sometimes employ two (or more) binaural mics positioned in different positions, so that in the studio, the multiple signals can be overlapped and interpolated to represent different head positions.

A binaural mic and a quad--binaural mic.

Tetrahedral microphone

A different approach to positional recording is to use an array of microphone diaphragms pointing in different directions (just like a 360°camera uses multiple camera lenses pointing in different directions). The most common version of this is called a *tetrahedral* mic which uses four mics.

This produces something similar to the binaural mic, but the sound can be rotated on any axis after the recording without any change in sound quality. For 360° video, this can be configured to match the listener's head position so the sound properly updates whenever she turns her head.

Tetrahedral mics replicate the sound exactly as it is heard from a specific position in the room. In order to accurately correspond the audio with the camera's position, place your tetrahedral mic as close to the camera as possible. If you mount a mic rig like this directly on top of (or underneath) the VR camera, it should be easy to hide the rig during the stitching process.

Also, tetrahedral mics are extremely sensitive, so they must always be suspended in a shock mount, otherwise small vibrations such as those caused by someone walking on the floor near where the camera is mounted can cause unwanted interference in the audio signal.

A tetrahedral mic outputs four individual audio channels. It's critical that the recorder saves the four channels at precisely identical audio recording levels. So, be advised to use a device with digital level settings (such as the Tascam DR-40). With an analog recorder (like the Zoom H6 with it's manual level dials) it's too easy for one channel to get set to a slightly different audio level which would distort the positional information.

Core Sound and Soundfield have sold tetrahedral mics for decades, (CoreSound also has an octohedral version) but with VR generating renewed interest in spatialized recording, there are now many options across a wide range of price points. Zoom's H3-VR is less than $300 and specifically designed for 360 video

Core Sound's Tetramic and Octamic with 4 and 8 capsules respectively.

Stitching: Combining multiple images/videos into one panoramic image/video (also sometimes refers to the seams in a panoramic image).

Shock mount: A microphone holder engineered to absorb physical bumps or vibrations to prevent movement from disturbing the audio signal.

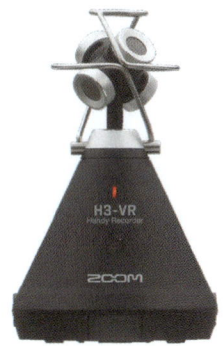

The Zoom H3-VR

The Audeze Planar Magnetic mic uses large-diaphragm condensers to capture a larger dynamic range.

recording. Sennheiser and Rode both offer mid-priced options. Other companies have tried to differentiate themselves, such as Audeze with it's large-diaphragm model, and Twirling with a tetrahedral mic that plugs directly into a smartphone.

The recordings from the tetrahedral mics are joined together into a special multichannel signal called an ambisonic recording. Later during post-production, (after converting from A-format to B-format) the sound can be carefully tuned and manipulated.

Important: Be sure to note the tetrahedral microphone's orientation during the shoot: Is the label forward or backward? Is the microphone inverted or right-side-up? This information is essential for aligning the direction of the sound when you get to the final mix.

Other multi-channel mics

There are several other mic options available for even more precise and high-quality sound. Mics such as the Dysonics RondoMic, The Zylia 8160, and the Schoeps ORTF-3D use many more sensors (and propietary decoding software) to process the recordings.

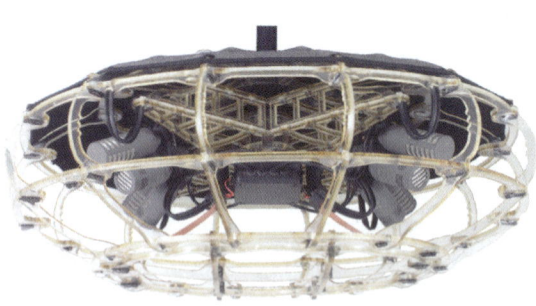

The Zylia 8160 Mic, The Schoeps ORTF-3D, and the Dysonics RondoMic.

Summary

For the best results, you'll need to implement a combination of audio-capture methods. A static positional mic at the camera's location may be great for capturing the sounds in the immediate environment, but it's less likely to clearly record more distant sounds (a dog barking, for example) or even the dialogue of people are talking in your scene. So, in addition to the positional mic recording environmental sounds, you'll want to add lavs or other mics to record any additional important sounds that are part of your scene.

The goal is to ensure that in the editing room you'll have all the elements needed to recreate the environment in the most immersive and realistic way. The downside is that you may have to manage a large number of discrete audio tracks, all of which need to be properly labeled, managed, ingested, synchronized, sweetened, and panned appropriately for your final mix.

Because of all this, I think it's more essential than ever to bring along a professional sound recordist on your VR shoot—someone with multiple microphones for recording different types of audio, who knows how to properly set levels, and who can organize all those different elements so your editor can effectively reassemble them in the editing room.

Levels: The adjustable sensitivity settings of microphones. Levels are set (and changed as necessary) to best capture the vocals of an actors performance.

A zone-based stereo camera mounts pairs of camera sensors positioned with a precise (and sometimes adjustable) interocular distance.

An omnidirectional stereo camera that uses an array of cameras evenly spaced and generate the stereo separation programmatically. (Image courtesy YI Technologies)

Spherical: Video that is displayed in a seamless 360 degree sphere.

Chapter 29: Stereoscopic recording

If you really want your 360° video to be deeply immersive, transporting the viewer to another location that feels real and authentic, you must shoot not just "in the round," but *stereoscopically* (aka *in 3D*) too.

Shooting stereoscopic 360° video requires different, specialized cameras that capture two images from slightly different angles (just as human eyes do) for each frame of video. Later, these two images are combined in an HMD to create the illusion of depth.

For the purposes of 360° video, there are two kinds of stereo rigs:

Zone-based stereo camera: whereby a series of paired cameras are mounted together. Each pair of cameras captures two side-by-side images (left and right) and then the left cameras are stitched together, the right cameras are stitched together, and the two stitched files are combined to create stereoscopic output. [7]

Omnidirectional stereo camera: This type uses a single camera body arranged in a ring with multiple lenses (and multiple image sensors) that provide enough overlap between adjacent lenses to allow for a computationally generated stereo image in all directions.

Unfortunately, recording in stereo can make shooting a lot harder. For starters, stereo requires a more complex, usually larger camera rig. Managing the media from a mono 360° camera is complicated enough. Stereo doubles the number of

7   One drawback to these rigs is that the stereo effect is focused on a narrow range directly in front of the cameras. Objects off to one side will not display effective stereo separation.

camera sensors, making media management exponentially more complex (as described in Chapter 32: Ingesting footage).

Additionally, with a stereo rig you must keep objects even farther from the camera or risk creating a hyperstereo effect where people and objects can look miniaturized. Stereo also increases the likelihood of parallax errors. And it introduces other limitations such as the need to keep the horizon level.

An additional, and not insignificant, downside to stereo: Because the data for both "eyes" must be squeezed into a standard frame for some distribution methods, stereo video may be displayed at half the resolution of mono video!

And, as if all that weren't bad enough, stereo 360° video is far

Hyperstereo effect: An optical distortion that makes the viewer feel gigantic. Occurs when the interaxial distance of stereo cameras appears greater than ordinary human distance based on the relative distance to the subject.

Parallax: The optical effect where an object's position appears to differ when viewed from different positions, i.e. the left eye vs. the right.

monoscopic image

stereoscopic image

more likely to trigger motion sickness in your viewers than mono 360° is. Although it's widely agreed that good stereo is much more immersive than mono, bad stereo is far, far worse.

Given all this, why does anyone bother shooting in stereo at all?

Well, in many ways, watching mono 360° video is like having your head inside a giant globe looking around at the inside of that sphere. With stereo, the contours of that globe fade away, and the illusion of being in real space intensifies. Technically, the difference is subtle, but experientially it's huge.

Donning a cumbersome pair of VR goggles head is a lot to ask of your audience—shouldn't you do everything you can to maximize their experience? On the other hand, if you expect the majority of your viewers to watch in a magic window on a phone or computer screen, then there's really no reason to shoot in 3D.

Also, given that stereo video is harder to create than mono video, for your first baby steps into 360° content, it makes sense to stick with mono. Better to make the inevitable mistakes in your first few projects without taking on the extra work and complications of stereoscopy.

When you're ready to step up to stereo, consider the following guidelines:

Hit the sweet spot

The stereo effect is only noticeable when objects are relatively close to the camera. Depending on the camera, the sweet spot for 3D is between 3 and 15 feet from your rig. Closer than 3 feet you risk unfixable stitching issues. Much farther than 15 feet and the stereo separation becomes increasingly subtle.

Beware the transition from stereo to mono

Some cameras record stereo for part of the sphere and mono for another part. For example, cameras like the YI HALO and Facebook 360 shoot stereo in a cylinder around the center, and mono at the top and bottom.

These ingenious designs attempt to maximize the value of the stereo effect where you'll most want it, but they come with a downside: transition zones between the 3D and the 2D portions

Stereo separation: The slight variations in image from the two perspectives that enable 3-dimensional viewing. The closer to the camera, the larger the variations.

Chapter 29: Stereoscopic recording

of the sphere. Unfortunately, objects stuck right in that zone may not stitch properly. Be careful to avoid having important subjects fall on, or cross over, that seam.

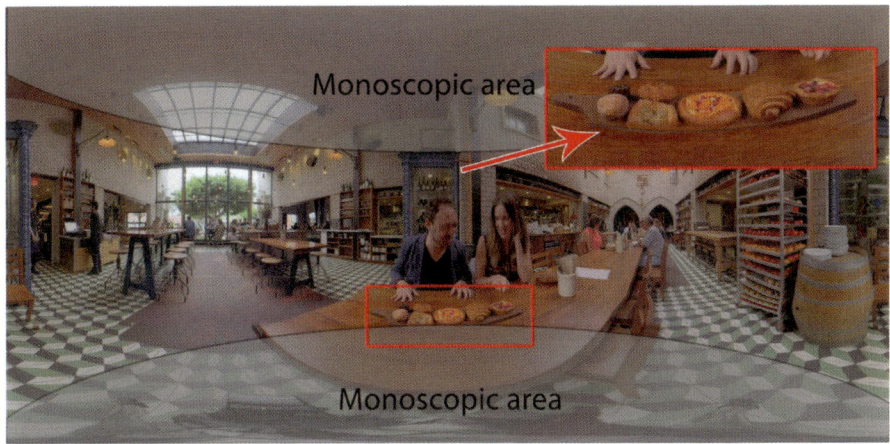

Maintain perfect level

When shooting stereo, keeping the camera level is vital. Ideally, you should mount the camera on an auto-leveling, gyroscope-balanced tripod head. If the camera pitches even slightly and skews the horizon, the stereo effect can be compromised, yielding footage that's unpleasant to watch.

Stabilize your shots

All 360° video benefits from a steady camera position. With mono footage, you can at least apply some stabilization in post to even out small bumps. But with stereo shots, digital stabilization can cause variations between the eyes that, again, ruins the stereo effect and make the resulting footage unwatchable.

Measure interaxial distance

Interocular separation (or *interpupillary distance*) describes the distance between the centers of human eyes. An adult male's is usually about 65mm (2.5 inches). When shooting with stereo cameras, you can control how far apart the lenses are, which is called interaxial distance.

Setting your interaxial distance to 65mm creates an effect that mimics natural vision. But there are times you may want to deliberately increase or decrease it for specific effect. Take care that each pair of lenses in your 360° rig maintain precisely matched distances.

Use a smaller interaxial distance for tiny objects (like for macro-photography) or to make the viewer feel like she is small and the world around her is huge. Increase distance to maintain a stereo effect when shooting massive or distant objects, or to simulate the effect that the viewer is large and the world around her is small.

Hire an expert

If you're intimidated by shooting in 3D, hire someone who knows what they're doing and overcome your fear. In fact, no matter what you do, I recommend hiring an experienced stereographer who can focus on managing your depth budget and configuring the camera's interaxial distances to maximize the 3D effect without causing discomfort for your viewers. Don't expect your director or cinematographer to handle stereographic tasks, which are complex and intricate, and best tasked to a specialist.

Depth budget: The amount of three-dimensional depth you can utilize in a scene without exhausting your viewer.

> **Note:** The post-production side of working with stereoscopic footage is covered later in the book.

Chapter 30: VR180

While 360° video enables the fully immersive experience we've been discussing throughout this book, there is a compromise type of immersive video that offers many of the benefits of 360 but also alleviates many of the drawbacks: limiting the video to only half the sphere. Or, in Google-speak: VR180.

Limited-sphere proponents argue that most so-called 360° shots don't take advantage of the full space, anyway. What's more, they say, a more limited range of view can significantly improve the VR experience, especially for narrative content.

Restricting the video to only half the sphere will:

Eliminate stitching: This may be the single best aspect of VR180; VR180 cameras use a single lens to capture the scene (there are actually two lenses, but that's to create a stereoscopic image). This means the biggest obstacle to going from shooting to viewing is eliminated. This also means no worrying about stitchlines while shooting!

Improve image quality: All 360° video is stored and delivered in rectangular frames. Those rectangles are then stretched onto a spherical canvas to be viewed, like an elastic washcloth being stretched around a round balloon. If you only need to stretch the washcloth around half of the balloon it doesn't have to be stretched as much. That translates into sharper images and/or smaller file sizes.

Help to control the viewer's focus: If the viewer understands that there's nothing to see beyond a certain distance from the center point, she can comfortably focus on the viewable area,

Stereoscopic: Video shot with two parallel cameras (or in the case of 360 video, multiple pairs of parallel cameras) Commonly referred to as 3D.

resting her neck muscles a rest and giving you, the creator, less space to fill.

Improve the editability of spherical video: One of the biggest obstacles to editing 360° footage is never knowing where a particular viewer might be looking at the point in the edit. If you cut to reveal some piece of new information in one area of the sphere, that might work fine so long as the viewer is looking straight ahead at the instant of the cut.

But if the viewer happens to be looking up, or to the right, or over their shoulder at the moment of the cut, she'll have a very jarring experience. This is why editing is so tricky (as explained in more detail in Chapter 40: Editing 360° footage). However, limiting the scope of view, greatly reduces the likelihood of your viewer looking in the wrong direction at a key moment.

If you happen to look directly down, often you'll see a logo where the camera was. But how often do you look down?

Go unnoticed by a large number of 360° users: The reality is that many people who watch 360° video never turn their head more than a few inches here or there. There are good reasons for this behavior: ingrained habits from years of watching traditional cinema, and the infrequent need for rapid head swings in our everyday life (unless you're paranoid).

Already, many productions cover the nadir (bottom) and/or apex (top) of the sphere with a logo (or a static background), believing that only a tiny number of viewers ever bother to look straight up or straight down; and that important action rarely happens in those quadrants.

Google has spearheaded this effort, creating special software tools for creating, working with, and viewing 180° footage, including the dedicated VR180 smartphone app.

> **Note:** 180° video also plays properly on YouTube, but is not automatically supported on other playback systems. In some cases, the 180° image is duplicated on the back half of the sphere. While this works as a way to display 180° video in software designed for 360° playback, it largely defeats most of the benefits that 180° video offers.

Google's intent (based on their ads and publicity around the VR180 technology) appears to be an effort to mainstream spherical video creation. They seem to be hoping that consumers with little or no filmmaking experience or know-how will choose to shoot VR180 as they document the important and sentimental moments of their lives, presumably instead of using the videocameras built into their smartphones.

Personally, despite my excitement for spherical video, I think this is a pretty unlikely development (unless or until manufacturers start building VR180 cameras into smartphones, which does seem utterly plausible in the near future). Buying a new camera, especially one with such a specific and limited function just for this purpose seems a pretty significant hurdle for most consumers.

Consumer VR180 Cameras: Lenovo Mirage, Yi Horizon and Lucidcam

However, VR180 does provide a wonderful opportunity and alternative creative medium for ambitious filmmakers like yourself! One of the nice benefits of Google's implementation of 180° video is that it supports (and expects) that the video is stereoscopic. So, while the images are limited in their lateral scope, they make up for it by seeming deeper and richer.

There are currently a number of VR180-specific cameras on the market. They are mostly aimed at a consumer audience, and are intended to be point-and-shoot with few options or customizable features. They also feature automatic wireless synching with Google's VR180 app, making distribution and exhibition of VR180 work that much easier.

A few manufacturers are trying to straddle the line, offering convertible cameras that can do VR180 but that can also shoot (mono) 360° video by moving the lenses from side-by-side to face in opposite directions.

Convertible VR180 cameras: (top) Vuze XR, (bottom): Kandao QooRoo

Professional VR180 cameras: (left) Z CAM K1 Pro, (right): iZugar Z2XL 180.

And finally, there are also a few options for professionals interested in VR180, including the Z CAM K1 Pro, and a rig from iZugar featuring (relatively large) micro 4/3 sensors and 220° lenses.

Of course if you want to edit, finesse, or otherwise modify your VR180 video before uploading it, you can easily do that too. However, there are some extra steps you may need to take (depending on the camera you use). This is covered in Chapter 47: Editing VR180 Footage .

Chapter 31: Shooting 360° with a flat camera

Some producers have been experimenting with generating 360° content using traditional cameras. There are several different approaches, and each can be beneficial for different reasons.

Shoot quadrants one at time

If you have complete control over your set, and if you can ensure that no objects ever cross the stitch lines between the different camera angles, you can simply point the camera towards the north quadrant and record that portion of the scene by itself. Then, rotate the camera 90° and record the east quadrant, and so on.

The results are the same as if you had used four cameras recording simultaneously, but by recording one section at a time, you have tremendous added flexibility on set. For starters, you can shoot with a state-of-the-art, high-resolution camera (with all the customizable controls DPs are accustomed to on traditional shoots). Such a camera would otherwise be too cumbersome and difficult to convert into a 360° rig. You can use lights and have crew and other equipment right there behind the camera. You can run multiple takes for each quadrant and combine the best take of each quadrant into one final shot. After the four quadrants are stitched together, the viewer will experience them simultaneously.

You can use this same technique with less-expensive 180° cameras such as VR180 cameras. Taking a VR180 camera and rotating it to shoot a scene in multiple takes is a way to get all the benefits of VR180, but with a full 360 result. Of course you will still need to manually stitch the two resulting shots.

Stitch lines: The seams in a 360° video where footage from one camera has been combined with another.

Shoot each quadrant, then rotate the camera and shoot again.

VR180: A subset of spherical video where only the front half of the sphere is recorded. Learn more in Chapter 30: VR180.

Use a nodal rig

In order to prevent parallax issues, it's helpful to use a nodal rig (or nodal slider) to rotate the camera between shots of the different quadrants. A nodal rig is a camera support device that moves in two dimensions as it rotates so the focal plane of the camera can remain constant. If you attempt to rotate the camera using a traditional tripod head, it's very difficult to ensure that the new camera position will line up precisely with the previous one, which can introduce parallax issues when stitching.

Record a depth map

Even more ambitious is the idea of using a LIDAR (light detection and ranging) camera or similar devices such as the XBox Kinect. These devices record the spatial placement of the objects in the room, creating a depth map and tracking how a subject moves within a space. That data can be combined with the visual output of a flat cinema camera to create a three-dimensional image of the subject. That footage can then be combined with CGI to create an experience closer to full VR than other 360° video.

Use Photogrammetry

This is a method of extracting three-dimensional data by comparing multiple (flat) images of the same subject taken from different angles. This data can then be assembled and projected into a spherical shape similar to 360° video. In practical application, this technique can be used to create photorealistic backgrounds for images captured using the depth map method described above. Photogrammetry can also be integrated with 3D computer-generated subjects to create realistic scenes.

Note: These techniques begin to overlap with some of what's being done with volumetric cameras (which are described in Chapter 9: Specialty Cameras.

Parallax issues: The phenomenon that occurs when the position of an object viewed from slightly different positions is inconsistent.

LIDAR: A system of detection that 'bounces' light off objects to record the layout of a space; the laser equivalent of RADAR.

CGI (computer-generated imagery): Synthetic images created by computer.

Volumetric cameras: Cameras that capture the spacial layout of a scene, rather than just recording the light that comes through the lens, representing the scene in a digital, 3-dimensional space.

158

Part III: Post-Production

As the previous chapters have shown, the production phase in 360° video can feel more complicated than traditional moviemaking in some ways, but simpler in others. The same holds true for the post-production phase. 360° video requires several additional steps before you can even get to the editing process, but for most projects the editing itself is quite a bit simpler than it is in flat video. And some post-production tasks are mostly the same whether your video is flat or spherical.

This section covers most of the phases of a project after shooting, up until the point where you have a completed edit. (The process of getting your edit ready for final distribution is covered in Part IV: Finishing.) Although, we'll spend a bit more time on topics that are specific to 360° content, we'll touch on all aspects of post-production, to give a thorough and clear picture of the overall workflow, and the tools involved.

Speaking of tools: A number of software manufacturers sell tools specifically designed for 360° video post-production. Some of these tools are plug-ins that add functionality to the commonly used editing and compositing applications like Adobe Premiere and After Effects, or Apple Final Cut Pro and Motion, and some are standalone apps. In the coming chapters, we'll reference specific products when they are applicable to the task being described, but that is not meant to be a comprehensive list of possible solutions.

SD card: (Secure Digital) A compact, portable memory card typically used in cameras and sound recording devices.

Take: Individual instances of a shot; a take = each time the camera is started and stopped.

Ambisonic: Pertaining to audio reproduction that captures the spatial acoustic qualities of recorded sound.

Chapter 32: Ingesting footage

Transferring files from a 360° camera to your computer is far more complicated and precarious than from a flat camera. First of all, remember that 360° video requires a lot of data and that moving it around efficiently requires fast and large drives. Also, most 360° cameras have multiple sensors (and lenses), and each sensor records to its own SD card. Keeping track of which card belongs to which camera sensor—and which take on a card corresponds to the same take on the other cards—can be daunting.

Further complicating the ingestion process is the fact that many cameras use generic (and sometimes identical) names for SD cards. And on top of *that*, the files on the cards are named with seemingly meaningless (and sometimes identical) codes of letters and numbers.

Add stereo (3D) into the mix, where some camera are recording the left eye's image and others are recording the right eye's image—or throw in audio files that were recorded to a separate device (sometimes with multiple tracks, including ambisonic tracks)—and you can see how mind-bogglingly complex footage ingestion can get.

The key to getting the job done without losing your mind (or valuable footage) is to get organized. Fortunately, there are a few simple rules of thumb you can follow to transfer video and audio files to your computer in an orderly and sanity-preserving fashion:

Slow down and do it right

The best advice I can offer is to implore you to allocate this critical job to a dedicated person and give that person the space

160

and time needed so the files can be properly copied, grouped, and labeled. Ensure that each file can easily be traced to the specific card and camera, and time of day.

Label the folders carefully and consistently

As each memory card is copied to the hard drive, rename the folders with a consistent, easy-to-parse code, and include the following essential data:

`CameraName_CameraNumber_CalendarDate`

If you have more than one card dump in a single day, also add the card number. So, for example:

`Jaunt_Lens01_Mar21_Card01`

Or if you have only one type of camera, you could substitute the camera location or scene name:

`Bedroom_Lens03_Mar21_Card01`
`MargeInterview_Cam01_Lens03_Mar21_Card01`

If you have multiple cameras shooting simultaneously, you'll want to add the camera number, too:

`PastaFight_Cam01_Angle1_Lens03_Mar21_Card01`

And if your camera has separate right and left eye lenses, you absolutely must include that information:

`Dinner_ Left_Cam01_Lens03_Mar21_Card01`

And so on. You can abbreviate further to make the names shorter:
`(Dinner_L_C01_L03_Mar21)`

But unless you're certain that the person handling the files in post will understand your notation, it's safer to be more explicit and avoid any potential confusion.

Note: Although you could attempt to rename the individual video files (within the card structure), there are a number of reasons not to do so. Some cameras store metadata about the files in separate, corresponding text files, and changing the names of files can break those links. What's more, renaming individual files would require viewing each file to determine which shot it came from—which isn't always obvious (for instance, for the output of a camera pointed at the floor).

Use offloading software

Although you can drag the contents of your memory cards onto a hard drive, software like 360CamMan from 360Rize is specifically designed to automate the process of copying SD cards from multiple cameras to a hard drive (including customizing the filenames as described above). It also reduces the risk of errors (human or otherwise), and simultaneously copies to multiple destinations.

Note: Many cameras come with their own custom software for ingesting the files and setting them up for stitching. Those are covered in the next chapter.

Ensure that the cameras are synced to real time

Unfortunately, the majority of 360° cameras do not support configurable timecode. That means you need to synchronize your cameras to real time. Why? Imagine the not-uncommon situation in which your files are mislabeled or otherwise mixed up. If you have an accurate timestamp on each file from multiple cameras, you'll be able to determine which files were recorded at the same hour, minute, and second. So before you shoot, don't forget to properly set the date and time on each of your cameras.

Stitching: Combining multiple images/ videos into one panoramic image/video (also sometimes refers to the seams in a panoramic image).

Timecode: A numerical code that identifies videos by the hour, minute, second, and frame in the format HH:MM:SS:FF (e.g.. 23:59:59:23).

Do it all at once

Copying the files from SD cards to a hard drive can be time-consuming. And especially on a small, fast-moving production you may be tempted to try to squeeze in some copying here and there during location changes or in between set-ups. Resist this urge. Copy the files only when someone can babysit the whole process and carefully rename the folder after each card is successfully transferred.

Create multiple backups

Be sure to back everything up to multiple hard drives in case any one drive falters or fails. You're likely to need to re-use the SD cards for the next camera set-up, and you never want to only have a single version of the files that represent all the hard work that went into your shoot.

Phew! Managing this data is daunting enough to deter most people venturing into this morass.

Fortunately, camera manufacturers are aware of this nightmare and many offer software solutions to simplify or automate footage ingestion (described in the next chapter).

Stitched: Multiple images/videos combined into one panoramic image/video.

Chapter 33: Software for ingesting footage

Nearly every camera manufacturer includes software to simplify one or more steps in the ingesting process. At minimum, the included apps group all the files that correspond with a single shot and then allow you to preview a stitched still frame so you can name the files to correspond with their content.

Kodak PixPro software.

Most consumer cameras provide software that automatically converts your footage into stitched clips (with little or no options or controls to finesse the stitch). Some cameras have Wi-Fi and transmit the footage directly to a connected smartphone. Others require you to load the cards onto a computer.

These apps don't typically require your SD card folders to be properly named (though there's little harm and some benefit in doing so anyway). These tools read metadata in each camera file to figure out which pieces go together and then group them accordingly, presenting a list of shots (with a corresponding stitched preview frame) for you to name and comment.

Smartphone-only tools are okay if you're planning to directly upload your raw footage to YouTube or another service. However, if you want to refine or edit your shots you'll need to transfer the files to a computer.

Tip: To keep the footage at the highest possible quality, skip any options in the camera's proprietary software to "enhance" or "optimize" your files. This ensures the most flexibility during the post-production process.

As one example of how this works, Kolor (owned by GoPro) created a special ingest tool to work with the Omni camera.

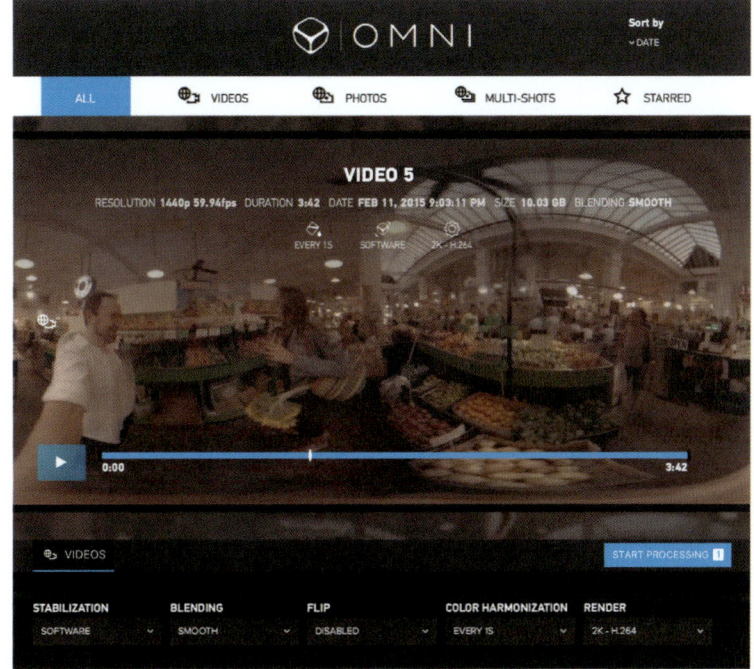

Kolor's Omni Importer software for the GoPro Omni camera.

GoPro Omni Importer is essentially just an alternative and simplified interface for Kolor's stitching software—Autopano Video Pro (AVP)—specifically designed to work with footage from Omni.

Like the other professional tools, Omni Importer doesn't require your SD card data to be properly named or pre-organized. Just place the copied versions of all the SD cards into one master folder on your hard drive and point the Omni Importer to that master folder. The software analyzes the files and organizes them into a list of shots.

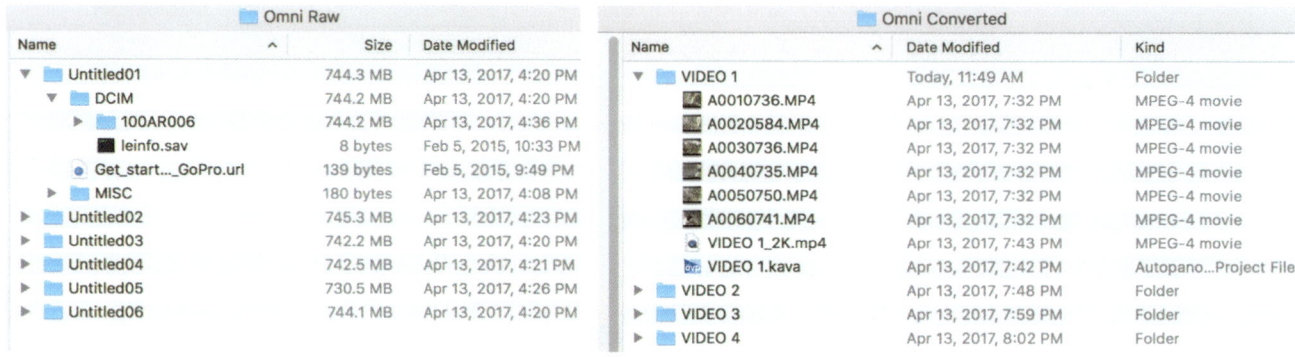

The raw contents of the SD cards.

After processing, the files are organized into shots.

Omni Importer lets you apply a small number of basic adjustments and then generates quick stitches directly on your computer. (Beware, this can take a LOT of time!) When you process the quick stitches, the software conveniently copies all the source data into new folders, organized by shot, and with a project file that allows you to open the shot directly into AVP and work on the fine stitching.

Sidebar: Using Theta with a Mac

Ricoh's Theta V is a fantastic 360˚ camera to learn on. Although it doesn't have the quality of more professional cameras, the Theta's tiny size means there are negligible parallax issues. And its two lenses leave you with only one stitch line to worry about. It's lightweight, it's inexpensive, and it's easy to monitor (on the companion smartphone app).

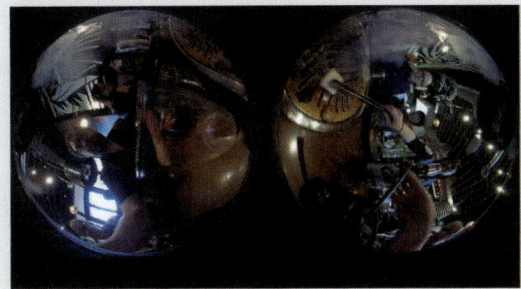

What the camera records

The stitched result.

However, if you're on a Mac, stitching the footage requires overriding Apple Photos importer. If you don't take care, you may wind up with files that can't easily be stitched and the benefits of this great camera may seem undone by this minor technical obstacle.

Read the following steps before you connect your Theta to your Mac:

1. Connect the Theta to the Mac with a USB cable. The Theta appears on your desktop as an external device and Apple's Photos app automatically launches.

2. When Photos asks if you want to import the images, click Cancel (or quit Photos).

3. From your Applications folder, open the Image Capture app.

4. In Image Capture, import the files from the Theta. (Remember where on your hard drive you save them.)

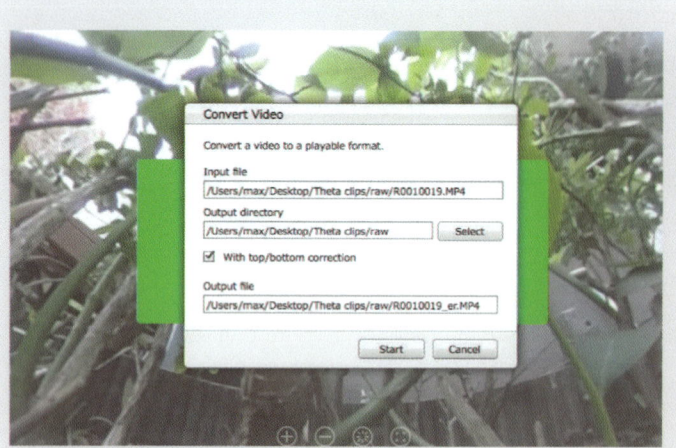

Ricoh Theta app.

Dual-fisheye source files: A single video file that contains the combined footage from two fisheye-lensed cameras, usually positioned side-by-side.

Latlong (latitudinal-longitudinal): Stretching a spherical image into a flat rectangle (similar to the way a world map represents the spherical Earth). Also called equirectangular.

Note: At this point you can delete the original image files on your connected Theta device, by dragging them to the Trash. (It's easier to delete image files from the camera while it's connected to your Mac.)

5. Eject the Theta device from the Mac desktop, then disconnect the USB cable.

6. Launch the Ricoh Theta app.

7. Drag the image files from the folder where you saved them into the Ricoh Theta app window.

The Theta app automatically converts the dual-fisheye source files into latlong projections, suitable for editing loading onto a Google Pixel or another smartphone, or uploading to YouTube or another 360°-aware video sharing service.

Note: Before uploading to a video sharing service, you need to inject spherical metadata. (See Chapter 60 to learn how.)

Chapter 34: Stitching overview

Before you can begin editing your footage as you would in a traditional video project, you need to convert your ingested and organized image files into stitched panoramas. If you're not using a camera that automatically stitches your files for you (as described in the previous chapter), this step can be surprisingly complicated.

The overall goal of combining the various source files into one final output requires a number of individual steps. Depending on the method you use to perform this action (described in Chapter 35: Stitching methods and tools), some of these steps may be automatic or otherwise hidden from you. The steps are not necessarily performed exactly in this order, but all of these steps must be performed:

Step 1: Synchronize

First, you must synchronize the multiple source files (in case the camera start-stop times weren't perfectly coordinated), so that, for example, frame 10 of camera A lines up with frame 10 of camera B, and so on. If the files aren't synced, the individual pieces of your patchwork may never properly line up.

Step 2: Remove lens distortion

Next, you need to remove the distortion created by the wide-angle lenses used in 360° cameras. Such distortion causes objects in the center of the frame to appear tiny and objects near the edge of the frame to appear large. The most extreme wide-angle lenses are called fisheye lenses, where the entire scene is captured in a circular image saved in the middle of the rectangular sensor.

Apply a reverse distortion to neutralize the distortion build into the shot.

> **Tip:** Most software has preset distortions for this purpose labeled with the name and focal length of specific lenses. For this, it's important to know which lens your camera utilizes.

Step 3: Stabilize

In some cases, you may need to apply image stabilization— which must be done on the individual camera shots before the files are stitched. If you try to stabilize the stitched master file, you'll create seams or other errors around the edges of the latlong boundary.

Step 4: Match colors

To create a smooth, continuous-looking stitched file you need to ensure that the brightness and color settings are matched across all the camera source files. This can be challenging if you're shooting in an environment where the lighting is inconsistent in different directions (such as a room with a bright window on one side and a dark hallway on the opposite side).

Image stabilization: A process to reduce shakiness caused by an unstable camera.

Latlong (latitudinal-longitudinal): Stretching a spherical image into a flat rectangle (similar to the way a world map represents the spherical Earth). Also called equirectangular.

Stitch lines

The sun is creating a glare on one lens causing a color mismatch across the stitch lines.

170

Step 5: Stitch

The bulk of the stitching process involves positioning the pieces in a way that mimics the cameras' relative vantage on set. And then you need to clean up the overlapping areas to make the scene look like a single, continuous shot in 360°. Unfortunately, as it turns out, that's a lot easier said than done.

Remember the Understanding parallax sidebar earlier in the book? Each camera in your array sees the world from a slightly different point in space. Therefore, objects won't appear in exactly the same place across the different cameras. If you align the overlapping areas of the images to make an object close to the camera line up, then objects further from the camera will be misaligned (called ghosting) and vice versa.

Ghosting visible on the faces of the subjects.

You can reconcile these misalignments by stretching or shifting parts of one individual image in one direction, and other parts in other directions. You can cut out overlapping parts in one of the images, and then using special software (such as Mistika VR, or Movavi), adjust the control points between the two views to create a natural-looking composite.

Composite: The post-production process of combining two or more images. Could be as simple as a title superimposed over an image, or as complex a digitally generated explosion rotoscoped over a filmed miniature spaceship in front of a hand-painted painting of outer space. Also can refer to the result of that process; a composite, or a composite image.

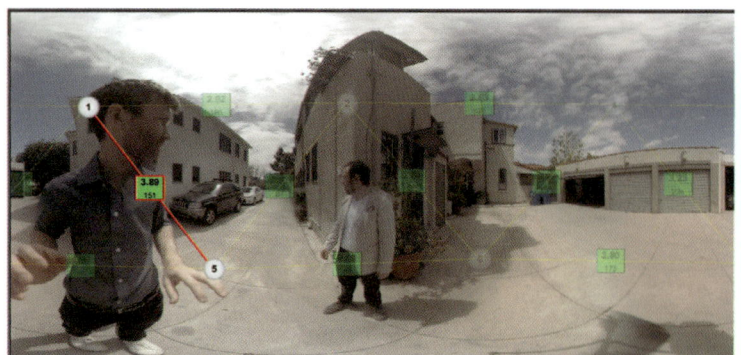

Left: shows which stitch line is being worked on. Right: Each dot is a point mapped in both images and aligned.

Keyframing: A process to create animations by identifying parameter values (such as an object's size or its position in the frame) at differing points in time, and interpolating the intervening values.

Important: If objects are too close to the camera, the shot may never stitch properly. Similarly, if objects move across the stitch line, you may need to perform elaborate keyframing animations to force the stitch lines to change over time, corresponding with the movement of the objects. And in some cases, it's impossible to get a perfect looking stitch without painstakingly compositing the multiple images by hand in a tool like Nuke or After Effects.

Step 6: Set the horizon

After the image is stitched, you (or your software) need to determine where the horizon is, and if necessary, realign the stitched image to make the horizon straight and level.

The right image shows the straightened horizon.

Step 7: Adjust vertical lines

Similar to adjusting the horizon, you should ensure that vertical lines are straight up and down. This often will automatically fix any horizon issues as well.

The colored bars show lines that should appear vertically straight. The right image shows the corrected image.

If you're working with stereoscopic source material, stitching is even more difficult. You'll need to create stitched versions of both the left-eye image and right-eye image, and then align those two images to define the proper interaxial value to yield the desired 3D effect. To learn more about working with 3D footage, see Chapter 46: Editing stereoscopic footage.

Because stitching can be processor-intensive, most projects employ an offline/online editing model: First, a low-res quick stitch is created for all of the source footage. Next, after the footage is shaved down to just the few moments you plan to use in the finished piece, that smaller chunk of footage is re-stitched with more precision to get the best-possible final results.

Interaxial: The mechanic equivalent of Interpupillary; the distance between the lenses of a camera in stereoscopic photography

Offline/online: The process of dividing editorial work into two stages: Offline, where creative decisions are made using proxy versions of the full-resolution files, and a subsequent online edit where the high-res files are conformed to match the offline version.

Chapter 35: Stitching methods and tools

There are three basic ways to stitch panoramic files:

- *Manually*
- *With software assistance*
- *Computationally (fully automated)*

Each method has advantages and drawbacks, described below.

Manual stitching

The act of stitching is essentially just creating a type of composite. In fact, you can create a basic stitched file—performing most of the tasks described in the previous chapter—using any robust compositing application. That said, the manual approach isn't necessarily for the faint of heart; it's enormously time-consuming and technically challenging.

Fortunately, you can automate or simplify aspects of the manual stitching process using commercially available plug-ins, including Cara VR for Nuke and Karta VR for Black Magic Fusion.

But even with the shortcuts the plug-ins provide, good results are difficult to achieve. The big benefit of manual stitching is that it's a totally open environment, which gives you (or, if you're smart, the professional stitcher you're going to hire) unlimited control over every detail of every shot. So an experienced and talented compositor/stitcher can achieve better results than you'd achieve using either of the more automated methods described below, especially for tricky or problem shots.

Software-assisted stitching

You can also use software products designed to automatically

Composite: The post-production process of combining two or more images. Could be as simple as a title superimposed over an image, or as complex a digitally generated explosion rotoscoped over a filmed miniature spaceship in front of a hand-painted painting of outer space. Also can refer to the result of that process; a composite, or a composite image.

stitch your files. Many of these tools are camera-specific. So, for instance, if you shot using Z CAM S1 cameras, there's a tool from Z CAM called WonderStitch that you can use to stitch those files. If you shot on the Insta360 Pro, there's a software tool from Insta360 to stitch those files. But the Z CAM app won't (easily) stitch the Insta footage, and vice versa.

Z CAM WonderStitch stitching software.

Several software tools can be used universally, such as Autopano Video Pro (AVP) or Assimilate Scratch VR. Another tool, StereoStitch, is specifically designed for working with stereoscopic footage.

Although these tools make stitching vastly easier than the manual method, they're not simple to operate. And to make matters worse, stitching requires significant computing power, especially when working with high-resolution originals. Even with the latest, fastest computer with a powerful graphics card, stitching can be very slow-going, with a lag that makes it hard to interact with the software in a fluid, intuitive way.

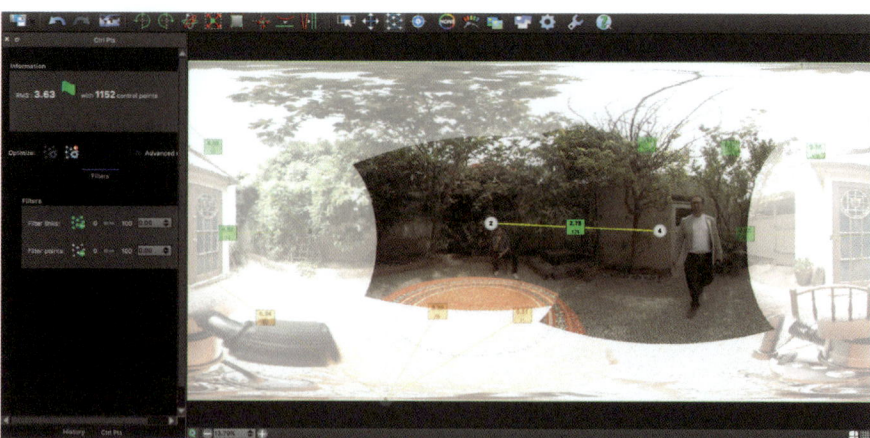
Kolor Autopano Video Pro stitching software.

Interestingly, the vast majority of stitching tools are based on a single, 18-year-old open source toolset called Panorama Tools (and its derivative, PTGui). Different manufacturers have added their own user interfaces and supplemental features, but the basic stitching algorithm is exactly the same under the hood.

Computational stitching

Another approach is to throw a massive amount of computer power at the stitching problem. Facebook 360 and Google's Jump platform are the big players in this category. Both Facebook and Google have developed algorithms to stitch multiple camera views together and create high-quality stereoscopic results requiring no human input whatsoever. To use these systems, you need only upload your footage to the Facebook or Jump servers, wait for the files to be processed, and then download the finished masters.

This approach to stitching is incredibly promising, but (not surprisingly), it comes with a number of drawbacks. First of all, the computational power required is enormous. The stitching effort must be distributed across a large number of networked computers, and at present only a few companies (Google and Facebook) have this kind of massive hardware capability.

Secondly, these specialized algorithms work only with a few predetermined 360°camera rig designs (ones that comprise a large number of individual cameras). Google's Jump platform stitches footage shot with a 16- or 17-camera Jump-certified camera rig (GoPro Odyssey or YI HALO). and Facebook's algorithm stitches footage shot with their own system.

Thirdly, and this is the kicker: Computational stitching services are far from perfect. Due to the size and nature of the cameras and algorithms, there are limitations. Objects close to the lens may not stitch properly. (Jump promises that they can stitch as close as 3 feet or even less if there is clear separation between the foreground and background.) What's more, even for objects at the correct distance from the camera, sometimes certain patterns or movement in the sphere can cause errors that mix the background and foreground elements together.

And because you've got no manual control, there's very little you can do to fix any issues that arise. (When stitching manually, you might optimize the results so that the some objects look better even if it makes other objects look worse.)

Presumably, these algorithms will continue to improve. But currently if you want perfect results, some shots may still require hand-stitching. Alas, humans are still needed for something!

Chapter 36: Stitching quality

During post-production, you'll deal with two types of stitching:

Quick-stitching: Creates a low-quality stitched output files with enough fidelity to facilitate basic editorial decisions. Quick-stitched files are fast and dirty, to be used during initial shot selection and editing.[1]

Fine-stitching: Creates a high-quality stitched output files for use in your final product (replacing the rough quick-stitched files you used to assemble your edit). Fine-stitching is essentially a finishing task, with the aim to make all the seams as invisible as possible.

The quick stitch shows a number of obvious problems.

The fine stitch remedies these errors.

Whereas fine-stitching is processor-intensive, quick-stitching is typically less of a resource hog. In fact, you can easily output quick-stitched files on a modern computer or even on many smartphones (albeit at low resolutions). Plenty of tools even perform real time quick-stitching for livestreaming 360° content.

1   Jump also provides "proxy" stitches which are clean stitches but at lower resolution than their final fine stitched output. They differentiate these from quick-stitched files which have more stitching errors.

(Learn more about this in Chapter 64: Livestreaming.) Yes, modern software automates much of the quick-stitching process, but in most cases, you'll still need to perform a few tasks to get usable files. Before stitching, you'll need to make sure the multiple camera views in each shot are properly synced. And after quick-stitching, you'll need to set the horizon. Additionally, your quick stitch output will likely contain obvious stitching errors where the camera views overlap; color discrepancies between angles, and other anomalies that you'd never include in the finished piece.

Quick stitch files should be sufficient for editing, though there's no absolute definition of what constitutes a quick stitch versus a fine-stitch—it's more of a continuum. You may find some quick-stitched shots perfectly suitable for final release, and other times you may want to put in some extra work to make your quick stitches more accurate or complete, to better judge the content within the shot.

Tip: Before you begin shooting, it's a very good idea to create a quick stitch of a test shot on set. You won't get a perfect view of how the finished shot will look, but you can gauge how your blocking is (or isn't) working; whether the subjects are positioned at the correct distance from the camera; and whether any action crosses a stitch line.

You may be able to rotate the axis slightly to adjust where the stitch lines appear and help prevent action from occurring in exactly the wrong place.

Quick stitching: Generating a rapid, albeit potentially imperfect, stitch of 360° footage. In multi camera rigs, this may be achieved without utilizing information from every camera's lens.

Latlong (latitudinal-longitudinal): Stretching a spherical image into a flat rectangle (similar to the way a world map represents the spherical Earth). Also called equirectangular.

HMD (head-mounted display): goggles or a headset designed to optimize 360° video viewing.

Magic window: A method of viewing 360 content where a rectangular frame acts as a portal to the larger, spherical recording. The viewer can navigate to a different perspective by scrolling (on a computer), or by tilting the viewing device (on a smartphone or tablet).

Chapter 37: Viewing 360° video

After quick-stitching your files, you need to view the footage in a way that allows you to evaluate it effectively. While experienced 360° creators may be able to make sense of the latlong versions, it's important to view the files the same way your audience will. And that means either in an HMD or in a magic window.

Adobe Premiere and Apple's Final Cut Pro both have built-in tools that allow you to view the stitched video in a connected HMD, or in a magic window on screen. Other popular software will likely support it in the near future (directly or through free plugins).

Most likely, on a given project you'll need to view your 360° footage using more than one method. The common viewing methods are described below in more detail.

HMD preview

Previewing footage in a VR headset is ideal for simulating your viewer's experience, but donning and doffing an HMD over and over as you work can be cumbersome and impractical. For that reason, you'll probably view your footage this way only occasionally—perhaps after completing a rough cut, or at other milestone stages of the editing process.

Previewing footage in an HMD is also the only way to see footage in stereo (3D). If you shot in stereo (and have stereo quick stitches like the ones provided by Google's Jump Assembler), it may make sense to review all of your footage in a headset to ensure there aren't any issues making any of your shots unusable.

Magic window preview

The magic window method is a great compromise that allows you to see the action in your scenes closely enough to read facial expressions, to evaluate takes, and to identify where the scenes should start and end.

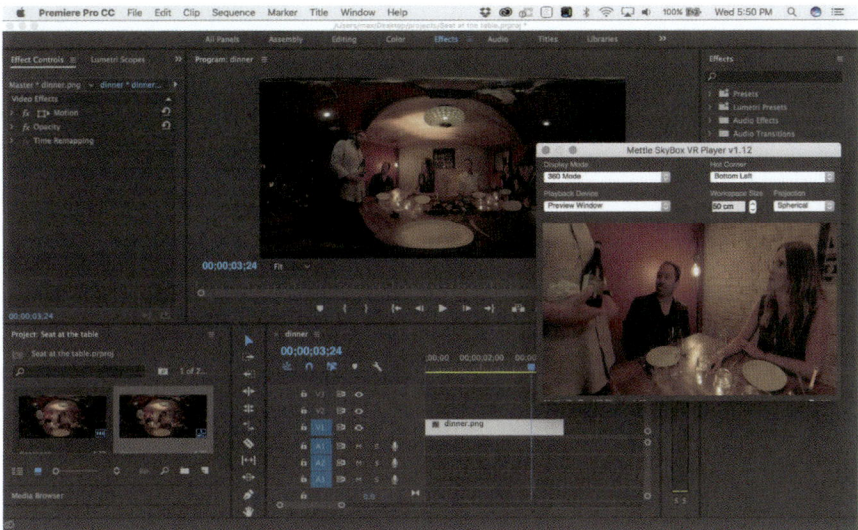

Adobe Premiere's program window shows the latlong while the floating preview window shows the HMD view.

The magic window appears as a separate window floating over your editing system and displays the video projected spherically (but that means you can only see part of the image at a time). You can scroll around within that view to see what the scene looks like when a viewer turns her head.

The only problem with viewing a scene in a magic window is that it's easy to become fixated on one portion of your scene and neglect the rest of the sphere. So, although viewing in a magic window can be very useful, be careful not to use it exclusively (unless you're actively scrolling around the view as you watch).

Projected spherically: Video that is displayed in a seamless 360 degree sphere. Also called rectilinear.

Latlong view

(Also known as equirectangular view) This is how your footage looks without any special treatment. After you know the contents of your footage well, you can probably work successfully in this view, at least up to a point. It's expedient—a latlong image allows you to see the whole of the sphere in a simple rectangle. However, the image is so distorted that the majority of details in the content are too obscure to view in a meaningful way.

If you've got the screen real estate, a popular way to work is to view both the latlong and magic window preview simultaneously.

In addition to the latlong, there are a number of other ways to examine your footage on a computer screen. These methods, which can be useful for specific aspects of the post-production process, are covered in the Spherical Video Projections sidebar on the following pages.

Sidebar: Spherical video projections

A 360° camera is usually a group of cameras with wide-angle lenses that project an image onto each of the cameras' sensors. The stitching process combines those images into a single file that contains the video of the entire sphere.

When viewed during playback, the audience sees only a portion of the sphere at a time—and that portion changes dynamically as the viewer turns her head. (The amount viewed at any one time is based on the field of view of the playback device.) This is called a *spherical* (or sometimes *rectilinear*) projection.

Stitching: Combining multiple images/videos into one panoramic image/video (also sometimes refers to a seam in a panoramic image).

Field of view: The angle of space viewable from a given lens position.

In this example, six camera originals are combined to create one spherical image.

This is perfect for giving a viewer the experience of being surrounded by the scene, but while you're working with the files, you often need to view the contents of the entire sphere all at once. Just as a world map represents the spherical Earth in a flat, two-dimensional image, you can view your spherical video as a flat image as well.

The most common method of flattening a spherical image is known as an *equirectangular projection* (sometimes also referred to as *latitudinal-longitudinal* or "latlong" for short).

A latlong provides the advantage of seeing the entire image all at once, and allows you to work with your footage in software created for flat video. As a creator, you'll quickly get used to seeing the video this way, and you'll soon be able to envision the flat image as a sphere.

A latong (equirectangular) projection of the spherical source.

However, latlong viewing has some key drawbacks: Because critical detail in the flattened image is distorted and appears small in the sphere, latlong imaging is not very useful for reading performances, human-scale actions, or any nuanced details of a scene.

Fortunately, there are additional ways of displaying spherical video on a flat screen. For example, you can convert the spherical video field of view to a cube, and then "unwrap" the cube into six equal-sized panels. Although somewhat useless for watching the video, *cubic projection* (sometimes called a *cubemap*) has the benefit of being undistorted.

A cubic projection is extremely useful for digitally modifying the shot, such as adding a dinosaur to your scene or painting out parts of the sphere where the tripod is visible (often called rig removal).

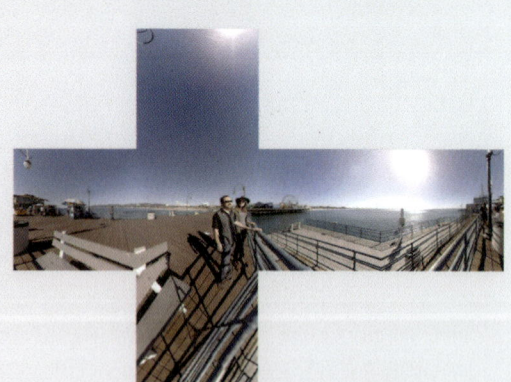

A cubic projection of the spherical source.

Notice how in the image below, the camera baseplate (the white box) at the bottom of the equirectangular image appears very large (just like the way Antarctica appears artificially large on many world maps). The same area in the cubemap reveals that baseplate is, in fact, a very small area.

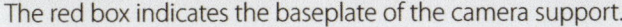

The red box indicates the baseplate of the camera support.

In the cubemap, it's much smaller.

There are other ways of displaying spherical data, but those are not particularly useful for video intended to be viewed in a magic window or HMD. Instead, they're used for including spherical content in an otherwise flat video.

These graphics show the spherical image represented as a "ring," a "little planet," and a "hurricane."

Chapter 38: Project settings

When creating a project in Adobe Premiere or Final Cut Pro (the two most commonly used apps for editing 360° video), you need to ensure that your timeline (called a *sequence* in Premiere and a *project* in Final Cut Pro) is configured properly before adding spherical source files. There are a number of settings to check:

Projection

Projection refers to the way a spherical image is stored in the rectangular video file. This is how you let the software know that your files are spherical. In Premiere, there is a VR tab at the top of the New Sequence window. Set Projection to Equirectangular.

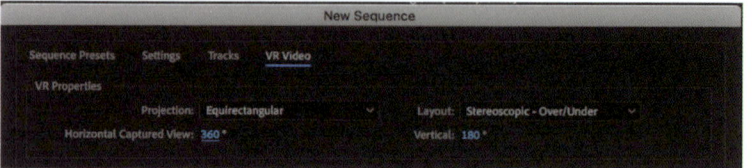

In Final Cut Pro, in the New Project sheet, set Video format to 360° and then you can set Projection Type to Mono or Stereo.

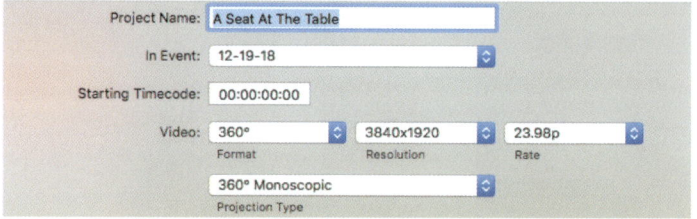

Important: You must also configure the projection settings of your individual video files. In Premiere, use the Interpret Footage window; in Final Cut Pro, look in the Info pane of the Inspector.

Frame rate

Frame rate refers to the number of frames per second (fps) in the video stream. Common frame rates for 360° video are 30 fps and 60 fps (which is usually actually recorded at 59.94 fps).

In general, you should set your editing system to match the settings in your camera. (Recommended frame rates are discussed in Chapter 22: Camera settings.) However there are cases where you might override that setting and instead edit in the frame rate used by your intended playback system. For example, if your main audience is going to watch on the Samsung Gear VR which works best at 30 fps, you can edit at 30 fps, even if your footage was shot at 60 fps.

> **Note:** Some 360˚ video creators advocate shooting at the highest frame rate possible, in the interest of creating the smoothest motion for playback. Although higher frame rates do create smoother motion, some people think high frame rates look unnatural, primarily because the majority of filmed content we've been exposed to for years is captured at rates of 24 fps or 30 fps.

It's important to understand that the playback rate of your video is not equivalent to the *refresh rate* of the device displaying the video to your viewer's eyes. Most manufacturers have determined that refresh rates less than 90 fps (or 90 *hertz*) can cause disorientation and sometimes motion sickness. This is why PC-based headsets like the HTC Cosmos and Oculus Quest require a very high-powered graphics card to play smoothly.

Frame size

Frame size refers to the pixel dimensions of the video image. Even though 360˚ video is viewed in a spherical projection, the frame size (of a stitched file) refers to how the image is stored in an equirectangular projection.

In most cases, you should configure your project settings in your editing software to match the settings of your camera. If you

Spherical projection: Video that is displayed in a seamless 360 degree sphere. Also called rectilinear.

Stitched: Multiple videos that have been combined into one panoramic video.

Equirectangular: Stretching a spherical image into a flat rectangle (similar to the way a world map represents the spherical Earth). Also called latlong (for latitudinal-longitudinal).

shot your project using several different cameras, go with the settings of the camera used to shoot the majority of the footage. However, there are exceptions to this rule. Some 360° cameras generate stitched files at extremely large frame sizes, such as 8K or higher. Trying to edit an entire sequence at this frame size will likely tax even a robust computer. It may be better to work at a reduced frame size and then only use the high-res versions when you assemble your master file .

It's also important to be aware of your intended output format. For example, if you know you're planning to distribute primarily for a device with a maximum frame size of UHD (3840 x 1920), there's not much benefit to working at a higher resolution, even if your footage was shot at a higher resolution than that.

Note: If your program includes compositing such as green screen or other special effects, there is a benefit to rendering those composites at the highest possible resolution, even if the result will eventually be converted to a lower res for final output. Also, if your content is not time-sensitive (like sports, or news, or culturally based stories), you might choose to work at a higher resolution in an attempt to future-proof your show, so it will still look its best, even on future generations of playback hardware.

Aspect ratio

Aspect ratio (sometimes called *DAR* for display aspect ratio) refers to the relative dimensions of a video image. For example,

Common aspect ratios.

HD video uses a 16:9 aspect ratio (1920x1080 or 1280x720). 360°
video is stored in a 2:1 aspect ratio (3840x1920 or 4096x2048).
If you attempt to work in a 16:9 video frame size (for example,
3840x2160 as opposed to 3840x1920), you'll either have black
bars at the top and bottom of the latlong (which translates to
black areas at the apex and nadir of your sphere), or, alternatively
your image will appear slightly stretched as pictured to the right:

Stereoscopic frame sizes

When working with stereoscopic footage, both the left-eye
image and right-eye image must be stored in a single file for
editing and for distribution. With two eyes worth of video, you're
forced to either squeeze twice the data into a 2:1 video frame, or,
alternatively, work in a square video frame, such as 3840 x 3840.

Tip: In a top-bottom configuration, the left image is always
stored on top and the right image on the bottom.

The square frame preserves more resolution but creates a file
that's twice as big. Some playback systems can't handle that
frame size or the higher data rate required. So some creators
opt instead to squeeze the data into a single 2:1 file, which
unfortunately amounts to throwing away half the resolution of
the image.

Stereo footage can be stored in either a side-by-side format, or
in the top-bottom format described above. At first blush it might
seem intuitive to put the two sources side-by-side, because that's
how our eyes are positioned on our head. However, because
our horizontal field of view is much larger than our vertical
field of view, it's actually smarter to stack the two channels in
the top-bottom format. That way, only the vertical resolution is
compressed.

When a 2:1 latlong clip is placed in a 16:9
window, it must either be letterboxed (top) or
stretched (bottom).

Stereo in native 1:1 (square) aspect ratio.

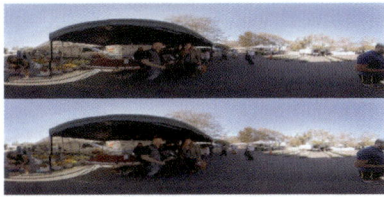

Stereo compressed into 2:1 aspect ratio.

Sidebar: Understanding VR resolution (or: why does my video look so bad?!)

Because 360° video is stretched out from a latlong file and projected onto a virtual sphere for viewing, even high-resolution files can appear soft and blocky during playback. To better understand why VR resolution often seems so low, remember that during playback the data from the image must cover a sphere all around you, but you're only looking at a small portion of that sphere at any given time.

Original latlong image.

View inside the HMD.

In fact, most VR viewers display a field of view between 90–110°. That means you're viewing only about ¼ of the image at any given time—or put another way, the source image must be approximately 4 times larger than your screen resolution in order to appear fully sharp.

So, if the resolution of the device you're viewing is 2560 x 1440 (as on a Samsung Galaxy phone) and your field of view is 96° (as on the Samsung Gear VR, which converts the Galaxy into an HMD), the video file should ideally have a resolution of approximately 5080 x 2880. Unfortunately, this is larger than the maximum 4096 x 2048 resolution that Gear VR supports.

This already-compromised resolution gets dramatically worse with stereoscopic images. In some cases stereo data for both eyes is stored in that same file, which cuts the resolution in half!

So, no matter how good your camera resolution may be, playback resolution is often limited by the viewing hardware, and (at least with the current generation of viewers) it can look pretty crappy. But this is changing rapidly. Recently, YouTube increased their capacity to accept up to 8192x8192 for stereo files.

Ironically, footage viewed in a magic window environment (on a phone or a computer) may look sharper, at least in cases where the playback device supports higher-resolution files because your eyes are farther from the screen, which improves perceived resolution.

Stereoscopic: Video shot with two parallel cameras (or in the case of 360 video, multiple pairs of parallel cameras) Commonly referred to as 3D.

Magic window: A method of viewing 360° content where a rectangular frame acts as a portal to the larger, spherical recording. The viewer can navigate to a different perspective by scrolling (on a computer), or by tilting the viewing device (on a smartphone or tablet).

Chapter 39: Setting the center point

Regardless of how your camera was positioned during production, you can redefine the center point of each shot during post to align critical action in the scene to "north." North is what appears directly in front of the viewer based on the direction they are facing when they began playing the video.

Latlong (latitudinal-longitudinal): Stretching a spherical image into a flat rectangle (similar to the way a world map represents the spherical Earth). Also called equirectangular.

In a latlong image (and in your editing application) north is the very center of the screen. It's crucial to consider what lies at this location because this helps establish the point of focus for your viewers. Although you can't control where your viewer will look at any given moment, you can trust that she'll be less comfortable craning her neck to one side than sitting comfortably and looking straight ahead. Therefore, you should position the critical action in the sphere so it resides at that most comfortable viewing position.

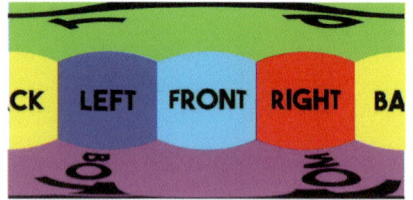

This image shows where the different quadrants (sextants, really) appear when viewing a latlong image.

Offsetting the center point is probably the most common adjustment you'll make to your 360° footage. In fact, it's not unusual to adjust every shot this way. The center point is established during the stitching process, but it can be changed in the edit room, as long as you're using a 360°-aware editing program like Adobe Premiere (By adding the *VR Rotate Sphere* effect) or Final Cut Pro (in the Orientation section of the Video Inspector, for any clip who's Projection Type is set to Equirectangular. For more, see Chapter 38: Project settings).

You can change the X (tilt or pitch), Y (pan or yaw), and Z (roll) axes, but in practice, you're almost always rotating around the Y axis (which is akin to panning the camera). It's rare to change the X or Z axes—lest you skew the horizon, or make the viewer feel like they're lurching forward (see the *correct tilted images* topic below).

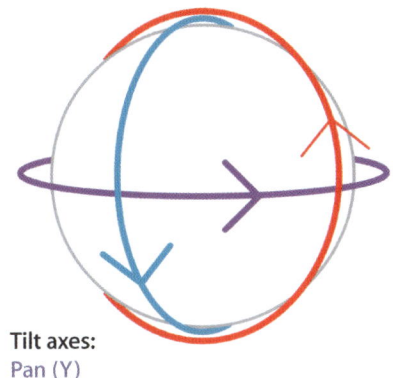

Tilt axes:
Pan (Y)
Tilt (X)
Roll (Z)

Here are several reasons you may want to adjust the center point:

Control viewer's focus

If your goal is to emphasize some actions within the sphere but put less emphasis on other actions, offset the center to align the primary action to north, or rotate the image to move secondary actions away from that center point.

By moving the center point of the image, you can change the focus of the scene.

Align action across edits

You can also adjust the center point to ensure that critical action lines up across edit points. So, for example, if the action in shot one shows a man emerging out of a manhole (at due north) and then walking to his left to pick up an errant banana, you can assume that most viewers will follow his movement; when the shot ends, they'll be looking at that banana spot, slightly to the east. Shot two's center should be offset so that the primary action (a woman playing a sousaphone) aligns with that location where most viewers' eyes will be at the cut point, rather than true center.

The following diagram presents a more realistic example: In the first shot, the people walk from the center of the frame towards the left (west), then the next shot picks up with the people aligned at that position, and then the people walk farther to the left into the south quadrant. The third shot picks up with the people in that new position. At this point the viewer would have to be looking almost all the way over her shoulder to see that main subject of the shot.

The left image shows the starting frame of the shot and the right image shows the ending frame. The red line indicates the center point of the subject within the shot (which changes over time as the subject moves). The green line shows the center point at the beginning of the shot.

If each successive shot leads farther and farther toward one side, your audience will soon tire of turning their necks, and you may lose their attention completely. So be sure to correct for this kind of center-point drift. After making several consecutive center-point changes, you may find that you need to go back to the earlier clips in your Timeline and offset the center point of the first shot in the sequence in the opposite direction so that any drift that occurs in subsequent shots doesn't lead the viewer too far from north. Ideally this risk can be mitigated through thoughtful blocking and choreography.

In the following diagram, the first shot has been deliberately off-set towards the right, so that by the time the third shot appears, it's not quite as far to the left.

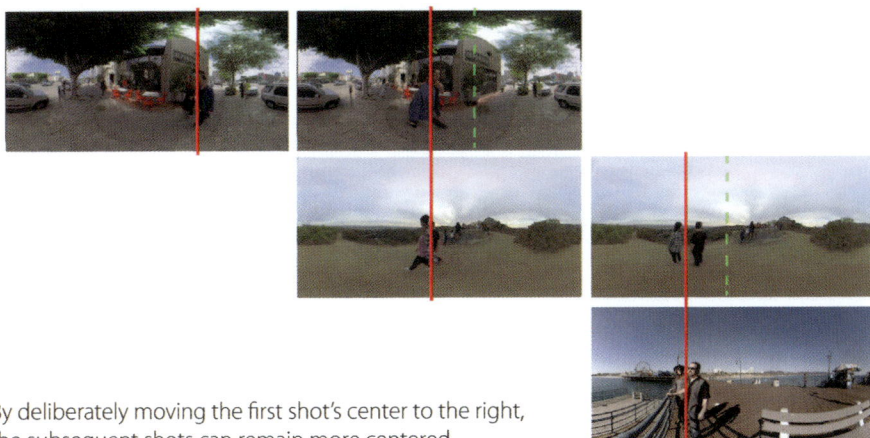

By deliberately moving the first shot's center to the right, the subsequent shots can remain more centered.

New playback technologies are being developed that allow you to reassign the center point to north at each cut point. So you can prepare all of your shots so the primary action is dead center, but when the video cuts, that center point appears directly in front of the viewer's eyes, no matter where she may be looking. Automatic orientation resets like this can prevent drift, but be careful because in some situations, it can disorient a viewer who may be looking over her shoulder when the camera abruptly resets its view to north. When they unwind their neck, they're going to be looking exactly where you didn't want them to.

The top image shows the uncorrected image, the bottom shows the straightened horizon.

Correct tilted images
If stitching (or poor camera placement) yields video that appears tilted (either side-to-side or forward-back), you can true the image by adjusting the tilt (X) or roll (Z) axes. This is far less common than adjusting the Y.

Inserts: Close-up shots of an object or detail previously seen in a wider angle.

Cutaways: Shots of an object within the location of the scene, but not seen in the previous shots, such as seagulls during a beach scene, or the cheering crowd at a concert. Cutaways provide editing options and help to enhance the sense of presence in a scene.

Quick-stitched: Rapid, albeit potentially imperfect, stitching of 360° footage. In multi camera rigs, this may be achieved without utilizing information from every camera's lens.

Chapter 40: Editing 360° footage

When people think of editing, they mostly think about montages of different shots, or of intra-scene inserts or cutaways, say, from a wide shot to a close-up on a detail within the scene. Neither of these techniques is particularly well-suited to 360° video (I'll discuss why in the following chapter), but there are many other aspects of editing that are essential for 360° video, just as they are for the traditional stuff.

Most aspects of editing are similar to those for traditional media, but each step in the process needs to be done with the unique requirements of 360° video in mind.

> **Note:** The editing techniques described here can be done in any basic video editing application, though I recommend a 360°-aware editor that allows you to view the video in an HMD or magic window (as described in Chapter 37: Viewing 360° video).

Step 1: Sync audio and video

Most 360° productions require the use of lavaliere and other microphones that aren't recorded directly onto the camera. One very early step in the editing process is to align those audio recordings to the quick-stitched video footage to ensure that the clips you watch have all the relevant audio.

Your 360° video clips may have camera audio attached to them, which can be very helpful for the synching (especially if you're using a synching tool that compares audio waveforms like Plural-Eyes). But after your high-quality production audio is aligned to the video clips, it's probably a good idea to turn off or disable the camera audio.

Step 2: Select takes

One of the most fundamental aspects of video editing—360˚ or flat—is choosing which sections of the source footage to use. This process entails sorting through multiple takes and choosing the best (or most appropriate) version of each shot. For fiction projects, this step is typically about finding the best performance. However, even when you identify the killer take where your actors nail it, other issues such as missed blocking can play a spoiler role, making the footage unusable. For nonfiction projects, a scene might be shot from a variety of vantage points, and your job is to decide which of those angles makes it into the final piece.

You can probably weed out a lot of footage based on production notes or other elements obvious even when viewed in the latlong format. However, it's essential to watch your footage in an HMD to ensure that you don't overlook subtle details or issues that can ruin (or recommend) a shot.

Unfortunately, because 360° video is usually shot as a series of long takes, that means more opportunities for mistakes or technical problems that can undermine a shot. While for the most part you can't use the beginning of one shot and the end of another, there are some cases where you can cheat by combining quadrants from different takes. See Chapter 43: Split screens to learn how.

Step 3: Mark clips

The next step is to identify the start and end points (usually called In and Out points) of the shots that you want to include in your edit. 360˚ clips often have long handles that must be trimmed (because after starting the camera, the whole crew had to run and hide before the scene began).

Takes: Individual instances of a shot; a take = each time the camera is started and stopped.

Blocking: The positions and movement of actors in a scene.

Latlong (latitudinal-longitudinal): Stretching a spherical image into a flat rectangle (similar to the way a world map represents the spherical Earth). Also called equirectangular.

HMD (head-mounted display): goggles or a headset designed to optimize 360° video viewing.

Handles: Extra footage before the beginning and/or after the ending of the used portion of a shot.

Step 4: Assemble clips

After you've got the best sections of your clips selected, it's time to put those shots together to create a coherent finished piece. Some 360° videos are just a single, unedited shot—relying on the viewer's ability to look around and observe different aspects of the scene (as well as well-thought out choreography and blocking) to convey the range of elements that comprise the story. Other times there may be multiple scenes or locations, which need to be assembled sequentially, perhaps with simple fades between them. And in some cases you may choose to incorporate intra-scene editing—just like in a traditional film.

No matter what your show requires, the next chapter offers some suggestions about how to make the best of editing in 360°.

Chapter 41: Editing tips and techniques

There are many ways in which editing 360° video is similar to editing traditional footage; fundamentally you are still assembling source footage to be watched by a passive viewer. You want to find the footage that best conveys the tone and meaning that communicates your chosen theme; avoid unnecessary repetition and redundancy; provoke your audience to consider the world from a new perspective; and engage and entertain them in an economical and effective way.

But there are many ways in which editing 360° video asks you to answer different questions, like how to move a viewer from one location to another when you're not sure where they may be looking. And you may have to come up with different answers to familiar questions, like how to control rhythm and pacing in an environment where every cut creates a physical reaction for your viewers.

In many ways, the rules of how to work with this sort of footage are simply as yet unwritten. And how to communicate most effectively in this medium is still very much up for debate. Still, there are a handful of suggestions that may help you approach the editing process or at least get you asking yourself the right questions.

Set the pace

Many 360° video creators believe it's important give your viewers extra time to adapt to each new scene. In other words, when the magic of editing transports them to a new location, it's a good idea to give the audience five or ten seconds to look around and get their bearings before important action starts.

This consideration can affect how you choose to mark your clips—you might want to add more "idle" time at the head of some clips than you would for traditional cinema. This breathing room after a scene change is more important for viewers new to the medium than for VR veterans who know the drill. So, depending on your target audience, this might or might not apply.

> **Tip:** Ideally, you should account for this time when shooting, so that acclimation time is not "idle" but instead contains subtle, non-critical action that aids in welcoming the viewer to a location, such a moment of a chicken pecking at seeds on the ground before the farmer steps out and begins describing her harvesting techniques. Or a mouse scurrying across the floor of the haunted house bedroom before the lunatic murderer bursts through the door. (Basically, anything involving a small animal.)

Cut between scenes

Few 360° projects use cuts within scenes that take place in a single location. Still, any project that includes multiple locations require some kind of transition when the action moves from one place to another.

Cuts (edits): The point where one shot ends and another shot begins.

The most commonly used device is a *dip-to-black effect* (sometimes called *fade-out/fade-in*), This is a gentler transition than a hard cut, as it gives the audience a moment in complete darkness to disengage from one scene before diving into the next one. But there are plenty of opportunities for direct cuts between scenes, especially as viewers get more comfortable with watching 360° media.

Such cuts should be artful, and you should be mindful of where in the sphere the viewer is likely looking at the end of the outgoing shot. Think about elements that can smooth the juxtaposition from one place to another—for example, geometric patterns (like the vertical lines of an office building's windows matched up with the vertical lines of a jail cell) or a burst of color that links two scenes together.

Contrarily, you can use a cut to deliberately generate contrast between two locations—for example, cutting from a dimly lit, dark-colored bedroom to a brightly lit, white-walled museum lobby. Or from that highly geometric, straight-edged museum to an ornately twisted jungle of vines. Yes, this might be momentarily disorienting for the viewer, but in the right context, such disorientation can be used purposefully.

Lead with audio

Another way to acclimate viewers to a new scene is to let the sound for the new environment fade in a moment or two early, over black, to prepare viewers for what they're about to see. This is in effect a type of split edit, where the audio leads the video. This can work to shorten the amount of time you need to wait before beginning the action (as described above in the "Set the pace" section). And it can also work as a way to suggest some juxtaposition between two scenes, where the audio for the new location appears while your body still feels like it is in the old one.

Split edit: An editing technique in which the audio and visual components of a shot do not transition at the same time; so the sound occurs before the picture appears, or the sound lingers on after the picture has cut to a new shot.

Keep it moving

Whenever you need to cut from footage shot with a moving camera, the next shot should also be a moving shot. The same rule applies to cutting from a static shot: the follow-up shot should also be static. (Otherwise, you'll test your audience's resistance to irritation—and maybe even nausea). Ideally camera movement should begin mid-scene (and with minimal acceleration, as described in Chapter 26: Moving shots). That way, the viewer can adjust to the perspective change organically, having first gotten their bearings in the space before any movement begins. Similarly, let camera movement slow to a stop before cutting back to a static vantage point. This guideline is helpful in flat cinema, but violating it in 360° video is an E-ticket[2] straight to motion sickness.

Preview your cut

No matter what editing you do, it's essential to preview your show in an HMD as often as possible. The timing and placement of edits can feel totally different in a headset than it does when watching it in a magic window on the screen. It's easy to get overconfident and start cutting strictly by viewing the latlong images. I can tell you from experience that this is a mistake!

Keep in mind that all of these techniques are limited to seated experiences where the viewer has no agency other than simply turning their head. As the medium evolves and experiences become more dynamic and you can get up and walk around within a scene, many of these techniques could become irrelevant or even dangerous.

HMD (head-mounted display): goggles or a headset designed to optimize 360° video viewing.

Magic window: A method of viewing 360 content where a rectangular frame acts as a portal to the larger, spherical recording. The viewer can navigate to a different perspective by scrolling (on a computer), or by tilting the viewing device (on a smartphone or tablet).

Latlong (latitudinal-longitudinal): Stretching a spherical image into a flat rectangle (similar to the way a world map represents the spherical Earth). Also called equirectangular.

2   Ask your dad.

Chapter 42: Intra-scene editing

Some creators insist that Intra-scene editing (where you cut from one perspective to another perspective within the same location and time) has no place in VR, primarily because you don't know where a viewer may be looking at the moment of the cut. Suddenly "teleporting" viewers across the room can be extremely disorienting—especially when following traditional editing patterns such as cutting back and forth between OTS MCUs.

Still, there are occasions when your 360˚ scene has one very clear point of focus. Under those circumstances, it's reasonable to assume that most viewers will be looking in the same direction, so if you cut to another angle (following the common rules and techniques used in flat cinema, such as the 180° rule, match cuts, split edits, and so forth) any audience member familiar with TV or movies will naturally follow along without much confusion.

And as this new medium grows up, the visual language of cinema will also evolve to keep up. There are already a few edit types that are becoming established.

Leap cuts

An editing technique that can be especially useful in spherical video is a cut from one vantage point in a location to another point in the same scene (sometimes triggered voluntarily by the viewer). Known as a *leap cut*, this technique works especially well if you alert viewers to the new vantage point (by highlighting that spot) before they "leap" to it.

For example, imagine a video that captures the experience of watching a football game from the front row of the mezzanine tier. When viewers look down to the field, a graphical highlight

OTS MCU (over the shoulder medium close-up): Shot that include part of a character in the foreground (often out of focus), with the principal subject framed from the chest to the top of the head. This is one of the most common types of shots for dialogue scenes.

180° rule: A cinematography technique to ensure eyelines remain consistent across edits. It works by drawing an imaginary line between principal subjects on set, and keeping all coverage of those subjects on one or the other side of that line.

Match cuts: Edits where action within the scene is continued in real time across an edit point; such as seeing a door begin to close from one angle, and then continuing to close from another angle.

Split edits: An editing technique in which the audio and visual components of a shot do not transition at the same time; so the sound occurs before the picture appears, or the sound lingers on after the picture has cut to a new shot.

hovers at the sideline of the 50-yard line. Viewers can then click on that highlight to leap down to that new vantage point without suffering any disorientation.

While that example suggests a video where the user controls when the cut happens, you can accomplish a similar effect with predetermined cuts: Imagine a shot from inside a moving car as the vehicle pulls up and stops at an intersection. On the sidewalk, a white light shines up from the ground. Suddenly the video cuts, and you (the VR audience) are now standing in the beam of light, watching the car pull away from the intersection.

Temporal jump cuts

The *jump cut*—an abrupt transition from one shot to another—is another type of edit that works in both flat video and 360° video. Jump cuts can be moderately disorienting (and in traditional cinema, that's often their purpose). One trick that works especially well in 360° video is a strictly *temporal* jump cut—where the camera vantage stays exactly the same (remains locked-off), but *time* jumps forward with the cut. Because the point of view is exactly the same across the edit, no matter where the viewer might be looking, the cut will make sense. But you still get the benefit of cutting to compress time or to contrast two events (occurring in the same space, but at different times) in order to guide the story.

An extreme example of this is the animated VR short, *Pearl*, where the vantage is fixed on the dashboard of a car. From that point of view, you witness a complex story of a musician passing his creative torch to his daughter over the course of many years. The film lasts less than five minutes.

Locked-off: Static. Refers to the adjustable parts of a tripod being locked in place.

Directional edits

The traditional *split edit* can be extra confusing in VR. In a split edit, the audio transitions to a new shot at a different time than the picture. However, if you take advantage of the overlap, you can use a split edit to great effect in 360° video. The position of the leading sound can trigger not just an anticipation of a cut, but can direct your viewer's eyes to a particular location in preparation for that edit.

For example, If you want to ensure that after a cut your audience is looking due north (to be sure they don't miss an important story detail) make a motivated sound emanate from that location (someone talking, a door slamming, etc.) The sound will draw their eyes, and then, a half second later, cut the picture to the new shot. This will effectively reset (most) viewers' points of view.

You could even have a sound that moves into position just as a cut occurs, to move the viewer's attention in a more gradual way. This works if you have some expectation of where the viewers are most likely looking in the outgoing shot.

So for example, if you have a main character lead the viewers over to 90° east in one shot and you want to pull your viewers back to due north for the next shot, begin a sound associated with the incoming shot can emerge at 45° (NE) and over the course of a quarter or half a second, rotate it into position to align with the picture.

This triggers the viewer's eyes to move so they are subconsciously pulled to look in the desired direction just as a new image supplies the justification for the move.

Gaze-guided cuts

You can even cede a bit of editorial power to your viewers. In VR, it's possible to cue different shots based on where the viewer looks. So, for example, if the viewer is looking north, the cut point might continue the story of what's happening in front of her; but if she's looking west at the cut point, the transition could take her away on a different journey. (The case described in the leap cuts section above could be an example of this.) You would need to employ a game engine like Unity to create the final deliverable, but from a production standpoint you could easily accomplish an effect like this.

Chapter 43: Split screens

A traditional split screen is used to show two simultaneous actions— two sides of a telephone conversation, for example, or multiple musicians during a performance. Those techniques are just as valid in 360° video. But in VR, split screens can also be used in other ways: to surreptitiously combine the best aspects of multiple performances; to facilitate intra-scene editing without traditional cuts; to hide the evidence of the crew and equipment in the scene; and so on.

Here are a few unconventional ways to use split screens in spherical video:

Divide the quadrants

Because the available field of view in 360° video exceeds the amount viewers can see at any one time, you can take advantage of split screens in a whole new way. Different quadrants of the sphere can contain disparate contents, related or otherwise.

In this scene, turning your head will take you into an entirely new location.

The boundaries between the sections can be firm or permeable, and the contrast between the subjects can be subtle or extreme. As your viewer turns his head, he enters different experiences. This provides a fascinating alternative to editing for a way to play images off of one another.

Combine performances

You can split the screen to show an identical vantage point at different points of time. For example, you might block your actors carefully so they remain in separate camera views and don't cross stitch lines and then swap out camera views during stitching. Your assembled shot might use take 2 of the north quadrant where the fair princess awaits, and take 22 of the east quadrant, where the clumsy prince attempts to woo her.

Alternatively, you can split the screen to record a complicated sequence one quadrant at a time, then combine the quadrants later to create a rich tapestry of action. For example, you might record the action in the north quadrant while the director and crew stand behind the camera; then, leaving the camera untouched, move the crew to the north quadrant and record again, this time with the action going on only in the south quadrant. You get the benefit of focusing on one aspect of the scene at a time, and you get to stay on set and observe the performance as it happens. Assembling the two takes is no more difficult than any stitching (so long as you keep any movement away from the stitch lines).

You don't even need a 360° camera to the shoot the scenario described above. Media Monks created an entire 360° movie like this for Etihad airlines, using a 6K flat cinema camera and rotating the camera 90° after each shot to capture each quadrant one at a time. This approach allowed the crew to work

Stitch lines: The seams in a 360° video where footage from one camera has been combined with another.

with a familiar, powerful, and customizable cinema camera (and the crew could remain on set during shooting while still being "invisible" to the lens). But even better, the resulting footage had absolutely no parallax and, thus, perfect, undistorted stitching. The only compromise was that none of the action could cross the four stitch lines.

Hide the crew

As mentioned above, you can also use split screen techniques to "disappear" your crew, or lights or other evidence of filming. If you shoot your *visual room tone* shot after the actors leave, you can, for example, simply swap out the south quadrant with the view of the empty set to erase your crew from history (but not from your payroll). To learn more about visual room tone, see Chapter 25.

Chapter 44: Transition effects

Cross-dissolve: A transition effect where two clips fade into each other.

In Chapter 40: Editing 360° footage I describe the dip-to-black effect as one of the most common tricks to get from one scene to another in a spherical video, but there are plenty of other visual effects you can implement to artfully move from one location to another. For one thing, a trusty cross-dissolve works pretty well.

Wipes: A transition effect where the image displayed slides offscreen, revealing the new scene behind.

Page peels: A transition effect where the image displayed appears to fold off the screen, resembling the turning of a page in a book.

Latlong (latitudinal-longitudinal): Stretching a spherical image into a flat rectangle (similar to the way a world map represents the spherical Earth). Also called equirectangular.

HMD (head-mounted display): goggles or a headset designed to optimize 360° video viewing.

Effects common to (a certain sector of) traditional video such as wipes, page peels, and the like, don't translate particularly well to a video with no frame edges. But others, like certain kinds of iris or zoom effects that are focused around a single point in the image, can translate to 360° video rather well.

Unfortunately, because most editing programs treat latlong videos as if they were actually rectangular, the built-in transition effects can reveal the edges of that frame, generating unacceptable edges or distortions within your sphere.

In the image below, the first frame shows a traditional wipe applied to a spherical shot. While the circle appears round in the latlong, when viewed in an HMD it would appear distorted. Also, it gets incorrectly cut off by the edge of the frame. This would appear as an unnatural hard edge to a viewer.

A traditional iris applied to a latlong image.

An Iris specifically designed for 360° video.

In the frame on the right, an Iris transition specifically designed for 360° has been applied. While it looks distorted in the lat-long it will appear round in a headset, and it continues across the edge of the latlong frame so it will appear complete when viewed in a headset.

360°-aware transition effects are available in Adobe Premiere in the Immersive Video section (thanks to their 2017 acquisition of Mettle's Skybox Studio). These include zooms, irises, and wipes (one gradient wipe lets you create a wipe of virtually any shape).

The 360°-aware gradient wipe transition effect.

But remember: A key goal of 360° video is to generate a deep sense of physical immersion; having the whole world suddenly fall apart into a swirl or a checkerboard pattern isn't likely to help sell that illusion. Still, there are plenty of spherical projects that don't need to go "full Holodeck." Seasoning your transitions with a little variety may be a great way to spice up your show.

Latlong (latitudinal-longitudinal):
Stretching a spherical image into a flat rectangle (similar to the way a world map represents the spherical Earth). Also called equirectangular.

Chapter 45: 360˚ visual effects

Your editing software likely comes with dozens of special effects to modify the appearance of your videos. Some of these effects can be used on a 360˚ clip, but many cannot. Any effect that modifies the edge of the frame, or uses the edge to hide changes it makes to the image, won't work in a 360˚ shot, which has no edges. The "edge" of a latlong image wraps around to the other side when the video is played in a headset.

Effects like blur (used for removing noise) and sharpen (used for improving soft focus) work by spreading the pixels out in certain areas of the image. In ordinary video, some modified pixels may get pushed off the edge of the frame, but in 360˚ video any pixel pushed off the left edge of the frame must appear on the right edge, and so forth.

If you apply an ordinary filter to 360˚ video, you'll wind up with a visible line down the back of your sphere where these pixels got shifted.

This image was blurred and then the center point was shifted to the right so you can see the line that was created when an ordinary blur filter was applied to a latlong clip.

212

If instead you use a special filter designed for use with 360° video, you'll get the blurring or sharpening effect you desire, but without spawning that distracting line.

This image was blurred using a 360°-aware filter. No line appears.

Both Adobe Premiere and Final Cut Pro provide specific tools for performing these kinds of effects.

If you want to perform more complex effects, such as adding a computer-generated dinosaur to your 360° video of Times Square on New Year's Eve, you'll need to work with different specialized tools. Although you may be able to get the job done in a compositing tool like Nuke or After Effects, consider using dedicated 360° tool like Imagineer System's Mocha VR. Mocha provides motion tracking, advanced rotoscoping and masking, and other features that successfully cross over the back of the image just like the blur examples above.

In order to effectively composite objects into the 3D space of stereoscopic 360° video, you'll benefit from the depth map data that is available if you utilize the Jump platform.

Motion tracking: A technique for recording the movement of an object within a scene, to hide or paint that object or to affix a composited element to a corresponding position.

Rotoscoping: Digitally modifying video by tracing objects within the image one frame at a time.

Masking: Blocking a portion of the image.

Composite: The post-production process of combining two or more images.

Depth map: Digital data representing the distance of the objects in the scene from the camera.

Stitched: Multiple videos that have been combined into one panoramic video.

Chapter 46: Editing stereoscopic footage

Everything that's hard about 360° video is twice as hard with stereo. After all, in 3D video, you're dealing with *two* stitched images for *every* shot—a left-eye channel and a right-eye channel. And there are plenty of other reasons why stereo is challenging (see Chapter 11: Shooting 360° video for the gory details). Not surprisingly, the post side of stereoscopic 360°production can be similarly challenging.

Stitching stereo footage

Zone-based stereo camera: a rig utilizing pairs of cameras pointing in different directions.

Omnidirectional stereo camera: a rig with a large number of cameras arranged in a ring (like the Facebook 360, or GoPro Odyssey).

Depending on whether you're using zone-based stereo cameras or an omnidirectional stereo camera, your workflow will be different. With a zone-based camera, you basically have to do all the stitching you'd do for a mono set-up, and do it twice; once for each eye. And be sure you don't swap the left and right channels—otherwise, your viewers may suddenly feel cross-eyed! Using a tool like Assimilate Scratch VR can ease this added level of file management.

With an omnidirectional stereo camera you're dependent on a computational stitching system like Jump. In that case, your workflow is significantly easier. The service will provide you with rendered top-bottom stereo files that you can mostly just treat the same way you would deal with monoscopic shots. The only limitation is that there is little you can do to override the results of the stitching service.

Editing with stereo pairs

Subsequence or compound clip: Multiple clips which have been grouped into a single object for ease of workflow within an editing program.

For the editing process, if you've got two separate files I recommend sticking them (stacked left-eye channel on top of right-eye channel) into a subsequence or compound clip in your editing software. That way, you can move the two clips as a single object.

Keep the subsequence square (for example, 3840 x 3840) so the two files remain at full resolution.

Monitoring stereo footage

I discuss the reasons and methods for monitoring footage during the editing process in Chapter 37: Viewing 360° video. For the most part, you can monitor your stereo footage in mono, by either looking at only one channel, or using one of the preview methods described in that earlier chapter. (Most of the previewing tools allow you to define the input as stereo and the output as mono, and they will only display the left channel.)

When you want to see the actual stereo effect, there's really no other way around it: You have to view the footage in a headset. You can probably do most of your editing while monitoring only in mono, but if you've added titles or graphics, you'll want to be sure that your convergence settings are correct. And there's no way to check that other than viewing in stereo.

Sure, working in stereo makes your life harder, but isn't that true for anything truly worthwhile?

Convergence: The amount of stereo separation between the left and right channels that controls the stereo effect.

VR180: A subset of spherical video where only the front half of the sphere is recorded. Learn more about creating VR180 footage in Chapter 30: VR180.

Chapter 47: Editing VR180 Footage

VR180 is mainly positioned as a primarily consumer-oriented format, where most users will shoot footage and then upload it directly from the camera to the VR180 app for viewing. However, Google wisely created a simple software tool to allow intrepid VR180 filmmakers to do all the editing work that you might do in any other spherical production.

The tool, VR180 Creator[3], is free, cross platform (Mac, Windows & Linux) and only does three basic things for videomakers:[4]

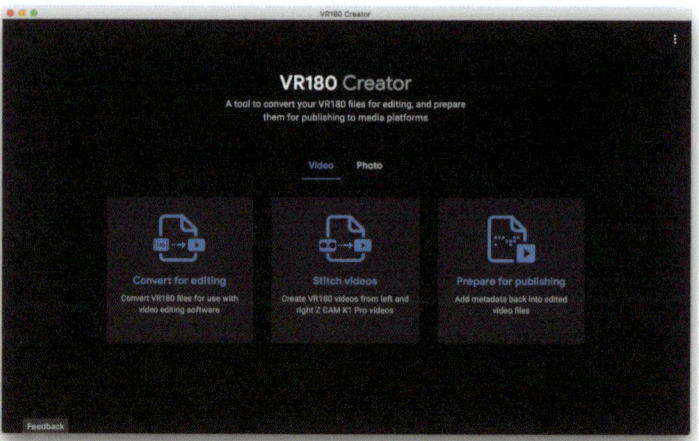

Convert For Editing

This is how you transform your VR180 source files into standard latlong files so they can be edited and manipulated like any other 360° footage. Simply choose your source files, select your settings (use the in-app help buttons to help you decide), and click Convert.

Latlong (latitudinal-longitudinal): Stretching a spherical image into a flat rectangle (similar to the way a world map represents the spherical Earth). Also called equirectangular.

---

3   https://vr.google.com/vr180/apps/

4   It also includes a few features for working with still images, but those are not discussed in this book.

This creates a new set of files with all the data within them. Import those files into your 360°-aware editing app and you're ready to do any of the editing tasks described in the previous chapters.

At this point you *could* wipe your camera or otherwise discard your original files, though an appropriately paranoid, or risk-averse producer would likely keep them in a safe place as a back-up.

Stitch Videos

This isn't actually doing any stitching as described elsewhere in the book. All this does is combine a left camera file and a right camera file into a single latlong file. This is needed for pro VR180 cameras like the Z CAM K1 Pro and the iZugar Z2XL. Be sure to verify the frame rate (30 or 60fps, depending on your shooting settings) and again, follow the in-app instructions for converting the files.

Prepare for Publishing

This step is only necessary if your video editing app doesn't automatically inject 360 metadata (both Premiere and Final Cut Pro do this, so long as you use the correct settings within those apps).

If you've got a spherical file ready to upload to YouTube (or publish elsewhere) and you're not certain if the metadata has been injected, simply choose that file within this section of the VR180 Creator app, assign the stereo layout and field of view (which should match the settings you chose when converting the original footage) and click Export. This will create a duplicate of your video file that includes the required metadata.

217

Chapter 48: Combining mono and stereo footage

As described in the Chapter 4: Choosing a camera, many productions wind up using multiple cameras over the course of a project. That often means having a mix of stereoscopic and monoscopic footage that needs to be combined for the final output.

First of all, you need to decide whether your final output will be stereo or mono. There are plenty of reasons to stick to mono output, as described in Chapter 46: Editing stereoscopic footage. But if you used a stereo-capable camera for some of your shots, you probably want to take advantage of those stereo images in your show. One way or the other, you need to pick a lane when you create the sequence for the master file in your editing application.

Monoscopic.

Stereoscopic.

Mono images are usually saved in an equirectangular format with a 2:1 aspect ratio. Stereo images contain two mono images (one for each eye) stacked on top of each other, resulting in a square (1:1) aspect ratio.

> **Note:** Many playback devices still require delivering a 2:1 image—even for stereoscopic files. If you want to edit directly into a 2:1 sequence, change the vertical (Y) axis of the stereoscopic files to 50% so they'll fit. (For more details on displaying stereo images, see Chapter 46: Editing stereoscopic footage.)

The specific frame size you use for your project should be determined based on the playback device you plan to distribute to. If you're producing a show to be viewed on multiple devices, use

Equirectangular: Stretching a spherical image in a flat, rectangular format. (i.e. the way a world map represents the spherical Earth).

Aspect ratio: The display ratio of resolution pixels along the x axis to the y axis (i.e. HD video of 1920 x 1080 pixels has a 16:9 aspect ratio).

Playback devices: The method for displaying a video. (i.e. HMD, magic window, etc.).

Frame size: The pixel dimension of a video element (i.e. HD is 1920 x 1080).

Crop out the bottom (right-eye) instance to leave a 2:1, single-image file.

the highest resolution of the selected target devices, then export separate files in the various sizes for delivery.

If you have only one or two stereo shots and you want to flatten them to use in a mono sequence, that's easy enough to do. First of all, many stereo-capable cameras such as the YI HALO or Z CAM V1 can output full-resolution mono versions of your shots, and you can just use those versions instead of the stereo versions.

Or, if all you have is a stereo shot, you can use the footage from just the left-eye channel by scaling the stereo shot so that the right eye channel is cropped out of the final image.

Latlong (latitudinal-longitudinal): Stretching a spherical image into a flat rectangle (similar to the way a world map represents the spherical Earth). Also called equirectangular.

If you want to use a mono shot in a stereoscopic project, simply duplicate the mono shot so the same exact image appears in both the top and bottom halves of the latlong.

Just be extra careful that the duplicated shots are lined up precisely in time. If you accidentally dragged one a few frames to the left or right when duplicating it, the two eyes will be out of sync with each other which is very uncomfortable to watch.

Viewing mixed content like this is actually quite unobtrusive. Depending on the specifics of the content you can usually sneak a few mono shots into a mostly stereo show without your viewers even noticing. If the show is mostly mono, interspersing a stereo shot here or there may be a little more distracting, but it's not likely to upset your viewers in any significant way.

Chapter 49: Audio post for 360° overview

When thinking about how best to construct the audio for your project, it helps to start at the end of the process and then work backwards. Imagine yourself as the viewer watching your spherical video. Now close your eyes. What are the elements that make up the soundscape of your world? Which elements have a specific location in space and which seem to be coming from all around you? Which elements are critical to your story (such as a person's voice or a ticking clock)? Which are potential distractions such as traffic outside or silverware clatter in a restaurant? Is there music? Is the music practical or just ambient score?

Mixing for 360° video isn't very different from mixing for surround sound. You start with mono elements and then pan them so they seem to emanate from the appropriate part of the room. The door slam on screen left comes mainly out of the left speaker. The voices of the actors in close-up come out of the center channel, and so forth.

With a surround mix, those positions are fixed to the physical speakers. If you're watching the movie wearing headphones, and you turn your head to the left, the sound moves with you, regardless of its source's location onscreen. With *spatialized* sound the audio is pinned to the objects onscreen. So, if you're facing the door on the left when it slams, it sounds like it's coming from in front of you; but if you were facing away from the door when it slammed, the sound would seem to come from behind you.

> **Note:** Both surround and spatialized audio are considered "directional" audio. The difference is whether or not the playback engine adjusts the positioning of the sound based on your head position.

Practical (diegetic): Occurring in the reality of the scene; heard by the characters within the scene (as opposed to sound only heard by the audience). For example, music played on a radio.

Score: Music added to enhance the mood of the video.

Pan: Set the position in space for where audio appears to originate.

As you plan the audio mix for your 360° project, consider the following guidelines:

Know your audience

Not all viewers will be able to watch your program on a platform that supports spatialized sound (or while wearing headphones). So how you approach your audio mix should begin with a consideration of how your viewers are most likely to experience your show.

If, for example, you think most users will watch your video in a magic window on their cell phone, the audio might best be optimized for that 3mm mono speaker. (In which case, you'd probably want to apply a low-pass filter to add more bass, compress voices to punch them up, and forgo any spatialization data at all.)

If, on the other hand, you think most viewers will watch on an HMD in a controlled environment, or that your subject requires the precise placement of different sounds to help guide the viewer's point of focus, then you absolutely should create a spatialized mix—even if not everyone who sees your show will get to hear it.

Don't overdo it

As with your spin budget (which was discussed earlier in the book), you should similarly exercise some restraint when it comes to spatialized sound into your project. Good sound shouldn't draw attention to itself. Restrict your spatialized elements to things that are obvious sources of sound, like percussive bangs, or the voices of an onscreen subject. Depending on your output format, you can include non-moving mono or stereo tracks along with the spatialized data. Voice-over narration, nondiegetic music, and even some kinds of ambiances or room tone might be better left out of the directional spatialized mix.

Magic window: A method of viewing 360° content where a rectangular frame acts as a portal to the larger, spherical recording. The viewer can navigate to a different perspective by scrolling (on a computer), or by tilting the viewing device (on a smartphone or tablet).

HMD (head-mounted display): goggles or a headset designed to optimize 360° video viewing.

Spin budget: The accumulated total degrees of head movement you can ask of your audience over a period of time.

Nondiegetic: Sound that is untethered to anything occurring in the scene.

Sidebar: Working with ambisonic source

In Chapter 27: Recording audio for 360°, I discussed using tetrahedral (or other positiona-capable) microphones, which can be ideal for capturing the ambiance of a location, recording the sound directionally from the camera position.

The thing is, the output of tetrahedral mikes is usually recorded in *A-format:* which is four channels based on the positions of the individual mics. You need to convert A-format to *B-format* (also four channels, but with a different configuration) to properly integrate the audio into an ambisonic mix.

This conversion is straightforward, but requires subtle adjustments based on the specific characteristics of each mic. Most hardware manufacturers provide software designed for their specific hardware. Here are some important considerations when working with ambisonic audio:

Line it up: Because ambisonic audio is directional (in 360°), you need to line up the front and center position of the mic with the corresponding position of the camera. This is why it's so important to note the direction and position of the mic on set.

Follow the center: If you change which part of the video sphere is facing north (as described in Chapter 39: Setting the center point), be sure to change the orientation of the ambisonic audio track too. There's a detailed description of how to perform this rotation in the help for Jump.[1]

Integrate it into your mix: You can add the four channels of the B-format audio to your mix as four mono channels. So long as you always move and adjust them as a group, the pan settings of the file should remain intact.

1 https://support.google.com/jump/answer/6400185

Chapter 50: Basic sound design

Before you get to the fancy audio tricks that take advantage of 360° video's unique playback environment, you need to lock down the basics. The first steps to creating a successful 360° sound mix are no different from those in a traditional show. Although I don't have room to include a thorough description of the process, I'll summarize the basic phases:

Step 1: Assemble the various sound elements

As described in Chapter 27: Recording audio for 360°, you're likely to use a variety of mics and techniques to record your audio—camera mics, lavalieres, tetrahedral mics, and so on. As you assemble your edit, you'll lay in all these sounds to your timeline to align with the corresponding video. Be sure that all dual-system audio (audio recorded to a separate device from the camera) is properly synced with the stitched video clips.

Step 2: Edit the production sound for timing and clarity

As you build your edit, trim your clips to create natural timing. Listening to the various audio source clips for each scene you'll begin to get a sense of which elements have the clearest sound. For example, you may find that the recording from your camera mic is so much noisier than the lav that you want to turn the camera mic off entirely. Or, in some cases, the lav may sound too dead and you may want to keep some of the camera mic track as well to add a little more natural reverb to the sound. As you finish your video edit you'll see what sound elements are still needed.

Step 3: Record ADR

If any dialogue wasn't properly recorded on set, you may need

Tetrahedral: A microphone with four recording capsules that captures a rendering of the sound in all directions around the mic.

Synced (Synchronized): Matched to play back at the same time as the video.

Dead: An environment with little or no reflections or reverberations of the sound.

to perform *alternate dialogue recording* (ADR). This is where you play the video in a quiet studio and record the actors speaking their lines in sync with their performance in the video.

ADR is pretty common in 360˚ productions for a number of reasons. First of all, without a boom-mounted shotgun mic, it's not always possible to record clean audio on set. Also, ADR is hardest to do on tight close-ups, but since 360˚ video generally forces you to keep you subject a safe distance from the camera, you don't have as many close-ups. That means your ADR doesn't need to be as precise; so you're more likely to rerecord any sound, even if it only had slight problems.

Boom-mounted shotgun mic: A directional microphone (that captures sound in a conical field reminiscent of a shotgun's blast area) attached to the end of a long, light-weight pole.

Step 4: Add ambiances, and other textural elements
To create naturalistic soundscapes for each of your scenes, it's common practice to add a little background noise. Ambient noise can help cover up any necessary edits or cuts in the picture. You can use room tone, or you can use ambiance track from a sound effects library that matches the type of location you used (restaurant, park, police station, busy traffic circle, etc.). You might also supplement the ambiance tracks with additional sound elements—for example, a deep, throbbing refrigerator hum to add a little bit of menace to an interrogation room, or a ticking clock for that late-at-night-in-a-quiet-house scene.

Room tone: An extended clip of sound recorded in the scene location without any additional sounds included.

Given how critical environments are to the VR experience, it behooves you to pay extra attention to these audio elements. After all, your goal is to create lively, realistic, and authentic atmospheres, and persuasive audio will help bring your spherical scenes to life.

Spatialization: Mixing in post-production to distribute sounds into positions in a sphere around the listener.

Step 5: Add sound fx as required by the on-screen action

Because the mics used in production tend to be small, directional, and most likely pointed at the on-camera talent's mouth, they'll probably not record other key sounds that occur during a scene—for example, a soda can being put down on a table, a lamp clicking on, a dog barking, or a parade marching down the street in the background of your shot. It's an essential step in the editing process to walk through your video—moment by moment—and add sounds for absolutely anything that moves on screen[5]. These are the sounds that are most likely to require careful spatialization (as described in Chapter 51: Spatial placement).

Step 6: Record foley

Record voices or sounds unique to the action in the scene the same way you record ADR. Play back the video, and while watching, recreate (or simulate) the sound of the onscreen action. This is called foley, and it's commonly used for footfalls, grunts, and so on. Just like the other sound effects, these elements are likely to require spatialization in order to feel properly integrated into the scene.

Step 7: Add music

After all the other elements have been added, you can integrate music; both diegetic (sound that can be heard by the participants in the scene) and nondiegetic (score, or music heard only by the audience). Even if the music covers up a lot of the sound effects and ambiances, it's ideal to include those natural sounds—no matter how subtle.

5   Anything that moves even if it doesn't have an obvious inherent sound. So, a paper airplane flying through a scene might warrant a tiny humming sound, even though it wouldn't make a detectable sound in real life. Also, moving titles and graphics are often enhanced by including a corresponding subtle sound.

Step 8: Set the levels and add fades

After all of the other audio elements are in place, you need to adjust the volume level so that each element is appropriately audible.

While setting levels can be somewhat of an art, for a rule of thumb, aim to set the average levels of primary audio (such as dialogue) to -12dB. This gives the peaks room to be a bit louder and still not cause any overmodulation. Also beware: audio levels are additive, so the more sounds that occur at a given point in time, the louder that section will be. Your primary concern should always be to prevent sounds from hitting 0dB, which will create distortion in the soundtrack.

You also need to add (sometimes tiny) fades at the beginning and end of each audio element to prevent clicks or pops. Remember, sound is cumulative, so the more sound elements that occur at a given point in time, the louder the overall sound will be.

Ordinarily, this last phase would include panning too (for stereo sound or for surround sound), but because panning in 360° video is a little different, that topic is covered separately in the next chapter.

Peaks: Short bursts of loud sound in an audio track. These are visible in an audio waveform as lines that stick up higher than the average audio levels.

Overmodulation: when a sound is louder than the recording device can measure, the waveform will be clipped, distorting the sound unnaturally.

Chapter 51: Spatial placement

After you address all your audio basics (as described in Chapter 50: Basic sound design), you can use special spatializing panners to position sound effects and other motivated sounds in the sphere. Spatial panners work essentially the same way as surround sound panners do (identifying where the sound originates in the sphere). However, whereas surround data is fixed, spatial data moves around depending on where the viewer turns her head.

In a flat video, if there's a sound that doesn't have a specific origin point, it seems to come from everywhere at once which isn't very off-putting. But in VR, sounds that should be motivated but don't have a specific source point can be distracting, or even disorienting: "I see the dog to my left, but it sounds like it's right in front of me."

DAW (digital audio workstation): Software designed to process and edit audio tracks.

Higher-order ambisonics: Ambisonic audio with more than 4 channels.

There are a number of plug-ins for Pro Tools, Reaper, and other DAWs that add spatial panners to just about any audio-mixing software. Two Big Ears (owned by Facebook) is very popular (perhaps because it's free), but there are other options such as Ambi Pan, Audio Ease, and O3A plug-ins from Blue Ripple Sound (for working with higher-order ambisonics). These products range in price, along with a corresponding range of options and levels of precision.

Latlong (latitudinal-longitudinal): Stretching a spherical image into a flat rectangle (similar to the way a world map represents the spherical Earth). Also called equirectangular.

The best interfaces allow you to pin the sound to a coordinate in the latlong image, so you can easily affix the barking sound to the dog's face.

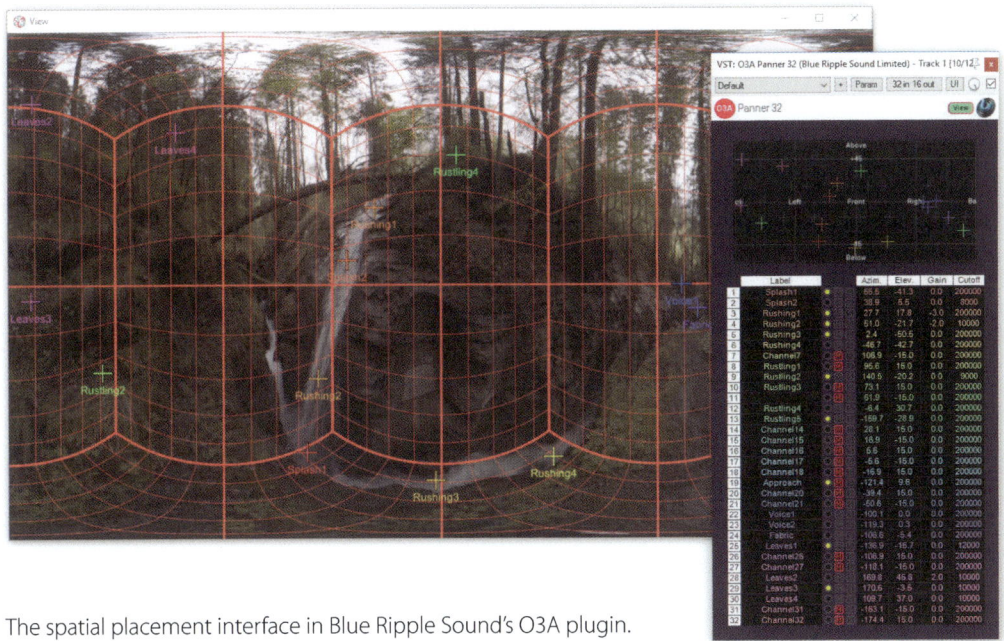

The spatial placement interface in Blue Ripple Sound's O3A plugin.

If the source of a sound is moving in space (such as an interview subject walking across a room or even a plane flying overhead), or if the camera is moving, or if both are happening at the same time, you'll need to animate the changing position of the sound element.

Many of these software packages facilitate this type of animation, allowing you to trace the movement of an object in space as it changes over time.

Chapter 52: Audio delivery options

OK, you've finished mixing and panning your audio. Now it's time to save the data. There are three or four commonly used formats for storing directional audio data, including two different flavors of B-format ambisonic:

- *B-format Furse-Malham (FuMa):* This is an extension of the classic B-format, and is used by a number of delivery services, although its use seems to be waning as SN3D gains popularity.

- *B-format SN3D:* SN3D contains similar data as FuMa, but the channels are arranged differently and it uses different weighting.

  SN3D is often conflated with the file format AmbiX, however AmbiX specifically refers to files using SN3D and stored in Apple's .caf file type, whereas SN3D data can be saved in a variety of formats.

  SN3D has been adopted by both Google (including YouTube) and Facebook as their preferred format for spatialized sound. However some delivery services identify AmbiX compatibility, but don't accept the .caf file format. Be sure to check your delivery service's requirements before uploading your files.

Panners: Controls that allow you to position the source of sound in space. In stereo environments sound could simply be panned from left to right, but with surround sound and spatialization, panning can be done in full three-dimensional coordinates.

Note: For the purposes of this book, I'm primarily discussing "first-order" ambisonic audio, which uses four channels, but there are also higher-order ambisonics (HOA). Second order ambisonics uses 9 channels, third order utilizes 16 channels, fourth order uses 25 channels and so on. The more channels you have, the more precision and fine placement of specific sounds you can create. Using panners such as those provided by Blue Ripple Sound's O3A plug in, you can mix up to third order ambisonics.

Dolby Atmos: Atmos has been in use as a surround format for many years. First of all, it's different than ambisonic audio in that it's object based rather than scene based. So, the more elements you have the larger the resulting files (this doesn't happen with ambisonics). Atmos is differentiated from 5.1 or 7.1 systems in that Atmos stores the positional data for audio based on the positions of objects an abstract sphere[6] rather than based on a specific speaker position. This allows Atmos data to be played on a 5-speaker setup in your living room or a 40-speaker setup in a movie theater. This also makes Atmos an easy fit for VR, where the position of the sound must move based on the direction the viewer's head is facing.

Surround: directional data can also be saved into a traditional surround sound format, and often it's saved this way as a "base-level" standard that can then be later converted into one of the dynamic formats above.

After you've integrated your directional data into your audio file, you need to link that file to your spherical video for final delivery. See Chapter 59: Muxing audio and video for details about that.

6   Atmos models are based on a partial sphere (more like a dome). Sounds don't originate from below the listener.

Part IV: Finishing

The final stage of the post-production process is often called *finishing*. It's considered a separate phase of post-production because the work is often performed by a different set of people (at least at the professional level). Finishing typically includes producing the final master file (incorporating and integrating the full-resolution versions of all the component shots); doing a final color grading pass; adding titles, credits, and graphics; and, when necessary, rendering output files for the project's intended distribution channels.

All of these steps are necessary for both traditional and 360° video. But 360° video requires that several additional tasks be performed in finishing: fine-stitching the shots and removing the rigs. Because the work must be precise, these extra tasks can be expensive or time-consuming. This is why you should attend to these steps only after you've whittled down your source footage to the exact number of frames that will appear in the final piece. After all, there's no point in color correcting or fine-stitching an entire three-minute shot when only 15 seconds of it will ever be seen by your audience.

Tip: Consider adding handles (extra footage before the beginning and/or after the ending of the used portion of a shot) to the beginning and end of each shot just in case you need to make minor adjustments to the edit during these final stages.

Chapter 53: Rig removal and nadir patching

To create a fully immersive experience, you need to hide all bogeys (evidence of equipment and crew) in your final cut. One of the most obvious examples of things you don't want your audience to see is the tripod your camera sits on. Unless you digitally erase the tripod, your viewers will see it whenever they look down toward the nadir of the sphere (or toward wherever your camera was rigged), and be reminded of the artifice of the experience. Fortunately, in many cases, removing rigs like this is quite easy.

The bottom image shows the tripod removed from the shot.

Most often, the camera is rigged from the floor or the ceiling, so the background (what's behind that tripod or rig) is static (unless the floor is made of glass and there's fish swimming beneath it).

Background plate: A duplicate set up of a shot with an unwanted object (tripod, interviewer, crewmember, etc.) removed.

Mocha VR lets you track and rotoscope in VR projects.

Rotoscoping: Digitally modifying video by tracing objects within the image one frame at a time.

In such cases you can composite a still image (background plate) over the tripod, and no one will be the wiser. (You can use this same method to fill in the top and bottom areas of footage from cylindrical cameras like the GoPro Odyssey or VSN Mobil's V.360, which don't have upward- or downward-facing lenses.)

Alternatively, you can employ motion tracking and advanced rotoscoping tools such as Mocha VR, which allow you to add or remove objects in your 360° videos as easily as in flat videos.

Important: If there are moving objects in the area you want to cover up, you may be better off using the split-screen method; replacing the camera views that see the tripod with alternative pieces of video. See Chapter 43: Split screens for more.

There are several ways to remove rigs from your shots. Or you can choose to leave them in, for a more *cinéma vérité* effect. When it's time to finish your production, consider the following options for dealing with bogeys and photobombing crew:

Hide your junk with a plate

If you followed the instructions in Chapter 25: Visual room tone, you'll have extra footage you can use to mask the portion of the screen containing equipment (or crew). You can add a plate over your primary footage quite easily in any compositing application.

Note: If you shot your plate with a different lens than the lenses on your 360° camera, you may need to apply an artificial lens distortion to the plate, to approximate the distortion created by the lenses on your 360° camera.

Tip: One apparent challenge with rig removal is that (in a latlong projection) the area containing the tripod is spread over a large portion of the image.

Latlong (latitudinal-longitudinal): Stretching a spherical image into a flat rectangle (similar to the way a world map represents the spherical Earth). Also called equirectangular.

Tripod legs

Replacing that large portion of your image would be difficult or at least time consuming. But if you convert the view of the image to a cube map, the same element takes up a tiny portion of the image, making it far easier to fix.

Cube map: A projection where a spherical image is viewed as a cube, and where the six faces of the cube are unfolded into a rectangle. The cube faces can be arranged in different ways for different purposes. In a cubemap, distortions present in a lat-long are corrected, giving an accurate scale to objects at the apex (top) and nadir (bottom) of the scene.

Tripod

Cubic projection (cubemap).

In the latlong, the tripod covers the bottom edge.

Convert to cubic; the tripod is now tiny.

Export a still image and clone the area.

Convert the cloned cubic back to latlong and paste the still image over the original video. The tripod is successfully removed.

Tip: 360Toolkit.co features free web-based conversions between latlong (equirectangular) images and cube maps. Or if you've got Adobe After Effects, you can use the VR Converter effect (in the Immersive Video effects category.

After you've removed the rig, convert the cube map view back to equirectangular for editing and output.

"Clone" neighboring areas

For simple cases, where the rig is in front of a uniform background (where there's not a lot of pattern or variation), you can get away with not even using your plate shots. The example images on the right illustrate the steps: Export a cubic still image of the shot you want to fix, and then use the clone-stamp brush in Photoshop (or a similar application) to cover the tripod legs with blobs of nearby pixels.

After you've digitally removed the rig (sometimes called *digitally painting it out*), import the image back into your compositing application and slap it over the footage. Because the rig-free still is an exact replica of the original footage, it should fit right on top.

The area you corrected will fit directly onto the original image.

Cover the rig with a graphic

If you don't have a plate shot, or if there's something in the nadir area that can't easily be covered up (like moving shadows or an actor's feet), you can opt to simply cover up the offending area with a logo or a compass graphic.

Adding a logo to the image to cover the tripod area at the nadir is a quick and easy solution.

If you look straight down in the headset, the nadir logo is visible (and legible).

There are tools built into Adobe Premiere and Final Cut Pro that allow you to quickly add a nadir patch and adjust the size, rotation, and position of the patch to quickly disguise any unseemly nadirs in your show.

Tip: Consider using a triangular nadir patch. If you're attempting to cover a tripod, a circle or square logo might not be the best shape (see example on next page).

Now, if a viewer looks down, at least she won't see the tripod (although I'm not sure if seeing a logo is any less distracting). Perhaps you can sell your nadir as ad space and recoup some of your production costs.

The tips of the tripod legs are visible.

A triangle-shaped logo will more easily cover a tripod.

Leave the rig in

In many cases, you may decide that it's simply not necessary to hide the rigs. Perhaps your project is nonfiction, and the presence of the camera isn't intended to be a secret. Or, hopefully, you have sufficient action going on in other areas of the screen (and your shots are short enough) that no serious audience member will bother to look down, anyway.

If your audience finds the floor more compelling than your action, you've likely got bigger problems than someone noticing the tripod!

Chapter 54: Adding titles and graphics

One of the most important things you can do to make a show feel finished is to add opening titles and closing credits. Titles and credits can be as simple as solid white letters superimposed over black or over part of the image. Or they can be as elaborate as animated 3D graphics (and beyond).

But titles and graphics aren't limited to the beginning and end of your project. You can enhance your show by adding them in many other places. For example, you can use lower-third style titles to identify interview subjects, locations, or the time-of-day. And you can add graphics such as arrows and thought bubbles to help your viewers understand what they're looking at, or to fill in blank spots in your sphere, or to control focus, and so on.

Lower-third: titles displaying an interview subject's name and title. Traditionally placed in the bottom third of the video screen.

Like everything else, titles and graphics require special treatment in 360° video. If you try to just slap a "flat" title on top of the latlong, it will appear distorted (and huge) to the viewer.

Latlong (latitudinal-longitudinal): Stretching a spherical image into a flat rectangle (similar to the way a world map represents the spherical Earth). Also called equirectangular.

Title applied in latlong

How it appears when viewed spherically.

To make a title or graphic appear correctly in 360° space, the image must be properly distorted when you add it to your editing timeline.

Both Adobe Premiere and Final Cut Pro (as well as their motion-graphics focused siblings After Effects and Motion, can

Title applied with proper distortion   How it appears when viewed spherically.

make this potentially complex process very simple. They include pre-built 360°-aware titles that will automatically work correctly, plus, if you're creating a graphic in another program, you can easily map it spherically. In Premiere use the VR Projection effect. In Final Cut Pro any flat clip added to a 360° project can be mapped onto the sphere by enabling the 360° Transform tools in the Video inspector.

Graphics resolution

You can see in the example above that warping process shrinks the graphic quite a bit. But to accurately control the shape and proportion, you should create your graphic at an identical resolution and aspect ratio as the latlong project. For example, in a project with a resolution of 3840 x 1920, your graphic should be sized at a resolution of 3840 x 1920. This ensures that the image looks the same to the viewer of the 360˚ video as it does to you when you create image (in Photoshop or a similar tool).

If you're working in stereo (3D), your graphic should still be created at a resolution of 3840 x 1920 (regardless of whether your project is 3840 x 3840 or 3840 x 1920. To learn more about project sizes, see Chapter 38: Project frame rate and frame size). The VR Projection effect allows you to specify stereo output and duplicates and positions the graphic appropriately.

Chapter 54: Adding titles and graphics

For stereo files, your title needs to appear in both eyes.

Graphics positioning

If you want a graphic to appear anywhere other than dead center in your output, not only do you need to reposition it on screen, but the distortion needs to change as well. If you're working in stereo, you can also adjust convergence, to make the graphic appear closer or further from the viewer.

Convergence: The point where the left and right eye projections meet in the screen to simulate the 3D effect.

> **Note:** For three-dimensional titles or graphics such as those created in a 3D modeling application, use a 360-aware application like Houdini to apply the necessary spherizing distortion. Houdini will output a pre-distorted (and if needed, stereoscopic) image with an alpha channel to dropped into your editing timeline on top of the main images.

Graphics animation

There's no reason your graphics have to be static. Like any other element, graphics can be faded in, blurred in, or enhanced with any other common effect. And the parameters of the Project 2D plug-in can be keyframed as well, so the graphic can move in space, too. Convergence can be changed over time, so (for stereo projects) you can make your title move toward or away from the viewer, as well.

Keyframed: Animations created by setting parameter values (such as an object's size or its position in the frame) at differing points in time, and interpolating the intervening values.

And there's no reason your graphic can't itself be an animation. In fact, using tools like the motion tracking feature in Mocha VR, you can create in 360˚ video nearly all of the compositing and special effects possible in flat video. The sky's the limit! Actually, the sky isn't a limit at all—let your alien spaceships pierce through it to land on the ground in front of your viewers!

Tip: Because viewers might miss a title or graphic if they're looking the wrong way at the wrong moment, consider placing duplicate copies of graphics in different directions in the sphere. That way, wayward gazers will see your flying titles no matter where they're gaping.

One graphic is positioned due north.   Another is positioned behind the viewer.

Dynamic title positioning

If you want a graphic to appear directly in front of the viewer, no matter where she's looking, Deep Inc.'s Liquid Cinema software lets you to add graphics (and other elements) onto a dynamic layer superimposed over the main video, and it uses the viewer's gaze to determine where that graphic appears. This expands the possibilities of how your program can be viewed (including swapping out assets for different languages or other variables). The only drawback to this solution is that it requires viewers to watch using Deep Inc.'s custom-made playback engine and hardware that supports eye tracking or gaze detection.

Chapter 55: Color grading

All video content can benefit a color-adjustment pass in which you evaluate and modify the contrast and color tone of each shot. This stage of post-production is typically called *color grading* or *color correction* (though often it's not at all about correcting problems).

There are usually four basic goals in the color grade process:

1. Improve the sharpness and clarity of the image (usually done by adjusting contrast).
2. Make sure any human faces appear a natural, appropriate color (and fixing this often improves the colors in the rest of the image).
3. Ensure that any shots from a single setting all look consistent and unified (even if they were filmed at different times or in different places).
4. Add a creative "look" to the footage to guide the audience's emotional reaction (such as "warming up" a cozy romantic encounter by tinting everything orange, or adding a blue-green high-contrast sheen to a sci-fi movie set in outer space).

I'm sure professional colorists would balk at this oversimplification. It's true that every show is unique. For some projects, some of those goals (or even *all* of them) may not apply—for example, when you're after a specific creative effect. But it's a nice, shorthand list to get you thinking about how you can use color grading to add professional polish to your production.

What follows are a few guidelines to consider as you color-grade your project:

Avoid shape masks

The good news is that most of the tools used for color grading traditional footage work just as well for 360° footage. The one exception is *square-edges masks* (sometimes called *power windows*). These are frequently used to make a change to the color or contrast of a certain region of the image without affecting the rest of it. For example, you could change the color of the sky by creating a window that begins at the horizon, or brighten the dark shadows in a hallway, using the door frame to guide where the power window should be applied.

Latlong (latitudinal-longitudinal): Stretching a spherical image into a flat rectangle (similar to the way a world map represents the spherical Earth). Also called equirectangular.

In spherical footage, these types of masks create problems. Straight lines appear curved in the latlong image, making straight edged masks tricky to execute. However, there are workarounds: You could, for example, change the projection of the image to a cube map or another view where the image is less distorted so that your mask might successfully match the shape of the horizon or door frame in the shot; or you could add the mask to an adjustment layer (in After Effects) and apply a *VR Plane to Sphere* effect (from the Immersive Video category) to that layer, matching the distortion to that of the video image.

Add a LUT

A common tool in color grading is the *look-up table* (LUT), a set of mathematical instructions for how colors should be represented in the image. This is especially important for footage that's deliberately shot to look "flat." Which is exactly what happens when you use the Protune setting in a GoPro camera (which I recommended using in Chapter 22: Camera settings).

The flat look is a deliberate reduction in contrast to preserve the maximum amount of data to work with in the bright and dark areas of the sphere. If, instead, you were to increase the contrast on the shot (so that everything below 90% gray is made pure black, for example), the image might look sharper and cleaner at first. But if you later wanted to enhance the detail in those dark areas, you'd be out of luck, because every pixel would be pure black.

Applying a LUT (which is a one-step command in most video-editing software) allows you to instantly assign a complex set of color and contrast settings to each shot. And there are hundreds of LUTs available for free on the internet, some designed specifically to compensate for the flat look of individual cameras (such as the GoPro set to Protune), and others artistic looks designed to emulate specific film stocks or apply other popular effects.

Good color correction requires more thought than simply slapping a LUT onto your clips. But a LUT is a great starting place and can help ensure consistency across a variety of shots.

Match camera output

For 360° video, there's another color correction task: making sure that the individual slices of the stitched shots are all perfectly consistent and uniform. But this is really more a piece of the stitching process than a separate process later. (For more information, see Chapter 34: Stitching overview.)

Stitched: Multiple videos that have been combined into one panoramic video.

Color can have tremendous impact on the way viewers respond to a particular scene, and good color grading is as much an art as composing a film's score. Is it essential? Not usually, but especially with VR where the goal is to create as immersive an experience as possible, color grading can be an invaluable tool.

HMD (head-mounted display): goggles or a headset designed to optimize 360° video viewing.

Chapter 56: Creating a dub master

After you complete all the steps to get your show to a fully finished state, it's time to output your work in preparation for sharing it with the world. However, different viewing methods require different settings and parameters, and you'll likely want to show your 360° video in more than one way (for example, as a link on Facebook and also as a file to be loaded onto a Daydream View HMD). So before you create specific files for the various devices (as described in Chapter 57: Creating delivery masters), it's a good idea to create a single master file that can then be used to create various outputs for the different avenues of exhibition. To borrow a term from traditional tape-based video production, we'll call this your "dub master" (i.e. the master from which you'll make your various copies or "dubs.")

Compression: A process of lowering overall image quality by reducing the amount of data in a file in order to make it more accessible to playback engines.

The dub master file should be the highest possible resolution and quality with the least amount of compression so you'll be sure to get the best-looking (and best-sounding) version of your show regardless of any additional processing required for the delivery masters.

Lossy: An artifact of data compression whereby visual information deemed unnecessary is discarded, resulting in noise.

For the most part, this is very easy. Your editing project should already be at the best possible frame size and frame rate for your source media (as described in Chapter 38: Project frame rate and frame size). Simply export (or *Share* in Apple parlance) a master file set to the same settings as the project and using the least-lossy compression method available to you.

Choose the right compression method

As you probably know, video files can be huge, and 360° video files are especially so. Compression allows you to reduce the size of files saved on your storage device, as well as to reduce bandwidth requirements for transferring those files across networks.

But compression comes with a cost: quality. Generally speaking, the more compressed the file is, the more artifacts or visual anomalies you'll be able to detect in the image. And even if the video might look "perfect" at first glance, because 360° video is usually viewed on a high-resolution screen mere inches from your eyes, even mild blurriness or blockiness is hard to miss.

Furthermore, small errors introduced by compression can be amplified when a file is re-compressed. So, if your original video is compressed in the camera (as most 360° video source is), and then it's compressed again to create a master file, and then it's compressed a third time to create the delivery file, the overall quality may be increasingly compromised.

Asynchronous compression schemes (codecs) like H.264/MPEG-4 create files that look good when played back in real time. But if you examine the file frame by frame, you'll see there's quite a lot of data missing. These formats are great for final output, but if you can avoid it, don't use them for your master file.

Avid's DNxHR and the Apple ProRes compression families are specifically designed for mastering, and the highest-quality versions successfully avoid any visible data loss, even after repeated encoding. These are your best bets for storing your master file.

Don't waste space
On the other hand, there's a limit to the benefit of these compression methods, and using a quality level significantly higher than your original source files serves no actual benefit, and may create an unnecessarily large file.

For example, if all your source footage was shot on a Ricoh Theta

4:2:0/4:4:4: One of the ways video is compressed is by removing color data that is less noticeable by the human eye. These numbers identify the "chroma subsampling" in different compression schemes (how that color data is removed). Lower numbers indicate more data is thrown out to make smaller files.

Aspect ratio: The display ratio of resolution pixels along the x axis to the y axis (i.e. HD video of 1920 x 1080 pixels has a 16:9 aspect ratio).

(which uses a 4:2:0 color space version of the H.264 codec), Apple ProRes 422 is a more than sufficient codec to represent all the data from the source (with room to spare). Using a 4:4:4 codec (like Apple ProRes 4444 or DNxHR *444*) would be total overkill. On the other hand, if you shot with the Nokia Ozo+, which uses a wavelet-based raw codec, you should absolutely output your dub master in a 4:4:4 codec capable of retaining all the data from the camera original.

Keep stereo square

If your source footage is stereoscopic (3D), keep your master in a 1:1 (square) aspect ratio (left eye on top of right, as described in Chapter 38: Project frame rate and frame size). This ensures that the maximum amount of data is saved in the file. Even though your final output may need to be crunched into 2:1 (for certain distribution venues), reserve that processing for the final step.

Create a mono version of your stereo project

You may also want to create a mono dub master based on your stereo dub master (for output venues like Facebook that don't support Stereoscopic video). In this case, you can simply nest your final 1:1 output sequence into a 2:1 project, offsetting the Y axis so that only the left eye is visible.

Output a second dub master and use that for creating your mono delivery versions. Creating this second file from the editing program (instead of in a second step after you've already output the 1:1 stereo dub master) potentially saves one generation of compression loss.

Chapter 57: Creating delivery masters

The lack of standards for the playback of 360° video is one of the most obvious examples of the immaturity of the VR industry. Nearly every device or service has different requirements, often with only slight variations from each other. However, if you use the wrong settings for a particular device, the system may not recognize your file, or you may have problems like poor image quality, stuttering playback, or no playback at all.

This means you'll likely need to render a number of different files, each intended for a different venue. The good news is that If you created a dub master (as described in the previous chapter), it's pretty easy to automatically generate the files needed for each of these output scenarios using a batch transcoder like Apple's Compressor, Adobe Media Encoder, or FFmpeg (a free, cross-platform, extremely simple and powerful file converter that unfortunately requires command-line instructions to operate).

Distribution options can be categorized into five basic types:
> • *Video-sharing sites that accept (or specialize in) 360° video*
> • *Curated 360° video sharing services*
> • *Manually distributing files for specific viewers*
> • *Custom video playback apps*
> • *Livestreaming*

These categories are described in detail in the next few chapters.

Most creators will want to use more than one of these. For example, you may want to upload a version to Facebook where the most people can see it, but also to YouTube where it can be viewed in stereo (and where it will be accessible on PlayStation and other systems). Plus, you may want a version specifically to be loaded locally onto a smartphone or standalone HMD so it can be viewed without an internet connection, and so on.

Spatialized: A soundscape where audio is positioned from specific locations in space around the listener.

For each of these cases, you need to create individual delivery masters to be uploaded to the respective sites. The settings required for each device/service are detailed in the following chapters. Additionally, see the instructions on how to combine your final video file with the spatialized audio (in Chapter 60: Muxing audio and video).

Purple Pill (a Dutch company that creates innovative standalone VR apps) identified what they found to be optimal settings for a variety of 360° video scenarios, and they released a free app called *VRencoder*[1] that adds a simple graphical user interface (GUI) for FFMpeg. It's a very rudimentary app, but it automatically converts your dub master to a number of possible preset outputs with just a few clicks.

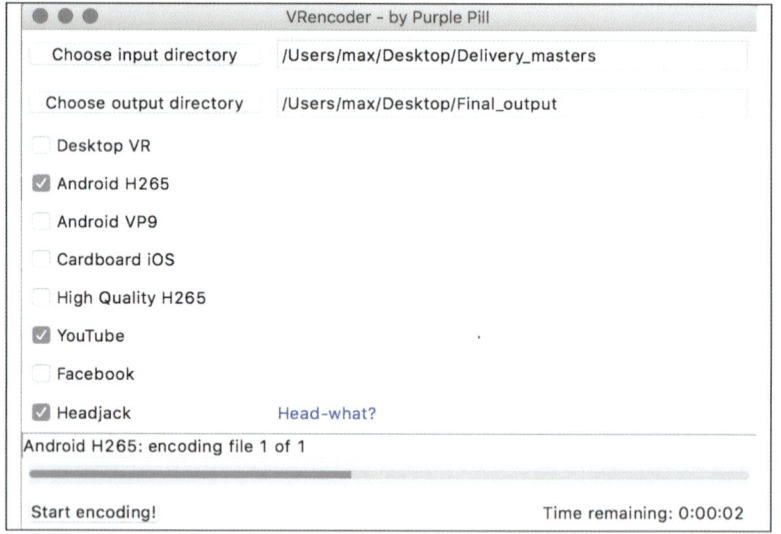

1   https://purplepill.io/vrencoder/

Chapter 58: Video-sharing services

The easiest way to share your 360° video is to upload it to public-facing video sharing services like YouTube, Facebook, Vimeo, and others. Each of these options has benefits and drawbacks. Most of these services allow your video to be viewed on both computers and mobile devices, either through a web browser or via a dedicated app. Many of the mobile apps can be used by themselves as a magic window, or, if you have a Google Cardboard-compatible headset, the app can be configured to show the two-up display.

Magic window: A method of viewing 360° content where a rectangular frame acts as a portal to the larger, spherical recording. The viewer can navigate to a different perspective by scrolling (on a computer), or by tilting the viewing device (on a smartphone or tablet).

Click the "cardboard" icon to enable dual viewer mode. so your video can be watched in an HMD.

> **Note:** Not all devices and not all browsers properly display 360° video, even for services that host it. For example, Apple's Safari browser (both mobile and desktop) still cannot display 360° video correctly (as of 2019). But no matter what, you must be sure to add the appropriate metadata to alert the playback system that your video is spherical (as described in Chapter 61: Adding spherical metadata).

Each video-sharing service has different recommendations and requirements for the file that you upload. Follow the descriptions in the following tables to ensure maximum compatibility.

YouTube

The most well-known video sharing site in the world, YouTube has embraced 360° video in a big way (which is not surprising because they're owned by Alphabet/Google, which is deeply invested in other aspects of VR). Not only can YouTube support stereoscopic video and ambisonic audio, but its ubiquity means that a 360° video uploaded to YouTube can be watched on nearly any device, including PlayStation VR, Oculus, HTC and other high-end HMDs, and will likely be available on any new VR hardware that emerges.

The specs below are the maximum allowed; YouTube is very flexible, and accepts a wide range of lower-quality files. However lower-quality files will appear correspondingly worse when viewed by your audience.

YouTube upload specs

Maximum file upload size:	128 GB
Maximum video length:	15 minutes (longer with a verified account)
File type:	MP4, MOV, AVI, VP9
Video codec:	H.264 (high profile), VP9
Bitrate:	66–85 Mbps
Frame rate:	60 fps
Resolution:	8192x8192
Stereoscopic:	Top-bottom format
Aspect ratio (dimensions):	2:1, 1:1
Audio codec:	AAC-LC
Audio channels:	Spatialized (AmbiX)

Facebook

The other behemoth player (also heavily invested in other aspects of VR), Facebook is more limited than YouTube in terms of the options available for 360° video. Currently, Facebook doesn't support stereoscopic video, and the maximum resolution is relatively small. This makes sense in that Facebook expects nearly all viewers to be watching the video within a Facebook news feed and not in a fully immersive HMD. They do however, support ambisonic sound, including a special *focusing* option where audio positioned in an area outside of the viewable frame of the magic window is attenuated.

Stereoscopic: Video shot with two parallel cameras (or in the case of 360° video, multiple pairs of parallel cameras) Commonly referred to as 3D.

HMD (head-mounted display): goggles or a headset designed to optimize 360° video viewing.

Facebook upload specs

Maximum file upload size:	5 GB
Maximum video length:	30 minutes
File type:	MP4
Video codec:	H.264
Bitrate:	20 Mbps
Frame rate:	60 fps
Resolution:	UHD (3840 x 1920)
Stereoscopic:	Not supported
Aspect ratio (dimensions):	2:1
Audio codec:	MP3 or AAC
Audio channels:	Spatialized (AmbiX or TBE format)

Vimeo

This site has always aimed to be the desired destination for more serious content creators, with a focus on quality and reliability, and their options for 360° video reflect that. The only drawback is that they do not currently support spatialized audio. Also, in order to exceed the 500 MB upload limit, you must purchase a monthly subscription.

Vimeo upload specs

Maximum file upload size:	500 MB (free) or unlimited (paid)
Maximum video length:	n/a
File type:	MP4, MOV
Video codec:	H.264, Apple ProRes 422HQ
Bitrate:	30–60Mbps
Frame rate:	60 fps
Resolution:	Up to 8K upload (displays at 4K)
Stereoscopic:	Top-bottom format
Aspect ratio (dimensions):	2:1
Audio codec:	AAC
Audio channels:	Mono or stereo

Samsung VR

Samsung has its own portal for hosting 360° video content, primarily intended for viewing on the Gear VR. Because Samsung serves the video to hardware that they manufacture, they have better control over the process to ensure high-quality results.

Samsung VR upload specs

Maximum file upload size:	25 GB
Maximum video length:	~5 minutes
File type:	MP4, MOV
Video codec:	H.264, HEVC
Bitrate:	Minimum 40 Mbps
Frame rate:	30, 48, 60 fps
Resolution:	3840 x 1920 or 3840 x 3840
Stereoscopic:	Top-bottom or left-right format
Aspect ratio (dimensions):	2:1 mono, 1:1 stereo
Audio codec:	AAC-LC
Audio channels:	Spatialized (AmbiX/ACN), 5.1 surround, binaural, quadraphonic

One big advantage is that Samsung VR supports the HEVC (also called H.265) codec. Newer and more powerful than the H.264 codec that is the industry standard, HEVC allows for higher-quality images at the same bitrate. Given the large file sizes of 360° content, this is a big win in terms of visual quality. Samsung VR also supports 1:1 aspect ratio for stereoscopic content, which means you don't have to throw away half your horizontal resolution. If you've got a Gear VR (and a compatible Samsung smartphone), you can also copy the video file directly to the storage on your phone as described in Chapter 62: Sideloading video.

Littlstar

A venture-backed startup that's attempting to become the YouTube of 360° video. Littlstar has already outlasted a number of potential competitors and has popular apps on all the major platforms, so you can view your content on virtually any device that plays 360° video. Their upload process is easy, and at least for now they seem to accept all submitted content. However, certain content is highlighted or promoted, which is likely the only stuff that's getting widely seen.

Littlstar upload specs

Maximum file upload size:	5 GB
Maximum video length:	n/a
File type:	MP4
Video codec:	H.264
Bitrate:	Unlimited
Frame rate:	60 fps
Resolution:	4096 x 2048
Stereoscopic:	Not supported
Aspect ratio (dimensions):	2:1
Audio codec:	AAC-LC
Audio channels:	FuMa or Atmos, binaural, quadraphonic

Dub master: A final version of your program ready for conversion into a distribution format. The term comes from the old days when videos were distributed on tapes or DVDs and a master was created to be used as the source for those duplicates or "dubs."

ProRes: A high-quality video compression format created by Apple that supports up to 8K resolution.

Jaunt VR

Your footage doesn't have to be shot with the Jaunt One camera to be hosted on their public channel, but they also don't accept just any submission. Jaunt VR has apps on all the major platforms and is quite selective in what content it publishes. One great thing about Jaunt VR: If your file is selected, you can submit the full-resolution dub master (at least if it's in ProRes). Then it's on them to compress it in the least-destructive way.

Jaunt VR upload specs

Maximum file upload size:	4 GB
Maximum video length:	n/a
File type:	MP4, MOV
Video codec:	H.264, Apple ProRes
Bitrate:	40 Mbps minimum
Frame rate:	24–60 fps
Resolution:	4096 x 2048 mono, 4096 x 4096 stereo
Stereoscopic:	Top-bottom Format
Aspect ratio (dimensions):	2:1 (mono) 1:1 (stereo)
Audio codec:	AAC
Audio channels:	FuMa, Atmos, Surround 5.1

Note: Some services reduce image quality to ensure that playback is smooth depending on the speed of your network. For best results, make sure the playback device is connected to a fast network and that the quality/resolution setting is set to the highest possible option.

Be sure to set YouTube's quality setting to the highest available resolution.

Chapter 59: Video-sharing options

Depending on the video sharing service you're using, there may be additional settings and options to improve or customize how your video is displayed. Because these services are continually improving and updating their offerings, these settings may change with little notice. Check the instructions for the service you're using to verify what options are available.

Here are a number of specific settings and controls you should consider:

Set the field of view (FOV)

Some services allow you to define how much of the image is viewable in the magic window, by setting a value for the field of view. (This doesn't affect playback in a headset, where FOV is determined by the specific hardware.) It's similar to setting a zoom level but doesn't actually magnify the video and lower the effective resolution. Vimeo (for example) lets you set the FOV to anywhere from 30–90° (with a default of 50). Choosing a number between 30 and 50 zooms in, enlarging the image. Setting a number between 50 and 90 zooms out. The larger the number, the greater the visible spherical distortion around the edges.

Change the center point

Some services also allow you to change the center point by entering X and Y coordinates. Like the FOV setting, this adjustment affects only viewers looking at the video in a magic window. (In an HMD, the center is determined by where you point your head.) If you've carefully chosen the center point for your video during the stitching and/or editing process (as I've recommended throughout this book), then you can safely ignore this setting.

Stitching: Combining multiple images/videos into one panoramic image/video (also sometimes refers to a seam in a panoramic image).

Poster Image: Use a still image from a high resolution camera and crop it to the aspect ratio as required by the service to which you are uploading. (The red areas in this image show the area being cropped.)

Latlong (latitudinal-longitudinal): Stretching a spherical image into a flat rectangle (similar to the way a world map represents the spherical Earth). Also called equirectangular.

Create a poster image

To watch your video, viewers will click or tap a thumbnail image. This image is called the poster image or poster frame, and it's usually a still frame from within the content of your show.

When viewers search for your program or open the primary page for your program on a video sharing site, they'll see this poster image. In many ways, the poster image is the single-most important piece of marketing for your show.

By default, most services automatically extract a poster image from the video itself, and for flat content, that's often sufficient. But with 360° video, that results in a latlong image where the main subject of the shot is tiny and distorted. Such an image isn't likely to convey the content and tone of your show.

Instead, create a non-spherical image to serve as your poster frame. Nearly all of the sites listed in the previous chapter offer the ability to upload a separate still image that overrides any auto-generated poster frame.

> **Tip:** If you try to zoom in on a frame of your spherical video to produce a non-distorted image, the resolution will likely be very low (and potentially pixelated), making it a less-than-ideal poster image. It's far smarter to anticipate the need for a poster and at some point during your production, take some high-res still photos with a DSLR (or even a high-quality cell phone camera). These images will be much better to use as your poster frame (as well as for any other promotional materials you create).

Consult the individual services for the recommended size and aspect ratio of the poster image.

Create a banner image

Littlstar uses an additional promotional tool if your content is displayed in their highlighted content: an image with the title text included, typically a bit larger than the poster frame. In practical terms, this is more like a traditional movie poster (in icon form). Littlstar provides a template to make it easy to adhere to their required specifications.

This image shows the Littlstar banner template with a custom graphic pasted in.

Creating a banner like this is a great idea even if you're not using Littlstar for distribution. You can use it anywhere you want to add a link to your video in place of simple text, even in a promotional email. And like the poster frame, the banner image (along with the title of the show) is your project's calling card and can make all the difference in determining who does or doesn't watch your work.

Spatialized: A soundscape where audio is positioned from specific locations in space around the listener.

Dub master: A final version of your program ready for conversion into a distribution format. The term comes from the old days when videos were distributed on tapes or DVDs and a master was created to be used as the source for those duplicates or "dubs."

Chapter 60: Muxing audio and video

Before delivering your work, you must create a single file that contains both your properly compressed video and the spatialized audio. This process is called multiplexing (or *muxing* for short) and must be done in a way that doesn't change (in any way) the contents of the video or audio components.

You can do this in one of two ways; you can mux your finished spatialized audio mix with your dub master and then create delivery masters from that (super-dub) file, or you can output your delivery masters first, and then mux the final audio into each of those individual files.

Either way is okay, but if you mux the audio with your dub master, be sure that any subsequent compression steps don't modify the audio component at all. Be sure to set the audio to *pass-through*, which is an option in some file-conversion tools such as Compressor.

If you output the individual (video-only) delivery masters first, you can mux those files with the final audio using a standalone multiplexing app such as Subler, Muxer, or Video Mux. These tools combine the two elements into a single file without modifying or recompressing either the video or audio components.

No matter how you do your muxing, be sure to add the required spherical metadata before uploading your files to any video sharing service as instructed in Chapter 61: Adding spherical metadata.

All-in-one option

The Facebook 360 Spatial Workstation comes with an app called FB360 Encoder.

This tool converts the output of a ProTools session (or another audio app using the Facebook 360 audio plug-ins) into the various ambisonic formats, and can do the muxing too (at least for a video formatted for Facebook or YouTube—it can only mux the AmbiX format). It even adds the spherical metadata for you!

AmbiX: A method of storing ambisonic audio data in the SN3D format.

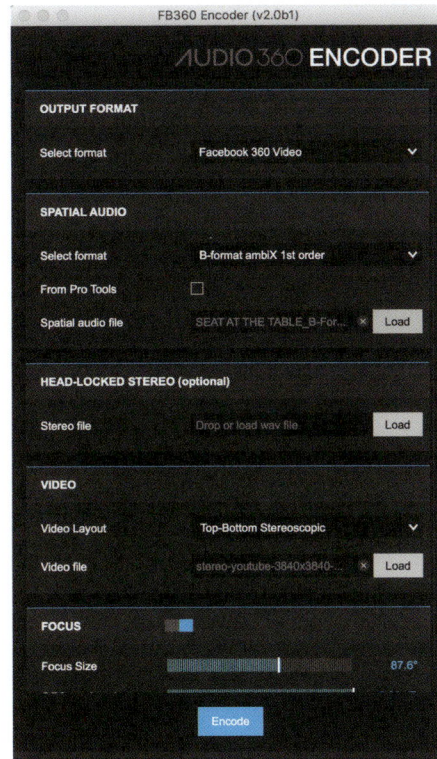

Spatialized: A soundscape where audio is positioned from specific locations in space around the listener.

Chapter 61: Adding spherical metadata

There's one more step to complete before you upload your video file to any of the video-sharing sites. You must add special tags to identify the file as spherical, whether it's monoscopic or stereo-scopic, and whether the audio is spatialized. The playback systems rely upon this metadata to ensure that 360° video is played back correctly. Adobe Premiere injects this information when you export a file, but if your video is sourced elsewhere, you'll need to add it manually.

Some video-sharing sites (like Vimeo and Facebook) also allow you to identify the video as 360° when you enter the video's title and description on their site after you've uploaded the file. But beware: YouTube doesn't provide this option. If you forget to add the metadata before uploading to YouTube, you'll need to delete the file and upload it again.

Here's how to add metadata to your file before uploading to YouTube:

1. Download Google's Spatial Media Metadata Injector app[2].
2. Open the app and in the window that appears, click Open.
3. Navigate to your delivery master file, then double-click it.
4. Select the checkboxes for the data you want to add ("My video is spherical," for example).
5. Click "Inject metadata."

    Your file is duplicated into a new file with the required metadata added.

---

2   https://support.google.com/jump/answer/7044297

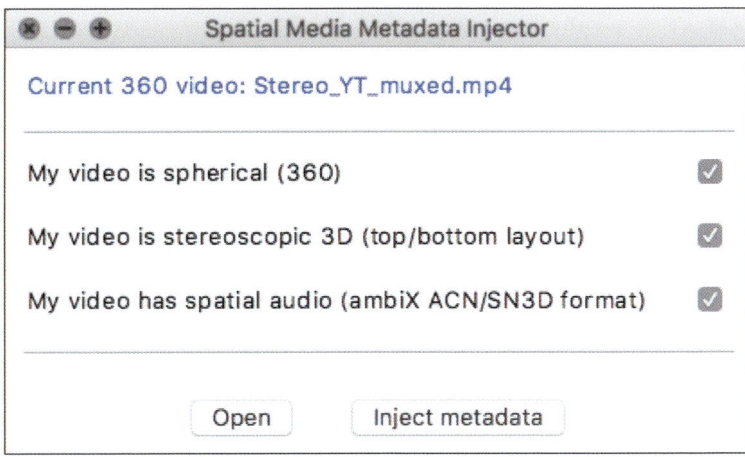

Google's Spatial Media Metadata Injector.

> **Note:** You must have enough disk space to safely dupli-cate the data before clicking "Inject metadata."

6. When the app finishes, quit and delete the original file.
7. Upload the new file to the video-sharing service.

Alternatively, you can add the metadata using Google's open source Python script.[3]

Python: An interpreted, object-oriented programming language similar to PERL, that has gained popularity for its clear syntax and readability.

> **Tip:** You can embed some of this data directly into the name of your file. This won't help YouTube identify your video properly, but it will for the Samsung and Oculus playback apps. And this method may be adopted by other vendors in the future. By appending the name of your filename with *360*, you are identify-ing it as spherical video. If the video is stereoscopic, you can also append it with *TB* (for top-bottom) or *LR* (for left-right).

3   https://github.com/google/spatial-media/blob/master/spatialmedia/

Chapter 61: Adding spherical metadata

Chapter 62: Sideloading video

In some cases, you may want to create a file for viewing directly on specific hardware such as Samsung Gear VR, Daydream View, Oculus Go, Quest or Rift, or HTC VIVE family. This is not a mass-distribution strategy, but it allows you to ensure the highest quality version of your video. Viewing your project directly on specific hardware, rather than streaming it, also eliminates buffering issues or stuttering playback caused by network congestion. Here's how to do it on a number of common hardware devices:

Samsung Gear VR

Both the *Oculus* app and the *Samsung VR* app can play local files while the Gear VR headset is active. For both apps, you'll first need to load the file onto the Samsung Galaxy phone that you use with the Gear VR device.

1. Connect your phone by doing one of the following:
   - *On a Windows PC:* Connect the phone via USB, and when the phone prompts you for the reason you connected the cable, choose Transfer Files.

   - *On a Mac:* Use the (free) Android File Transfer app[4], then connect the phone to your Mac using a USB cable.

2. On the phone, you can put the video files in one of the following places:
   - Create a folder called MilkVR Folder at the root directory of the phone. Video placed here appear in the "Sideloaded" channel in the Samsung VR app.

4   https://www.android.com/filetransfer/

- Create subfolders within the Oculus folder. Put 360 videos into Oculus/movies/360videos/ Put stereoscopic clips into Oculus/movies/360videos/3d/ (You can create these subfolders if they don't exist.)

You can also put the files directly in the Oculus/movies folder (instead of in the subfolders) if the filenames are appended with *_360* or *_360_TB* (for top-bottom stereoscopic). For example, `SeatAtTheTable_360.mp4`, or `SeatAtTheTable_360_TB.mp4`.

All video files in the Oculus folder are playable in the *My Videos* section of the Oculus Video app, or the "Local Files" section of the Samsung VR app. Regardless of which app you use, your video file should be set to the following specs listed to the right.

Note: If your device doesn't have an Oculus folder, you most likely do not have the Oculus app installed. Insert your phone into the Samsung Gear VR headset and follow the instructions to install the necessary apps.

Daydream View
To view files directly on a Daydream View, use the Jump Inspector app (downloadable from the Play Store). Connect your phone to a computer using the same steps as described in the Gear VR section above. Copy the files from the computer to the "Jump" folder on the Android phone. (You can create that folder if it doesn't yet exist). Files in that folder will be viewable in the Jump Inspector app. Use the specs listed to the right.

Note: Jump Inspector assumes your footage is stereoscopic (top-bottom). If your file is mono, append *.360.mono* to the end of the filename, and store it in a stretched 16:9 format. For more specific instructions, see Google's support page[5].

Gear VR specs

File type:	MP4, MOV
Video codec:	H.264, HEVC
Bitrate:	20Mbps
Frame rate:	30, 48, 60fps
Resolution:	3840x1920, 3840x3840
Stereoscopic:	Top-bottom or left-right
Aspect ratio:	2:1 mono or 1:1 stereo
Audio:	AAC-LC
Audio type:	Mono, stereo, spatialized, quad-binaural, 5.1 surround.

Daydream View specs

File type:	MP4, MOV, MKV
Video codec:	H.264 (main profile)
Bitrate:	20Mbps
Frame rate:	30fps
Resolution:	2048x2048, 2880x2880 or 3840x2160-stretched (See note in body)
Stereoscopic:	Top-bottom
Aspect ratio:	16:9 mono or 1:1 stereo)
Audio:	AAC, PCM, Vorbis
Audio type:	Mono, stereo, spatialized (1st order or 3rd order).

5   https://support.google.com/jump/answer/6400241

Oculus Go specs

File type:	MP4, VP9
Video codec:	HEVC, H.264
Bitrate:	20Mbps
Frame rate:	60fps
Resolution:	up to 4096x4096
Stereoscopic:	Top-bottom
Aspect ratio:	2:1 mono or 1:1 stereo)
Audio:	AAC-LC
Audio type:	Mono, stereo, spatialized, quad-binaural, 5.1 surround.

Oculus Go

Connect your Oculus Go to your computer via USB. You may need to put the device on your head and allow the computer to have access to the Go's internal storage. (Mac users, you'll need to use the Android File Transfer app as described in the GearVR section above.)

Once you can see the Go's file system on your computer, copy your 360° video file to the Movies folder on the Oculus Go. Be sure to, append the filename with _360 (for mono) or _360_TB (for top-bottom stereoscopic). For example, `SeatAt-TheTable_360.mp4`, or `SeatAtTheTable_360_TB.mp4`.

To view the files in the Go, go to Gallery > Internal Storage.

Computer-connected HMDs

For VR headsets that are connected directly to a computer, you simply need to store a video file on the host PC and open it via an app on the headset. There are a number of apps in the Steam, Oculus, or Viveport stores that enable this task. The simplest is *Virtual Desktop,* but there are many other apps that also work. Because these HMDs are connected to a computer, you can use a wide range of file specifications.

Tip: For all the same reasons I described in Chapter 58: Video-sharing services, you should create custom thumbnail images to go along with your files when sideloading. Create a .png file with the same name as your video and place it in the same folder with the video.

Chapter 63: Delivering custom apps

There are many reasons why you might want to distribute your video by embedding it into a standalone app.

You might want to add basic interactivity—for example, hot spots in the video so the viewer can leap cut to another location within a scene to change perspective, or cut to an entirely different scene. You could use this technique to create build-you-own-adventure stories, giving the viewer even more autonomy and agency to control the story they see.

You might want to mix 360˚ video and a computer-generated VR scene, perhaps creating a fully immersive VR experience in which a viewer using an HMD with positional tracking can walk around inside a synthetic environment but still see photorealistic 360˚ video at certain moments in the show.

You might want to take advantage of Liquid Cinema's dynamic title technology to create onscreen graphics that float above the 360° sphere, remaining in view, regardless of where the audience looks.

Or you might simply want to build an app so your viewers don't have to search for your videos on YouTube or Littlstar or through another portal where your immaculate piece might get lost amid videos with questionable quality (or worse, questionable content).

If you're trying to build a brand, and plan to release videos at a regular cadence, an app that delivers that content in one consistent space could become an important differentiating factor. As you build your library, your app could even search through your

Leap cut: An edit optionally executed by the audience by interacting with a hot spot in the frame.

collection and serve up different collections of videos to individual viewers based on their specific interests or needs.

Additionally, with your own playback app, you can control how the video is played back; for example, you might opt to force the viewer to download an entire file (rather than streaming it while it plays). Enforced downloads cause an annoying delay before the audience can watch, but eliminate buffering or stuttering that might interrupt the immersive experience. Or, alternatively, you could employ adaptive streaming based on the viewer's field of view (FOVAS or field of view adaptive streaming). This technique saves bandwidth (and correspondingly increases quality) by sending only high-quality video for the portion of the sphere the viewer is currently watching, and sending lower-quality video for the area in her peripheral vision.

You can build your app to take advantage of specific hardware like Daydream View or Oculus Quest, or go with a more generic playback system like Google Cardboard. The former will play only on specific devices but will provide a better user experience. The latter will play on a much wider range of devices but may not offer an experience much better than using a host like YouTube or Vimeo.

There are several companies offering no-programming app creation tools designed specifically for 360° video and VR. Headjack, and InstaVR are leaders in the field, offering simplified interfaces allowing you to quickly create apps of varying complexity, plus they hosts your video files for a subscription fee.

Pixvana Spin Studio provides not just (easy-to-use) app creation and hosting (with proprietary FOVAS techniques to maximize quality), but also takes care of stitching (from certain cameras) file management (which you know can be quite daunting if you read Chapter 32: Ingesting footage), and boasts collaboration, titling, and interactivity features as well. You can build your interactive app live, inside a headset. They're aiming to truly be an all-in-one solution for the post side of 360° and VR production.

Stitching: Combining multiple images/videos into one panoramic image/video (also sometimes refers to a seam in a panoramic image).

As your needs get more complex, it may make sense to hire a more versatile app developer, and here the sky's the limit. (Or rather, your budget is your only limit. Well, that and the extent of your developer's expertise.) Most VR apps are created in game engines like Unity or Unreal Engine, which have built-in capacities and APIs designed for creating complex interfaces around video elements.

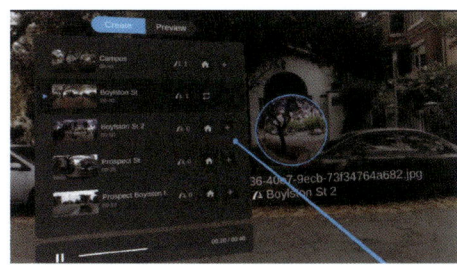

Pixvana Spin Studio's VR interface for building interactivity in 360° videos.

And for that happy medium between using an automated app creation tool, and hiring a private developer for a fully custom creation, there are several companies focused exclusively on creating custom apps for VR and 360° video such as Purple Pill (the creator of Headjack) and CubicleNinjas.

After your app is created, you can submit it to the Apple App Store and Google Play Store for use on cell phones; to the PlayStation Store for PlayStation VR; or the Steam store for viewing on HMDs like VIVE, Oculus, or Pimax. Or to all of the above!

Keep in mind that an app (even a simple one) needs to be designed carefully with well-thought-out user interface and user interaction procedures. Your app should be thoroughly evaluated and tested on every device and operating system you support. Also, be aware that the various app stores have different (sometimes contradictory) criteria and requirements that you'll need to adhere to.

Stitched: Multiple videos that have been combined into one panoramic video.

Chapter 64: Livestreaming

Most everything in this book has been geared toward the type of production where you shoot some footage and then evaluate and refine it before sharing it with your audience. But there are many situations in which your goal may be to send the output of the 360° camera directly to your viewers live—unedited and unrefined (though it still must be stitched for anyone to view it correctly).

Such projects might include high-profile news or sports events, broadcast simultaneously to a large audience; or something more intimate and personal sent to a single recipient (so your old, infirm aunt in Toledo can attend your wedding in real time without leaving her home). And there are many options in between. Facebook supports live 360° streaming directly to Facebook, so all your friends can stand beside you as your kid is born (or maybe just the friends to whom you gave the secret password).

Streaming 360° video is easy. Honestly, it's far easier than going through all the steps described throughout this book, which are intended to guide you toward a professional-looking, thoughtfully produced piece. If you're streaming your video, by definition you're winging it (at least to a certain extent), and timeliness takes priority over almost everything else.

Lossy: An artifact of data compression whereby visual information deemed unnecessary is discarded, resulting in noise.

In order to stream 360° video you still have to obey the laws of physics. 360° video files are very large, and to transmit them over the internet requires a high-bandwidth, fast connection or heavy, lossy compression (that reduces image quality) or both. Also, live streaming means no time for careful hand stitching, or even high-quality computational stitching. The video that goes out live will invariably have some visible stitch lines. But don't fret; let this free you from worrying too much about quality. After all, the point is the immediacy, not crisp, seamless resolution.

In addition to Facebook (mentioned above), YouTube and Twitter (via Periscope) also offer the ability to livestream 360˚ video (and the rest of the social media crowd can't be far behind). There are a number of consumer cameras (including the Ricoh Theta V and ALLie Home) that have partnered with YouTube to enable one-touch, direct streaming. After you configure the camera with your YouTube login information, you can simply turn it on, and a moment later your video magically appears on your YouTube channel!

The file is stitched locally in the camera (or more likely in a companion app on your phone or computer) and then the latlong file is uploaded via Wi-Fi[6] to a server, where it is multicast to whomever tunes in.

Latlong (latitudinal-longitudinal): Stretching a spherical image into a flat rectangle (similar to the way a world map represents the spherical Earth). Also called equirectangular.

Beware that these systems are pretty low-res. To get a higher-quality livestream, you can add a more powerful (and more expensive) live-stitching device. This could be dedicated hardware like 360 Designs Stitchbox; it could be a PC running Mistika VR software (although the PC needs to be fairly powerful, with multiple graphics cards), which takes in up to six video streams and stitches them together on the fly. The output of that can be fed directly to YouTube's (or Facebook's, or another service's) livestreaming link on a webpage.

The Teredek Sphere is a hardware H.264 encoder (described in Chapter 23: Monitoring on set) that (combined with it's iOS or macOS software) can stitch up to eight video streams[7] in real time. The benefit of this device is that it's small and can be

6   You may technically be able to upload using a cellular network, but it's unlikely to be fast enough, and I'd hate to see how quickly you'd eat up your phone plan's data allowance.

7   Each Sphere can accept 4 streams, but two can be daisy-chained to stitch 8 inputs together.

battery-powered, so it's especially great for remote or mobile productions. The Sphere comes with a $1000 livestreaming upgrade option that allows you to send its output directly to YouTube or another livestreaming service.

Nearly every camera manufacturer across a range of quality and options also offer livestreaming, but instead of (or in addition to) using YouTube's servers, they provide their own. Other than the fact that the website address you'll need to give your viewers won't be a YouTube link, the process is very similar.

Some of these devices do the stitching in the camera body and have a built-in Ethernet port to connect the output of the camera directly to a router. That's great if you're in a static, indoor location with internet access. Other devices require a companion app on your phone or laptop to do the stitching and transmit the latlong to the company's video server wirelessly.

There are also a number of companies (including Wowza, HugVR, and Visbit) focused solely on the hosting and distribution side of the livestreaming business. They promise more reliable, higher quality video streams, secure log-ins, and data analytics to report who is watching and for how long—along with other services that may be valuable to you depending on your project's needs.

Currently with most livestreaming products you can't transmit stereoscopic video or spatialized audio, and the maximum resolutions are limited (though all this is changing rapidly). But you can, with minimal configuration, turn on a 360° camera and see a stitched result live (almost) immediately. Which is unquestionably pretty cool.

Spatialized: A soundscape where audio is positioned from specific locations in space around the listener.

Epilogue

Writing this book has been a beguiling and humbling experience. I've thrust myself into a new world with unknown boundaries and an uninvented language. The inhabitants of this world have turned out to be some of the smartest and most inspiring people I've met. People unintimidated by the technical obstacles and creative uncertainties of an undefined medium, who nevertheless rush right in, unafraid of failure or embarrassment. They're driven by a dream of sharing the human experience—as widely and as immersively as presently possible. Some see a new way to create empathy; others a new way to teach, or just to tell stories. But underneath it all, there's a familiar child-like giddiness that seems to push the corners of their mouths up into a smile whenever they talk about their work.

But the process of writing this book has also been frustrating. Of course, I anticipated the continued development of tools and techniques and was not upset when I had to rewrite (or rethink) entire sections—sometimes more than once—as new products and titles came to market. (And I plan to update the book as frequently as possible to remain current over the coming years.) Maverick innovators continue to push (drag?) the state of the art forward, both in terms of solving technical obstacles and in terms of exploring and defining this new language. But it's slow going.

VR hardware is a hard sell outside the gamer community. Most people think of it as a novelty. For every great piece of content that has emerged, there are 25 that are head-scratchingly mediocre. Several of the most promising cameras that I was eager to review and include in the book remain stuck in beta or very limited availability, even a year after their originally planned ship dates.

And for all the billions of dollars being poured into the industry from all directions, it remains fragile. The truth is that there's a sweet spot where the technology is invisible enough and the content is compelling enough to attract a critical mass of people. Right now, we remain quite a ways from that spot (in both directions).

In writing this book, my hope is to do a small part to help the effort. To grease the skids and make the content-creation process easier (or at least easier to understand). And hopefully, I can gently nudge you, gentle reader, toward creating that irresistible content that will pull this medium into the mainstream, so more and more people get to enjoy that primal sense of delight of being truly transported into a new world.

Glossary

180° rule A cinematography technique to ensure eyelines remain consistent across edits. It works by drawing an imaginary line between principal subjects on set, and keeping all coverage of those subjects on one or the other side of that line.

2-shot A camera angle that encompasses two people in a scene.

2nd AC (2nd assistant camera) Crewperson responsible for operating the slate, keeping a camera log, and managing the raw film stock and footage shot.

4:2:0/4:4:4 One of the ways video is compressed is by removing color data that is less noticeable by the human eye. These numbers identify the "chroma subsampling" in different compression schemes (how that color data is removed). Lower numbers indicate more data is thrown out to make smaller files.

AD (assistant director) The crewmember responsible for running the set during production, ensuring the production runs on schedule and all requisite shots are captured.

ADR (Automated Dialogue Replacement) The process of re-recording dialogue by the original actor in post-production in a way that matches the recorded video. It is employed to correct sound issues or reflect dialogue changes (also called "looping").

Ambiance Background sound that captures an environment such as the general murmur of a crowd, birds and insects in a rainforest, or the pitter-patter of rain.

Ambisonic Pertaining to audio reproduction that captures the spatial acoustic qualities of recorded sound.

Ambisonic microphone A microphone that employs multiple sensors to capture a 360 sphere of sound (see also, tetrahedral microphone).

AmbiX A method of storing ambisonic audio data in the SN3D format.

AR (augmented reality The superimposition of video images onto a user's view of a real-world setting.

Assembly An extremely rough edit of shots that places them in the order they appear in the script.

Aspect ratio The display ratio of resolution pixels along the x axis to the y axis (i.e. HD video of 1920 x 1080 pixels has a 16:9 aspect ratio).

Background plate A duplicate set up of a shot where an unwanted object (tripod, interviewer, crewmember, etc.) has been removed.

Beats Units of action within a scene.

Below-the-line The budgetary field that accounts for 'non-creative' crew in film production (e.g. everyone except the producer, director, writer, cinematographer, composer, editor, etc.).

Block Position and choreograph actor movements in a scene.

Blocking The positions and movement of actors in a scene.

Blockiness An artifact of data compression whereby areas of the image look pixelated.

Bogey Adapted from military slang, a bogey a person or object who accidentally appears in the frame during a shot.

Boom-mounted shotgun mic A directional microphone (that captures sound in a conical field reminiscent of a shotgun's blast area) attached to the end of a long, light-weight pole.

Camera dollies Wheeled camera mounts, either on tracks or fully mobile, that facilitate smooth camera motion.

Cardioid Mic A microphone with a primary sensitivity in front of the microphone, but which also records audio to the left and right.

CGI (computer-generated imagery) Images created by computer.

Choreography Prescribing movement for actions that require precise execution, such as dance or combat

Close-miked Audio recorded with a mic placed very close to the subject (often directly attached to the clothes or body).

Closed-ear headphones Headphones that fully encompass the ear to reduce the interference of sound from the listener's environment.

Close-up (CU) A limited view that narrows in on a key feature of a subject: an actors face, a smoking gun on the floor, etc.

Color aberrations The optical consequence of a lens that fails to handle color waveforms equally. It can result in blurred images or noticeable colored edges or "fringes."

Color correction The adjustment of color in post-production to match different shots and enhance the picture.

Color fidelity The accuracy with which a digital camera captures the color of the photographed subject.

Color temperatures The apparent color of light measured in degrees kelvin (K), i.e. Daylight emits a blueish 5600K light, and Tungsten filaments (traditionally used in film lights) emit an orange 3200K light.

Composite The post-production process of combining two or more images. Could be as simple as a title superimposed over an image, or as complex a digitally generated explosion rotoscoped over a filmed miniature spaceship in front of a painting of outer space. Also can refer to the result of that process; a composite, or a composite image.

Composition Layout and relative position of the objects within a shot.

Compression A process of lowering overall image quality by reducing the amount of data in a file in order to make it more accessible to playback engines.

Coverage Multiple shots from multiple angles to capture the events in a scene (i.e. master shot, medium shots, close-ups, inserts, etc.).

Convergence The point where the left and right eye projections meet in the screen to simulate the 3D effect. Also, amount of stereo separation between the left and right channels that controls the stereo effect.

CRI (color rendering index) The measure of how close to true white a light bulb appears.

Cross-dissolve A transition effect where one clip fades out as another fades in.

Cubemap A projection where a spherical image is viewed as a cube, and where the six faces of the cube are unfolded into a rectangle. The cube faces can be arranged in different ways. In a cubemap, distortions present in a lat-long are corrected, giving an accurate scale to objects at the apex (top) and nadir (bottom) of the scene.

Cues A trigger for a action or line of dialogue.

Cutaway Shot of an object within the location of the scene, but not seen in the previous shots, such as seagulls during a beach scene, or the cheering crowd at a concert. Cutaways provide editing options and help to enhance the sense of presence in a scene.

Cuts (edits) The point where one shot ends and another shot begins.

Dailies The accumulated footage shot in a day on set (traditionally reviewed at the end of each day).

DAW (digital audio workstation) Software designed to process and edit audio tracks.

Dead An environment with little or no reflections or reverberations of the sound.

Depth budget The amount of three-dimensional depth you can utilize in a scene without tiring your viewer.

Depth map Digital data representing the distance of the objects in the scene from the camera.

Director of photography / DP Crewperson responsible for designing the shotlist and lighting state, advising on camera selection, and directing the camera and lighting departments on set.

DIT (digital imaging technician) Crewperson responsible for managing workflow of a production, ingesting and labeling footage from takes, monitoring image quality and color, and troubleshooting digital issues.

Directing action inward Framing a subject with action, people or objects that draws your attention to the center of the frame.

DK2 Developer kit version 2 of the Oculus Rift HMD, which works on Macs as well as Windows computers. The shipping "consumer version" (CV1) does not support Mac.

Downstage Closer to the audience/camera.

DSLR (digital single-lens reflex) A digital camera that uses a mirror to reflect the view coming through the lens onto the camera sensor, which enables the viewfinder to see the exact image the camera will capture (i.e. a professional still camera like the Canon 5D or Nikon D-series).

Dual-fisheye source files A single video file that contains the combined footage from two fisheye-lensed cameras, usually positioned side-by-side.

Dub master A final version of your program ready for conversion into a distribution format. The term comes from the old days when videos were distributed on tapes or DVDs and a master was created to be used as the source for those duplicates or "dubs."

Dutch angle When the camera is tilted slightly left or right, so the horizon appears to be diagonal.

Dynamic range The varying degrees of brightness that can be captured by a camera or displayed by a playback device. You can think of it as the number of grays that can be represented before areas of the image appear all-black (in the shadows) or all-white (in the highlights).

Equirectangular Stretching a spherical image into a flat, rectangular format. (i.e. the way a world map represents the spherical Earth).

Exposure The measurement of the brightness and range (latitude) of light being captured by the camera. Exposure is governed by camera settings that either control the overall amount of light that reaches the sensor (using aperture and shutter speed), or directly adjust the sensor's sensitivity to the light that reaches it (ISO).

Field of view The angle of space viewable from a given lens position.

Fisheye An extreme wide-angle lens, with image distortion occurring at the edges of the frame.

Flag A frame of solid black fabric used to partially block a light source.

Flatter Less contrast between the dark and light areas of the image.

Focal length A lens property; i.e. wide-angle or telephoto; different length lens lengths frame the subject differently, creating a different experience of a scene for the viewer. Also,can refer to the distance between the lens and its point of focus.

Foley The process of reproducing sound effects in a controlled environment synchronized to actions onscreen such as footsteps, or grunts.

Frame size The pixel dimension of a video element (i.e. 1920 x 1080).

G&E (grip and electric) The production departments on set responsible for the operation of grip and lighting equipment. They work under the director of photography.

Gaffer The chief electrician on set, responsible for contributing to and implementing the director of photography's lighting vision.

Gen-locked Using a signal generator to synchronize the shutters across multiple cameras so they all operate in precise alignment.

Global shutter A camera shutter that opens and closes all-at-once, exposing the entire sensor simultaneously (as opposed to a rolling shutter which opens a little at a time like a door opening).

Green screen A subject shot against a background of a particular shade of green so the background can be removed and replaced in post-production.

Handles Extra footage before the beginning and/or after the ending of the used portion of a shot.

Higher-order ambisonic Ambisonic audio with more than 4 channels.

HMD (head-mounted display) Goggles or a headset designed to optimize 360° video viewing.

Holodeck (from Star Trek) A chamber where a person is immersed in a holographic simulation of a physical environment indistinguishable from real life.

Hostess tray shot A shot captured by a camera rigged to the outside of a car's driver side, or passenger side window, supported by a device reminiscent of the trays used at drive-in restaurants in the '50's.

Hot-spots An active, or interactive area of the frame.

Hypercardioid / shotgun A microphone polar pattern that picks up sound primarily to the front, with less sensitivity to the side and rear.

Hyperstereo effect An optical distortion that makes the viewer feel gigantic. Occurs when the interaxial distance of stereo cameras appears greater than ordinary human distance based on the relative distance to the subject.

Image stabilization A process to reduce shakiness caused by an unstable camera.

Ingesting The process of capturing, transferring, and storing media in an organized manner in preparation for editing and output.

Insert Close-up shot of an object or detail previously seen in a wider angle.

Interaxial The mechanic equivalent of Interpupillary; the distance between the lenses of a camera in stereoscopic photography.

Interpupillary distance The distance between the pupils of the eye / lenses of a camera in stereoscopic photography.

Keyframing A process to create animations by identifying parameter values (such as an object's size or its position in the frame) at differing points in time, and interpolating the intervening values.

Latitude Similar to *dynamic range*; The range of brightness that can be captured by a camera usually measured in f-stops).

Latlong (latitudinal-longitudinal) Stretching a spherical image into a flat rectangle (similar to the way a world map represents the spherical Earth). Also called equirectangular.

Lavaliere mic A small microphone attached to a lapel or discretely hidden in an actors wardrobe.

Leading lines Subtly stimulating invisible lines that direct attention or convey meaning in a frame's composition.

Leap cut An edit optionally executed by the audience by interacting with a hot spot in the frame.

Levels The adjustable sensitivity settings of microphones. Levels are set (and changed as necessary) to best capture the vocals of an actors performance.

LIDAR A system of detection that 'bounces' light off objects to record the layout of a space; the laser equivalent of RADAR.

Lighting and grip equipment All the equipment required to rig and control the lights during production, including lights, lighting stands, C-stands, cables, silks, flags, sandbags, reflectors, etc. Grip equipment also encompasses auxiliary camera gear, such as dollies (& their tracks), cranes, jibs, etc.

Livestream Distribute video playback in real-time.

Locked-off Static. Refers to the adjustable parts of a tripod being locked in place.

Long lens (telephoto lens)
Magnifies objects in the distance, narrows the field of view, and optically 'flattens' an image.

Lossy An artifact of data compression whereby visual information deemed unnecessary is discarded, resulting in noise.

Lower-third Titles displaying an interview subject's name and title. Traditionally placed in the bottom third of the video screen.

Magic window A method of viewing 360 content where a rectangular frame acts as a portal to the larger, spherical recording. The viewer can navigate to a different perspective by scrolling (on a computer), or by tilting the viewing device (on a smartphone or tablet).

Marks A position on set (defined during blocking) where an actor is supposed to be at precise moments during a scene. On set, a mark might be a piece of tape on the ground to indicate where an actor should be standing.

Masking Blocking a portion of the image.

Master shot A shot, typically wide, that captures all the action across the duration of a scene.

Match cuts Edits where action within the scene is continued in real time across an edit point; such as seeing a door begin to close from one angle, and then continuing to close from another angle.

Medium shots A view sized from an actor's waist up to the top of her head.

Motion tracking A technique for recording the movement of an object within a scene, to hide or paint that object or to affix a composited element to a corresponding position.

Noise Undesirable variations of brightness and/or color in an image that typically occur when recording at high ISOs in digital cameras.

Nondiegetic Sound that is untethered to anything occurring in the scene.

North The point of origin where a viewer enters a 360° scene, also serves as a frame of reference for orienting discussions about the scene.

Offline edit An interim editing process where creative decisions are made using proxy versions of the full-resolution files (when processing the full-res files would otherwise be too cumbersome). Requires a subsequent *online* edit where the high-res files are conformed to match the offline version. (Also can refer to the result of that first step; the offline edit.)

Omnidirectional mic A microphone that picks up sound evenly in all directions.

Omnidirectional stereo camera A rig with a large number of cameras arranged in a ring like the Yi Halo or GoPro Odyssey).

Optically stabilized Includes mechanics that counteract camera-shake.

OTS MCU (over the shoulder medium close-up) Shot that include part of a character in the foreground (often out of focus), with the principal subject framed from the chest to the top of the head. This is one of the most common types of shots for dialogue scenes.

Overmodulation When a sound is louder than the recording device can record, the waveform will be clipped, distorting the sound unnaturally.

Paint out Digitally remove an object from a scene.

Page peels A transition effect where the image displayed appears to fold off the screen, resembling the turning of a page in a book.

Pan Set the position in space for where audio appears to originate.

Panners Controls that allow you to position the source of sound in space. In stereo environments sound could simply be panned from left to right, but with surround sound and spatialization, panning can be done in full three-dimensional coordinates.

Parallax The effect where an object's position appears to differ when viewed from different positions, i.e. the left eye vs. the right.

Peaks Short bursts of loud sound in an audio track. These are visible in an audio waveform as lines that stick up higher than the average audio levels.

Photogrammetry The use of photography to survey and map a location from a variety of angles.

Plate A part of a composite, usually intended as a background, though here it refers to a duplicate version of the main shot with the offending objects removed. The name comes from old-fashioned analog visual effects where the background was painted onto a sheet of plate glass.

Playback devices The method for displaying a video. (i.e. HMD, magic window, etc.).

PluralEyes Software that synchronizes audio and video files by aligning the audio waveforms of the different files.

Post (post-production) Work undertaken after principle photography wraps. Often refers to digital corrections.

POV (point of view) shot A shot that represents a character's perspective within the scene.

Practical Occurring in the reality of the scene; heard by the characters within the scene (as opposed to sound only heard by the audience). For example, music played on a radio.

Practical lights Lights that are illuminating a scene but that are part of the set, so they can be seen by the camera without revealing the artifice of the filmmaking act.

Production designer (PD) Crewperson responsible for all visual aspects of what is seen by the camera; (i.e. sets & locations, props, wardrobe etc.).

ProRes A high-quality video compression format created by Apple that supports up to 8K resolution.

Python An interpreted, object-oriented programming language similar to PERL, that has gained popularity because of its clear syntax and readability.

Quick stitch A rapid, albeit potentially imperfect, stitch of 360° footage. In multi camera rigs, this may be achieved without utilizing information from every camera's lens.

Rack-focus A shot where the camera focus is shifted during the scene (while the camera is rolling) to shift attention to a different subject or track a subject as it moves.

Refresh rate The frequency at which an image is drawn on screen during playback, expressed as the number of cycles per second (hertz). For example: 90hz.

Rig removal The process of compositing or painting out the camera support (tripod, dolly, slider, etc.) visible in the 360 image.

Resolution The number of pixels in an image, typically presented as a ratio of the total pixels on x axis to the total pixels on the y axis (i.e. 1920 x 1080 for HD).

Roll Term meaning "record," dating back to a time when physical film was rolled on an axle past the gate of a camera.

Room tone An extended clip of sound recorded in the scene location without any additional sounds included.

Rotoscoping Digitally modifying video by tracing objects within the image one frame at a time.

Rule of thirds The concept that divides a traditional film or television frame into nine squares to guide the optimal composition of subjects.

Score Music added to enhance the mood of the video.

SD (secure digital) card A compact, portable memory card typically used in cameras and sound recording devices.

Setup A camera position for a given scene. You might shoot more than one shot from a single set-up (wide shot and close-up).

Shock mount A microphone holder engineered to absorb physical bumps or vibrations to prevent movement from disturbing the audio signal.

Six degrees of freedom The ability to move left-right, up-down, and forward-backward (in addition to being able to rotate around the x, y, and z axes). Provides significantly more immersion than basic 360 video.

Slate A card or device positioned in front of the camera at the beginning of each shot to document all relevant shot information for easy identification during post. Usually operated by the 2nd AC, who reads the relevant information aloud and then activates the clapper bar to provide a synchronization point for audio and video files.

Slider A tripod 'head' mounted on a fixed track that enables the camera to smoothly move left and right or forward and back.

Sourced sound Sound elements that are tied to a specific object or source onscreen.

Spatialize Mix in post-production to distribute sounds into positions in a sphere around the listener.

Spherical projection
Video that is displayed in a seamless 360 degree sphere. Also called rectilinear.

Spin budget The accumulated total degrees of head movement you can ask of your audience over a period of time.

Split edit An editing technique in which the audio and visual components of a shot do not transition at the same time; so the sound occurs before the picture appears, or the sound lingers on after the picture has cut to a new shot.

Stealing a location Shooting in a location without first obtaining permission and/or the requisite permits.

Stereoscopic Video shot with two parallel cameras (or in the case of 360° video, multiple pairs of parallel cameras) Commonly referred to as 3D.

Stereo separation The slight variations in image from the two perspectives that enable 3-dimensional viewing. The closer to the camera, the larger the variations.

Stitch (stitching) Combine multiple images/videos into one panoramic image/video (also sometimes refers to a seam in a panoramic image, or the completed panorama itself).

Stitch lines The seams in a 360° video where footage from one camera has been combined with another.

Stops ƒ-stops are the measurement of, and mechanism for controlling how much light is let through the lens to reach a camera sensor (i.e. ƒ22, ƒ16, ƒ8, ƒ4, ƒ2, ƒ1.4, etc. Larger numbers mean less light)

Subsequence or compound clip Multiple clips which have been grouped into a single object for ease of workflow within an editing program.

Synchronize (sync or synch) Match audio and video to play back simultaneously.

Take Individual instance of a shot; a take = each time the camera is started and stopped.

Tetrahedral A microphone with four recording capsules that captures a rendering of the sound in all directions around the mic.

Timecode A numerical code that identifies videos by the hour, minute, second, and frame in the format HH:MM:SS:FF (e.g. 23:59:59:23).

Upstage Further away from the audience/camera.

Video assist A mechanism to watch in real-time what is being recorded by the camera.

Volumetric video recording A method of capturing a scene in which the spatial layout is recorded instead of just the light that comes through the lens, enabling representation of the scene in a digital, 3-dimensional space.

VR180 A limited-sphere, stereoscopic format created by Google and aimed at consumers

Wide-shot (WS) A expansive view that takes in the entirety of a scene or location.

Wipe A transition effect where the image displayed slides offscreen, revealing the new scene behind.

Zolly A shot where the lens is zoomed (focal length is changed) at the same time as the camera is physically moved (dollied) creating an optical effect where the background appears to shift around the subject.

Zone-based stereo camera A rig utilizing pairs of cameras pointing in different directions.

Index